W9-BWQ-952

CLASS CONFLICT AND COLLECTIVE ACTION

NEW APPROACHES TO SOCIAL SCIENCE HISTORY

Series Editor: *Stanley L. Engerman*
Professor of Economics and History
University of Rochester

Published in cooperation with the Social Science History Association

New Approaches to Social Science History is a series of books designed to encourage publication and dissemination of scholarly works of social science history and historically oriented social science. The series is a key element in the publications program of the Social Science History Association, an interdisciplinary organization formed in 1974 for the purpose of improving the quality of historical explanation by encouraging the selective use and adaptation of relevant theory and method from the social sciences and related disciplines in historical teaching and research. By facilitating freer interchange between historian and social scientist, a more systematic reintroduction of the historical dimension into social science work and the application of historical data to test social scientific theories can be achieved. The series includes both single-authored volumes and edited collections of original essays devoted to substantive research, theoretical issues, methodological concerns, and curricular development.

Louise A. Tilly, Charles Tilly
editors

CLASS CONFLICT AND COLLECTIVE ACTION

Published in cooperation with the
SOCIAL SCIENCE HISTORY ASSOCIATION

 SAGE PUBLICATIONS   Beverly Hills   London

For information address:

SAGE Publications, Inc.
275 South Beverly Drive
Beverly Hills, California 90212

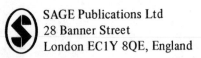

SAGE Publications Ltd
28 Banner Street
London EC1Y 8QE, England

Printed in the United States of America

Library of Congress Cataloging in Publication Data

Main entry under title:
Class conflict and collective action.

(New approaches to social science history ; v. 1)
Bibliography: p.
Includes index.
Contents: Introduction / Charles Tilly–The web of contention in eighteenth-century cities / Charles Tilly–Revolution and the rural community in the eastern Netherlands / Wayne Te Brake–[etc.]
1. Social conflict–Europe–History–Addresses, essays, lectures.
I. Tilly, Louise. II. Tilly, Charles. III. Title: Collective action.
IV. Series.
HN380.Z9S636   303.6'094   81-2701
ISBN 0-8039-1587-X   AACR2
ISBN 0-8039-1588-8 (pbk.)

FIRST PRINTING

CONTENTS

To BARRINGTON MOORE, Jr.

*In admiration and, when
possible, emulation*

PREFACE

Class Conflict and Collective Action is the inaugural volume in a new book series sponsored by the Social Science History Association with the goal of promoting a wider scholarly interchange between historians and social scientists. The series will include both single-authored works and edited collections of original essays devoted to applying social scientific methods to the study of historical issues, as well as to using the insights of historical research to broaden the perspectives of social scientific research.

The essays in this volume, with their detailed examinations of particular historical cases and their use of new data to evaluate explanations of individual and collective behavior, provide an excellent demonstration of the complementarity of historical and social scientific approaches in increasing our understanding of past events, social movements, and human behavior. Thus, *Class Conflict and Collective Action* is an appropriate collection for launching this young publishing program and, it is hoped, one which will stimulate and encourage the development of our interdisciplinary enterprise.

Rochester, New York   *Stanley L. Engerman*
                                                                 Series Editor

1

Introduction

CHARLES TILLY

COMPETING ACCOUNTS OF COLLECTIVE ACTION

"For the workers," writes Barrington Moore, Jr., in his grand reflections on *Injustice: The Social Bases of Obedience and Revolt,* "the
expropriation and rationalization of moral outrage has been a major part
of the capitalist experience" (1978: 502). Moore's own preface warns of
the condescension suggested by the attribution of "moral outrage" to
other people. Yet his searching discussions of working-class experience
make a case both for the centrality of a sense of injustice to popular
rebellion and for a tendency, within our own era, for large organizations to
become the exclusive vehicles for the expression of that sense of injustice.
Moore voices gentle, troubled skepticism concerning the extent to which
large organizations and mass movements actually quench their members'
thirst for justice. That is why he worries about the "expropriation and
rationalization of moral outrage." Thus, he breaks with two major traditions in the analysis of popular collective action: the one which treats
protest, rebellion, and related phenomena as unreasoned responses to
stress, and the one which chains together disparate actions as expressions
of the same, developing social movement.

The break is bold. In alternation and competition, the two views have dominated western thinking about popular collective action for more than a century. On one side we have a tension-release explanation: Extensive or rapid social change creates uncertainties, anxieties, and stresses which accumulate until people find the opportunity to vent them in violence, protest, and cathartic mass action. Norman Gash writes of Britain after the Napoleonic Wars:

> Riot and disorder were the immemorial reaction of the common people to distress and grievance. The highly localized outbreaks of Luddism, like the rural machine-breaking of 1816, arose from wider, more permanent features of British society: inadequate relief in time of unemployment, bad industrial relations, lack of accepted methods of wage negotiations, vulnerability of employers to forcible action, absence of an effective police, and the general weakness of the forces of law and order. Violence was common because it was an instinctive answer and because there was nothing to stop it in its early stages [Gash, 1979: 79-80].

On the other side we have a social-movement explanation: Haltingly but irreversibly, a set of people with a common problem, grievance, or hope become conscious of their shared fate, build organizations, create social movements for the pursuit of their aims. Thus, labor historians have most often organized their analyses around the development of "The Labor Movement." In their old, reliable history of "the British common people" from 1746 onward, Cole and Postgate inevitably paused to describe the swirl of agitation surrounding the career of London's John Wilkes in the 1760s and 1770s—just as I do in the next chapter of this volume. Closing that section (almost as inevitably) with the Gordon riots of 1780, they conclude:

> This sudden and short explosion blew the democratic movement into pieces. Wilkes disappeared from active politics. The operative liverymen and the richer merchants no longer formed a single block united against the Crown. The short and simple initial period, in which the democratic movement is concentrated under one leadership for the convenience of the historian, comes to an end. Henceforward it is scattered and various. But it is not for that reason weaker; indeed, the disappearance of the curious character who had for a short time been its dictator meant that before long the people of England would find their own leaders and not select them from the entourage of a peer [Cole and Postgate, 1961: 108].

For Cole and Postgate, the "democratic movement" provides the connecting thread for two centuries of British history.

Some analysts have played both sides at once—for example, by treating social movements as responses to unresolved tensions. Joseph Gusfield portrays an American temperance movement which appealed to the old, rural middle class: "As America became more urban, more secular, and more Catholic, the sense of declining status intensified the coercive, Populist elements in the Temperance movement" (1963: 7). Or, to return to Britain, we have J. T. Ward's pithy pronouncement on Chartism: "Hunger and regular wage-reductions, rather than any political theory, drove workers to revolt" (1970: 9; however, Brian Brown's account of early Chartist action, in this volume's fifth chapter, makes Ward's reductionism dubious). In such a synthesis as Ward's, sheer impulse plays a less important part than in the purest treatments of protest as tension-release. Nevertheless, even here the analyst refuses to take the movement's members on their own terms and searches for the displacement and transformation of other motives than those the members acknowledge. By focusing on a coherent, and somehow reasonable, sense of injustice, Barrington Moore parts with both traditions—tension-release and social movement—and with their combination as well.

To be sure, Moore does not part in total solitude. After World War II, Albert Soboul, George Rudé, E. J. Hobsbawm, and other students of the "little people" of rebellion and revolution began struggling to reconstruct the rationales of such apparently impulsive actions as food riots and machine-breaking. E. P. Thompson contributed his own distinctive account of the way the English working class created itself through combat with its enemies. Recently, Dirk Hoerder has reexamined the crowd actions of the American Revolution for signs of the implicit but coherent doctrine of popular sovereignty they expressed; John Brewer has conducted a parallel investigation of English popular ideology in the late eighteenth century; and Michelle Perrot has lovingly portrayed the complexities of nineteenth-century French strikes. These studies, and others like them, constitute a growing third stream in the analysis of popular collective action: taking the definitions and beliefs of the participants seriously; attempting to connect the action with the interests, grievances, and aspirations of everyday; and attaching great importance to the social structures which link the actors to each other, as well as to their rivals, enemies, and exploiters. Within this third stream, Moore's analysis stands out for its stress on justice and—especially—injustice as keys to popular action.

THIS BOOK

Most of the problems addressed by this book come from Moore's essay on injustice. Some of the book's co-authors show greater confidence than Moore in the efficacy of large-scale organization. Some of us insist that a sense of injustice is too pervasive, and rebellion too rare, for one to be a sufficient explanation of the other. Yet, on the whole, the book's analyses of European workers and popular collective action join Moore's in rejecting both tension-release and social-movement accounts of what the participants were about. In general, they involve a determined effort to reconstruct the rationales of the diverse forms of action they portray from the perspectives of the persons and places implicated in the action. For the most part, the analyses assume that collective action is historically specific—that its forms and social bases vary significantly from one time and place to another and show the cumulated effects of past experience. Recurrently, they turn on an old compelling question: How often, and under what conditions, does class conflict provide the basis of popular collective action? In all these regards, the historical studies in this book address the same basic questions as did Moore's inquiry. That they should sometimes use different methods from Moore's, and sometimes come up with different answers, only adds to the interest of the comparison.

After wandering around the world in search of ideas about "the social bases of obedience and revolt," Moore settled down to a detailed examination of the experiences of German workers in the heyday of industrialization. Our ideas have a narrower scope, while the cases we consider cover a wider range. Basically, the ideas come from two main sources: (1) thinking about the impact of capitalism and large-scale organization on the lives of different sorts of workers and on their capacity to control their lives, and (2) thinking about the character of collective action.

The cases at hand concentrate in western Europe—especially France and Britain—from 1750 to World War I. Often, the studies reported in the book ask how the development of capitalism and the growth of large-scale organization affected the fates of particular western European populations and altered the ways in which they acted together on shared interests. Not all the studies fit that pattern neatly: Samuel Cohn's investigation of labor discipline in British railway construction, for example, aims mainly at explaining the behavior of employers, not of their employees. But Wayne Te Brake's patient tracing of the class bases of political alignments in small-town Holland during the eighteenth-century Patriot Movement, Frank Munger's vast survey of the various forms of working-class contention in Lancashire from 1750 to 1830, and almost all the other papers deal with the ways in which ordinary working people coped with change—and, particularly, in what circumstances they managed to band together for action.

Class conflict and collective action? Any names we attach to our inquiries invite controversy. We dare to speak of "class conflict" because so many of the struggles portrayed in this book pitted sets of people who occupied similar positions with respect to the means of production—social classes, that is, or fragments of them—against others who occupied different positions. That usage opens us to the objection that the people involved did not cast their action in terms of class, were not truly aware of their class interests, or defined their enemies inaccurately. To these hypothetical objections we can only reply that such demanding standards for class conflict nearly banish class conflict from history; however engaging the vision of workers speaking articulately in class terms and acting decisively on the basis of an accurate assessment of their interests and enemies, the event itself has been rare indeed. We settle for a less demanding, and wider-ranging, conception of class conflict.

We choose the abstract term *collective action* over the familiar "protest" or "rebellion" for two reasons. First, the conventional vocabulary—not only "protest" and "rebellion" but also "disorder," "disturbance," and similar terms—prejudges the intentions and political position of the actors, usually from the perspective of authorities. The idea of collective action applies more or less equally to actors who are determined to tear down the system and those who seek minor reforms, to the outcast and the privileged, to the successful and the ineffectual. Second, collective action covers a wide range of behavior whose connections and common properties deserve attention: not only almost all behavior which authorities call "protest," "rebellion," or one of the other disparaging epithets, but also petitioning, parading, bloc voting, and any number of other ways of acting together which authorities tolerate or even encourage. In the history we are examining, a number of forms of action have crossed the line between illegal and acceptable behavior; witness the legalization of the strike in country after country. Why let the boundary of our subject matter depend on the attitude of the authorities? Collective action, for our purposes, consists of all occasions on which sets of people commit pooled resources, including their own efforts, to common ends. Our historical work consists of discovering which sets of people, which resources, which common ends, and which forms of commitment were involved in different places and times. Did the configurations change systematically with the advances of capitalism and large organizations?

The chapters in this book suggest a cautious "yes." Of course, they are not alone. Social movement historians normally tell their stories in terms of cumulative learning, of a maturing movement: the labor movement, the drive for suffrage or feminism, comes of age; Michael Vester's analysis of "the development of the proletariat as a learning process" in England from 1792 to 1848 is simply an extreme version of a standard analysis (Vester, 1970). George Rudé has long insisted on the difference between "pre-industrial" and "industrial" protests, with Chartism marking the British watershed between spontaneous, backward-looking direct action and organized, structured displays of strength (for example, 1978: 52-58). John Stevenson declares that the "great change which appears to lie in the period under discussion [1700-1870] is the growth of organised and pacific means of articulating demands" (1979: 316). Yet the papers we have collected here make their own contribution to the discussion, for they bring out the connection between alterations in the forms of contention and changes in the structures of production and power.

The following chapters make that contribution on the small scale and the large. On the small scale, they show us ordinary people fashioning or selecting means of action which fit their own interests, organization, and understanding of the world. Laura Frader, for example, lends insight into the correspondence between the proletarian condition of Coursan's vineyard workers on one hand and their rejection of socialist electoral politics for strikes and direct action on the other. She draws attention, furthermore, to the ways in which the organization of production in fairly large *domaines* worked by teams which were collectively responsible and collectively paid promoted unionization and mutualism among the day laborers. In a similar fashion, Wayne Te Brake's thoughtful consideration of enclosures in the Dutch province of Overijssel leads to a plausible explanation of an anomaly: that the same rural people who invaded the lands recently acquired by bourgeois landowners—and thereby demonstrated their determination to defend the old organization of the village—should align themselves with the reforming Patriot movement, and against the counterrevolutionaries, of the 1780s.

In the course of the book, such small-scale insights eventually join into an important large-scale observation: that the twin processes of capital concentration and proletarianization were transforming the interests and organization of most groups in western Europe from 1750 to 1914. That transformation altered their capacity and propensity for collective action, altering their choice of forms of action as well. In general, the confrontation between the expropriators and the expropriated become sharper, broader, and more visible. Proletarianization by no means created class conflict, but it did widen class conflict's scope. The artisans and peasants who played such important parts in eighteenth-century conflicts often resisted the effects of capital concentration and proletarianization vigorously. As the twin process moved on, however, wage workers and landless agricultural laborers who had little interest in maintaining the old organization of the craft or the village took up the cudgels against the capitalists. Frank Munger's tracing of Lancashire's contentious gatherings from the eighteenth to the nineteenth century shows that great change in motion. Brian Brown then caps Munger's analysis by demonstrating the prominence of proletarian interests, and of proletarians themselves, in the actions of Lancashire Chartism. George Rudé's "pre-industrial" and "industrial" forms of protest might better bear the labels "early capitalist" and "late capitalist."

REPERTOIRES OF COLLECTIVE ACTION

For the purposes of this book, however, it will be sufficient to distinguish eighteenth-century from nineteenth-century collective action—with the clear understanding of a gray zone between the centuries rather than instant transition. Let us think of the repertoires of collective action which prevailed in western Europe during each of the two centuries. The analogy of actors choosing among the limited number of performances with which they are familiar, and of audiences prepared to jeer, cheer, and understand the actors' interpretations, nicely captures the learning and circumscribed choice involved in all real-life collective action—at the risk of understating the seriousness with which real-life actors commonly take their parts. People *learn* how to strike, to invade fields, to burn in effigy, just as they fail to learn a great many other forms of action which they might, in theory, employ to advance their interests. What is more, each learned form of collective action acquires a sort of standing within some defined population as others learn to interpret it and react to it: The first strike is a mystery, the second an outrage, the thousandth a problem to be dealt with. We can thus speak reasonably of any coherent population as having a limited repertoire of collective action within which its members ordinarily make choices when they have collective claims to advance.

In western Europe, the prevailing eighteenth-century repertoire differed significantly from the modes of collective action Europeans employ today.

Its most dramatic recurrent forms were the food riot, concerted resistance to conscription, organized invasions of fields and forests, and rebellion against tax-collectors. Less visible, but in some ways more influential, were established public festivals and rituals during which ordinary people voiced demands or complaints, and stated assemblies of corporate groups—communities, gilds, religious congregations, and the like—which produced petitions, lawsuits, condemnations, and occasionally even deliberate acts of rebellion. Seen by twentieth-century eyes, these eighteenth-century forms of collective action have exotic features, such as the frequent use of costumes and disguises (men in blackface or dressed as women, for example), displays of effigies and symbols of the crowd's enemies, or the ritual sacking of a wrongdoer's dwelling. The recurrent adoption of the authorities' own expected means of action (in mock trials and executions, for instance, or in the seizure of grain for public sale which lay at the center of many food riots) communicated a kind of contingent subordination with which we are no longer familiar. These and other traits marked a distinctive eighteenth-century repertoire of collective action.

The repertoire which came to dominate nineteenth-century collective action looked quite different. Its most visible recurrent forms were the demonstration, the protest meeting, the strike, the electoral rally—essentially the means by which aggrieved Europeans today air their grievances collectively. Much more so than during the eighteenth century, participants in these and related forms of action tended to organize their presentations of claims around named special-interest associations; to assemble deliberately (and numerously, if possible) in symbolically significant public places; to address their message to the public as well as to the immediate objects of their claims; and to convey the message in writing via signs, banners, pamphlets, and badges.

It misses the mark to call these forms of collective action more "organized" than the eighteenth-century forms, although on the average they were certainly larger in scale. Their organizational bases simply differed. Nor is it accurate to declare that the later forms contrasted with the earlier ones by being more "political," although *national* politics certainly loomed much larger in the run-of-the-mill nineteenth-century action. For ordinary eighteenth-century people, food, taxes, and enclosed fields were the stuff of politics. From the eighteenth to the nineteenth century, the locus of relevant politics shifted. New organizational bases and new loci for the power-holders involved separating the later repertoire from the earlier.

But how did the forms of action themselves change? How and why did the food riot, the tax rebellion, the invasion of fields, the raucous street theater, and the other standard ways of voicing eighteenth-century demands give way to the strike, the demonstration, the public meeting, the electoral rally, and the other means of contention which came to predominate in the nineteenth and twentieth centuries? Changes in interest and organization alone are not clear explanations for the emergence of specific and widely used new routines. The harder we stare at the question, the clearer it becomes that something is missing.

The missing element is the political process. The chapters in this book offer many clues to the significance of the state, the structure of power, and the organization of routine politics in shaping and reshaping collective action. Frank Munger and Brian Brown themselves insist on the influence of governmental repression over the costs and benefits of different forms of contention. Louise Tilly's review of the conditions under which French women became involved in collective action begins with the reorganization of production from household to firm, but also accords importance to the shift of political power and resources from the local community to the national state. Judy Reardon's examination of French and Belgian workers in nineteenth-century Roubaix confirms the existence of economic divisions between the two groups, but then goes on to show how nationality itself could divide the working class. In the guise of parliamentary investigation and "external influence," government and the structure of power even peep around the corners of Samuel Cohn's resolutely economist and organizational analysis of labor discipline in the British railways.

These repeated references to politics do not, in themselves, amount to an account of how repertoires of collective action change. They point the way, however, toward a fuller appreciation of two political facts: (1) If people learn repertoires, they learn them as a function of the response of other parties to their collective action, emphatically including the response of government authorities. (2) Governments and power-holders themselves have interests in fostering some forms of collective action, tolerating others, and eliminating still others from the scene. To some extent, as a result, the differential response of authorities and power-holders to different forms of collective action reshapes subsequent action. Where the likely benefits from a repressed and a tolerated action are roughly equal, generally speaking, groups tend to press and to innovate within or just adjacent to the tolerated area.

Although this sounds like paradise for power-holders, they, too, face constraints: Repression costs plenty and diverts resources from other advantageous undertakings; and powerholders acquire vested interests in maintaining certain forms of collective action to the extent that they, their supporters, and their allies employ those forms. Twentieth-century ruling parties have often declared the opposition parties illegal and have sometimes made their declarations stick; but that way of behaving undermines the electoral process itself. In the Europe we examine in this book, governments based on broad bourgeois coalitions generally had trouble curtailing the use of the forms of electoral politics for the articulation of radical demands and complaints. Bourgeois blocs came to power with demands for the regularization of elections and the broadening of the electorate. They retained some commitment to civil liberties, to rights of assembly, association, expression, and opposition. They behaved as though the alternative to electoral politics was something worse. Skilled at organizing campaigns, speaking through the press, and appealing to the public at large, bourgeois blocs developed vested interests in maintaining the apparatus of electoral politics. Governments which depended on their support could only tamper with the apparatus very tentatively.

The expansion of electoral politics legitimated and rewarded forms of collective action which had previously been little known, dangerous, unproductive, or all three. Under a regime of elections, special-purpose associations, statements of programs, displays of strength, solicitations of popular support, and threats to withdraw support all acquired a legitimacy and effectiveness they had lacked under most eighteenth-century conditions. They compounded into the actions in the new nineteenth-century repertoire: the protest meeting, the demonstration, the rally, and the strike.

Did the mere introduction of electoral mechanics cause all these changes? I believe that the development of elections which made some small difference to the distribution of power did, indeed, promote the creation of electoral, quasi-electoral, and pseudo-electoral means of collective action. But the fundamental processes were (1) capital concentration/ proletarianization, with its widening of the division between owners and workers and its creation of bourgeois hegemony; and (2) the focusing of power in the national state, which necessarily decreased the extent to which the actions of local communities, landlords, gilds, churches, and other eighteenth-century holders of power determined the fates of ordinary Europeans. The combination of the two produced national electoral politics and gave them their importance. The concentration of capital and the growth of the national state, in the final analysis, set the stage for the decline of the eighteenth-century repertoire and the rise of its nineteenth-century successor.

Discovering the nineteenth century to be the age of capital and national states will strike some readers—demanding souls!—as less than novel. The novelty, if any, lies in recognizing the intimate connection of the alteration in collective-action repertoires on one side to the concentration of capital and the growth of national states on the other. In the course of these large processes, the interests and organization of ordinary people changed, the loci of power over their lives shifted, and their opportunities to act together in different ways altered. Ordinary people responded by creating and adopting new forms of collective action. The studies in this book deal with different aspects of that complex of change and creation.

WHAT IS COMING

Never fear! The essays which follow do not stagger along, burdened by abstract definitions and ensnarled in coils of concepts. My fellow authors do not spend their time in self-conscious elaboration and testing of the analysis I have just laid out. They fix their problems in time and space, then get on with the business of description and analysis. Some of the studies—notably those by Frank Munger on "contentious gatherings" in Lancashire and Samuel Cohn on labor discipline in British railway construction—read a bit more like social science than the others, since they draw deliberately on recent theoretical work and employ formal statistical analyses. Some of them—Brian Brown's study of Lancashire in the 1840s is the outstanding example—grapple openly with large questions of political and social theory. But even these self-conscious confrontations with very general problems occur in the course of sustained efforts to describe and understand the particularities of real people in stipulated places during delimited time periods. This introduction raises the level of abstraction only in order to identify the chapters' common ground, much as one clambers up a mountain to grasp the pattern of the whole valley below.

We have arranged the papers in a roughly chronological order. My contribution, "The Web of Contention in Eighteenth-Century Cities," sketches the repertoires of popular collective action in London, Charleston, and Paris toward the end of the eighteenth century, with an eye toward the dominance of new forms of contention during the nineteenth. In "Revolution and the Rural Community in the Eastern Netherlands," Wayne Te Brake traces the class bases of political alignments in small-town Holland during the Patriot Movement—a series of conflicts which R. R. Palmer has treated as an early phase of the western Democratic Revolution. Frank Munger's "Contentious Gatherings in Lancashire, England: 1750-1830" reports a dense, sophisticated analysis of the changing character of events involving popular collective action over a major period of industrial concentration and working-class mobilization. Under the title "Industrial Capitalism, Political Conflict, and Working-Class Contention in Lancashire," Brian Brown offers a concentrated, effective study of working-class action in 1842, a pivot of Chartist contention. "Keeping the Navvies in Line," by Samuel Cohn, presents an ingenious and informative treatment of the determinants of different sorts of work discipline—for example, the use of the truck system and long pay intervals—in the construction of British railways during the early nineteenth century. Judy Reardon's "Belgian and French Workers in Nineteenth-Century Roubaix" brings out the importance of foreign workers in the economy and, to some extent, the politics of a nineteenth-century mill city. In the course of her "Grapes of Wrath: Vineyard Workers, Labor Unions, and Strike Activity in the Aude: 1860-1913," set in a classic area of "industrial" winegrowing, Laura Frader grounds a careful portrayal of winegrower politics in an analysis of regional economic change. Louise Tilly's "Women's Collective Action and Feminism in France, 1870-1914" explores three overlapping problems: (1) how women got involved in various forms of French collective action from the Commune to World War I, (2) the conditions under which women acted on their shared interests *as women,* and (3) the extent to which French feminism represented and appealed to those interests. The book's conclusion, also by Louise Tilly, reviews the individual papers and draws out their implications for the history of class conflict and collective action.

In the preface to his book, *Injustice,* Moore reflects:

> Though the time may be rapidly approaching when a comparative history of Western industrial workers—and not just labor movements involving a small minority of these workers—may be feasible and profitable, this did not seem possible to me at the time I began serious work on this work, more than ten years ago. Most of the

secondary literature consisted of books about what theorists *thought* masses of ordinary workers felt, or else were rather detailed blow-by-blow accounts of the history of national labor movements [1978: xiv].

If our collection of studies helps make that comparative history more feasible and more profitable, it will have served its purpose.

2

The Web of Contention in
Eighteenth-Century Cities

CHARLES TILLY

FEARING THE MOB

"Dear Son," wrote the fussy old fellow in London to his son in New Jersey,

Since my last . . . nothing has been talked or thought of here but elections. There have been amazing contests all over the kingdom, £ 20 or 30,000 of a side spent in several places, and inconceivable mischief done by debauching the people and making them idle, besides the immediate actual mischief done by drunken mad mobs to houses, windows, &c. The scenes have been horrible. London was illuminated two nights running at the command of the mob for the success of Wilkes in the Middlesex election; the second night

We gratefully acknowledge permission from Yale University Press to quote extensively from W. B. Wilcox, editor, *The Papers of Benjamin Franklin, Vol. 15* (1972: 98-99, 129).

exceeded anything of the kind ever seen here on the greatest occasions of rejoicing, as even the small cross streets, lanes, courts, and other out-of-the-way places were all in a blaze with lights, and the principal streets all night long, as the mobs went round again after two o'clock, and obliged people who had extinguished their candles to light them again. Those who refused had all their windows destroyed. . . . Tis really an extraordinary event, to see an outlaw and exile, of bad personal character, not worth a farthing, come over from France, set himself up as candidate for the capital of the kingdom, miss his election only by being too late in his application, and immediately carrying it for the principal county. The mob (spirited up by numbers of different ballads sung or roared in every street) requiring gentlemen and ladies of all ranks as they passed in their carriages to shout for Wilkes and liberty, marking the same words on all their coaches and chalk, and No. 45 on every door; which extends a vast way along the roads into the country [Franklin, 1972: 98-99].

The time was April 1768; the writer, our future revolutionary Benjamin Franklin.

The Wilkes in question was the gentleman, journalist, rake, and demagogue John Wilkes. Wilkes had entered Parliament as Member for Aylesbury in 1757. In April 1763, issue 45 of Wilkes' paper, *The North Briton*, printed a veiled criticism of the King's speech at the opening of Parliament. For that article, Wilkes was briefly imprisoned in the Tower of London, and the executioner burned No. 45 publicly in Cheapside. In 1764, Wilkes was expelled from the House of Commons, sentenced to jail, then declared an outlaw. Now he had not only reprinted the infamous No. 45, but also printed a pornographic parody of Pope's *Essay on Man* (entitled, to be sure, *Essay on Woman*), and then fled the country. After spending four years in leisurely but increasingly debt-ridden exile on the continent, Wilkes slipped back into Britain early in 1768. He appealed unsuccessfully for a pardon, failed in a bid for one parliamentary seat, and then (in March of 1768) won election to a seat in Middlesex. Benjamin Franklin's letter to his son described the riotous Wilkite victory celebration of the twenty-ninth of March.

Wilkes' 1768 parliamentary campaign affronted the establishment in its direct appeal to the electorate—an appeal by an outlaw, no less. Despite the narrowness of that eighteenth-century electorate, the entire campaign smacked of popular sovereignty. It challenged the principle of virtual representation. It threatened the power of the authorities to place their allies and clients in Parliament and, by extension, in the government itself. The whiff of popular sovereignty did not please Benjamin Franklin either. In describing the Wilkite celebrations, Franklin used the language of the authorities. The word was not "crowd," or "assembly," or "gathering," but *mob*. Mobs are gatherings of dangerous people performing improper acts. Mobs make riots. Riots, in the language of the authorities, are collective actions (whether violent or not) whose impropriety justifies the use of force to terminate them. Related words in the eighteenth-century lexicon are *outrage* and *sedition*. The words are essentially political labels; they set a distance between the observer and the actors, mark a line between responsible and irresponsible means of pursuing interests. As such, the categories are important. They affect the way the authorities behave. In the eighteenth-century setting, their use deserves the closest study. But as categories for historical and sociological analysis, words such as mob, riot, outrage, and sedition obscure much of what is going on.

As it happens, over the past twenty years students of the eighteenth century have played the largest part in revealing what social realities lie in, and behind, the events authorities call riots or seditions. In Britain, we have only to think of the work of E. P. Thompson, George Rudé, Walter Shelton, and John Stevenson. In America, historians of the American Revolution such as Dirk Hoerder and Jesse Lemisch have made important contributions to "history from below." In France, the Revolution of 1789 has attracted the lion's share of the attention, with recent studies by Mona Ozouf and Lynn Hunt showing us that there are still important things to be learned about the revolutionary crowd. Yves-Marie Bercé, the ubiquitous George Rudé, and others have extended the analysis of popular collective action both before and after the revolution. Other western countries have produced similar historiographies; the study of the crowd in history has become something of an international enterprise. Social, political, and economic historians have shown us how to use the record of popular collective action to bring inarticulate ordinary people back into the history they lived and made.

LONDON'S POPULAR COLLECTIVE ACTION

Following the insights of this by now well-established historical approach, let us look more carefully at the popular collective action of London in 1768 before moving to observations and reflections on other eighteenth-century cities. By "popular collective action" I mean simply the various means by which ordinary people who share an interest, grievance, or aspiration band together to act in their common interest. Some of those means are hard to trace because they involve the routine use of personal influence and daily contacts, or because the actors deliberately hid their action from the authorities and thereby from the historical record. We can make a start on the problem by concentrating on contentious gatherings: occasions on which people assembled and made visible claims on other people via declarations, attacks, petitions, symbolic displays, or other means.

Contentious gatherings have a greater chance of entering the historical record than most other forms of popular collective action, since they are (almost by definition) observable, since observers find them interesting, and since authorities commonly seek to control them in one way or another. We can gain some sense of the web of collective action in general by examining the form and content of contentious gatherings in eighteenth-century London and other cities and then asking what the often exotic character of those gatherings has to do with the structure of the eighteenth-century city.

Let me stress again that many other scholars have taken up these problems—indeed, have worked over many of the same materials and events we are examining here. Furthermore, my own current research on these matters is still far from complete. This is not, then, a report of new and original research but a survey of where we stand and where we go from here. For the materials of popular collective action in eighteenth-century cities provide exciting opportunities for further reflection and research: opportunities to identify the links between what we loosely call "protest" and the routine ways in which people pursue their interests; to see how the particular geographic and social structure of the eighteenth century shaped the character of collective action; to specify the relationship between the large social changes going on in the eighteenth century and the local grievances which became visible in contentious gatherings; and, finally, to examine how the repertoire of available means of action was changing, and why.

When Benjamin Franklin witnessed the Wilkite electoral celebration of 1768, he had been in London representing the interests of several American colonies for over a year. Giant London had the wherewithal to impress even so sophisticated a provincial as Franklin. The metropolis was a sprawling agglomeration centered on the twin cities of London and Westminster. With three-quarters of a million people, greater London was then very likely the world's largest city. It served as Britain's capital, manufacturing center, and commercial metropolis. It commanded a thriving, if turbulent, empire. It was the hurricane's eye of eighteenth-century industrialization. The metropolis of the time was dividing itself increasingly into a commercial center based on the old City of London: a rich, fashionable West embracing parks, squares, avenues, and palaces; a crowded industrial East, especially rundown and dense near the busy docks of the Thames.

The window-breaking celebration of the Wilkites had extended from the City over to the fine houses and public buildings of Westminster. Franklin himself lived in Craven Street, off the Strand. That put him by the river, only a stone's throw from Charing Cross, not far from Whitehall—between Parliament and St. James's on one side and the commercial centers of the City on the other. It also placed him just off the primary path of frequent processions and marches. These commonly originated at Mansion House or some other symbolically charged location in the City and then proceeded, soberly or tumultuously, down the Strand toward Parliament or St. James's. Charing Cross was, in fact, the choice-point: south toward Parliament or west toward the royal palace. The Wilkites of 1768 broke windows at the Duke of Northumberland's, in Charing Cross, a few steps away from Franklin's house; they may well have rushed down Franklin's street as well.

Franklin's disdain for the London crowd was not a momentary aberration. In May 1768, Franklin wrote the following to Joseph Galloway:

> While I am writing, a great mob of coal porters fill the street, carrying a wretch of their business upon poles to be ducked, and otherwise punished at their pleasure for working at the old wages. All respect to law and government seems to be lost among the common people, who are moreover continually enflamed by seditious scribblers to trample on authority and every thing that used to keep them in order [1972: 127].

That same day (May 14) he wrote to John Ross:

> Even this Capital, the Residence of the King, is now a daily Scene of lawless Riot and Confusion. Mobs are patrolling the Streets at Noon Day, some Knocking all down that will not roar for Wilkes and Liberty: Courts of Justice afraid to give Judgment against him: Coalheavers and Porters pulling down the Houses of Coal Merchants that refuse to give them more Wages; Sawyers destroying the new Sawmills; Sailors unrigging all the outward-bound Ships, and suffering none to sail till Merchants agree to raise their Pay; Watermen

destroying private Boats and threatening Bridges; Weavers entering Houses by Force, and destroying the Work in the Looms; Soldiers firing among the Mobs and killing Men, Women and Children, which seems only to have produc'd a universal Sullenness, that looks like a great black Cloud coming on, ready to burst in a general Tempest [1972: 129].

Thus, the mobs of London, in Franklin's estimation, posed a serious threat to good government. Indeed, all these things had happened recently in London and vicinity. On April 22, a large body of coal heavers, according to *Gentleman's Magazine:*

> assembled in a riotous manner in Wapping, went on board the colliers, and obliged the men who were at work to leave off; so that the business of delivering ships, in the river, is wholly at a stand. . . . This riot was attended with much blood shed, the rioters having met with opposition fought desperately, and several lives were lost [1768: 197].

A week later their leaders met with city officials and made a provisional settlement of the dispute. On the seventh of May, "the sailors assembled in a body in St. George's fields, and went to St. James's, with colours flying, drums beating, and fifes playing, and presented a petition to his majesty, setting forth their grievances, and praying relief" (1768: 262). On the ninth,

> a numerous body of watermen assembled before the mansion house, and laid their complaint before the lord mayor, who advised them, to appoint proper persons to draw up a petition to parliament, which his lordship promised them he would present; upon which they gave him three huzzas and went quietly home. The same night a large mob of another kind assembled before the mansion-house, carrying a gallows with a boot hanging to it, and a red cap; but on some of the ringleaders being secured by the peace-officers, the rest dispersed [1768: 242].

That boot on a gallows, we shall meet again. On the following day,

> A large body of sawyers assembled and pulled down the saw-mill lately erected by Mr. Dingley at Lymehouse, on pretence that it deprived many workmen of employment. . . . The coal-heavers assembled again . . . this day and rendezvoused in Stepney-fields,

where their numbers considerably increased, and then they repaired with a flag flying, drums beating, and two violins playing before them to Palace-yard, where they were met by Sir John Fielding, who persuaded them to part with their flag, to silence their drums, and to discharge their fidlers; and then talking with their leaders, prevailed upon them to meet some of their masters at his office in the afternoon, and accommodate their differences [1768: 242-243].

That same day, according to *Gentleman's Magazine,*

the mob which has constantly surrounded the King's Bench prison in St. George's-fields, ever since the imprisonment of Mr. Wilkes, grew outrageous; the riot act was read, and the soldiers ordered to fire. Several persons who were passing along the road at a distance were unfortunately killed; and one youth about 17, son to a stable-keeper in the Borough, was singled out, followed, and shot dead, in an outhouse where he had fled for shelter [p. 242].

In the Wilkite legend, this event came to be known as the Massacre of St. George's Fields. Only a few days (and a few riots) later, Benjamin Franklin wrote his gloomy diagnosis of the capital's condition: enfeebled by sedition and infected with Wilkism.

The Wilkite fever was, in fact, still raging. At the end of April, Wilkes had gone to jail, had been released temporarily, only to be sentenced to 22 months in prison. During the judicial maneuvering, his supporters had thronged the streets, broken windows, and attended his every move.

Even pragmatic Americans, Franklin regretted to observe, showed a culpable sympathy for the mob. As he wrote to William Franklin in October 1768,

Wilkes is extinguished. I am sorry to see in the American papers that some People there are so indiscreet as to distinguish themselves in applauding his No. 45, which I suppose they do not know was a Paper in which their King was personally affronted, whom I am sure they love and honour. It hurts you here with sober sensible Men, when they see you so easily infected with the Madness of English Mobs [Franklin, 1972: 224].

Wilkes was not so easily extinguished as that. When Franklin wrote to his son, Wilkes was comfortably ensconced in the King's Bench Prison, keeping good company and biding his time. In 1769, while still in prison, he won election as a London alderman, found himself expelled from Parliament, then won four more elections to his Middlesex seat, only to be disqualified each time. On all these occasions and more, London crowds celebrated or acted out their disapproval in the streets. Wilkes was yet to become Sheriff in 1771, to be named Lord Mayor in 1774, and finally to reenter Parliament that same year. From those establishment positions, he continued to bombard the King and the Commons with protests and demands. He became a major British defender of American rights. Across the Atlantic, Americans treated Wilkes as an ally, a hero, and a symbol of liberty. On both sides of the ocean, "Wilkes and Liberty" became the rallying cry of opposition to royal policy.

AMERICAN VARIANTS

On the first of October 1768, for example, an electoral assembly of "Mechanicks and other inhabitants" took place in Charleston, South Carolina. After the choice of nominees for the provincial legislature, the electors gathered at a live oak in a nearby pasture, dubbed it their Liberty Tree, and drank many a patriotic toast.

> In the evening, the tree was decorated with 45 lights, and 45 sky-rockets were fired. About 8 o'clock, the whole company, preceded by 45 of their number, carrying as many lights, marched in regular procession to town, down King Street and Broad Street, to Mr. Robert Dillon's tavern; where the 45 lights being placed upon the table, with 45 bowls of punch, 45 bottles of wine, and 92 glasses [for the 92 Anti-Rescinders of Massachusetts Bay], they spent a few hours in a new round of toasts, among which, scarce a celebrated Patriot of Britain or America was omitted; and preserving the same good order and regularity as had been observed throughout the day, at 10 they retired [South Carolina Gazette, October 3, 1768].

Wilkes was, of course, among the many patriots hailed on that occasion. By then the equation had greatly simplified: 45 = Wilkes = Liberty = the colonial cause. Ben Franklin was right to think that Americans were applauding Wilkes' No. 45 but wrong to think they were unaware of its strong, subversive political message.

The officials and merchants of South Carolina were joining the opposition. On the South Carolina frontier, the substantial vigilantes who came to be known as the Regulators were establishing their own courts and governments in defiance of royal decree. In Charleston, both the provincial assembly and the merchants were following the lead of Massachusetts in asserting claims of provincial rights which bordered on claims of popular sovereignty. What is more, previously disfranchised citizens were demanding the right to take part in the election of the assembly which was to convene late in October—and which would approve the nonimportation agreement against British goods the following month. As Lieutenant Governor Bull reported on the 10th of September,

> it will be difficult to guess at the complexion of the New Assembly, which will be the Representative of a great Number of Constituents, who tho' freeholders (consisting of above 4000 sensible Men, half the strength of this province) have hitherto been considered as not having a clear right to vote in any particular Parish, from the uncertainty of boundaries between the Parishes. They have lately resolved to make use of this right, & been at the trouble of running the dividing lines far westward to ascertain the Parish in which their settlement is situated [Public Record Office, London, Colonial Office 5/409].

Although the lieutenant governor dissolved the new assembly as soon as it dared to join the nonimportation agreement, its election initiated a struggle between the king's lieutenant and the provincial legislature in which the provincials steadily expanded their claims to mint, to incur debt, to approve or disapprove taxation, to resist royal decrees, and to make laws on behalf of the colony's people. The struggle ended with the lieutenant governor's flight from the revolutionary armies a decade later. The conflict in the legislature ran on more decorously than the festivities in the streets, but they moved in parallel lines. John Wilkes symbolized the popular line.

Wilkes' dramatic personification of the principle of liberty has recently led Richard Sennett to see in Wilkism the stirrings of privatism, the beginning of the end of Public Man. "From this idea of individual personality as a social principle," writes Sennett, "came ultimately the modern impulse to find political measures worthwhile only to the extent that their champions are 'credible,' 'believable,' 'decent' persons" (Sennett, 1977: 105). It seems to me, however, that in his general argument and in the specific case of Wilkes, Sennett has joined the eighteenth-century authorities in mistaking a challenge to the narrowness of national politics for a threat to principled public politics in general. I am more inclined to accept John Brewer's recent interpretation of Wilkism as, at bottom, a principled challenge to indirect rule. Later I will also stress the role of the Wilkites in the development of a set of political techniques and precedents which cleared the way for a politics of large-scale popular mobilization via voluntary special-interest associations. Yet Sennett has his finger on something significant: the emergence in the later eighteenth century of a type of demagogue (in the literal sense of the word) who would become a prominent figure in the politics of the nineteenth century. It is that sense of things to come, as much as the colorful character of Wilkes the man, that draws historian after historian to reflect on his career.

The details of Wilkes' career—and the career of his reputation—are rich and fascinating. There is the ugly debauchee himself, one of the great political entrepreneurs. There is the implicit debate between virtual representation and popular sovereignty posed by his later career. There is, most important for our purposes, the rambunctious creativity of the eighteenth-century urban crowd. The handful of events we have already reviewed show us the frequent use of music and parade: flying colors, drums, fifes, violins, tendentious ballads. They show us the display of dramatic symbols, such as a gallows and a boot to portray the crowd's punning condemnation of the king's favorite, Lord Bute. They show us the chalking of the magic number 45, the forced illumination, the vengeful breaking of unlighted windows, and many more actions which, as cultural forms, belong unmistakably to the eighteenth century. If we followed Wilkes and his supporters further, we would also observe them organizing giant marches across London in which the pretext was the presentation of petitions to Parliament, staging elaborate tableaus (rich with symbols such as the number 45, the gallows, and the liberty cap) in public places, and performing in a variety of other ways which, to twentieth-century minds, touch on street theater, mardi gras celebrations, circus parades—or perhaps college pep rallies.

Lest we think that popular creativity was somehow confined to Wilkism, however, we have only to turn our observations of Charleston back two or three years to the time of the Stamp Act crisis in the American colonies. On the October 19, 1765, for example, a group of Charleston patriots erected in mid-city a twenty-foot gallows bearing three images: a devil, a stamp-tax distributor, and a boot surmounted by a head with a Scotch bonnet, an allusion to Lord Bute. At the end of the day, the crowd removed the figures from the gallows, loaded them into a wagon, marched them to the house of the probable local stamp-tax distributor, broke a few windows there, demanded the surrender of any stamped papers, found none, proceeded to the Green, and ceremoniously burned the effigies. "The bells of St. Michael's church," according to the South Carolina *Gazette,* "rang muffled all day; and, during the procession, there was a most solemn knell for the burial of a coffin, on which was inscribed, AMERICAN LIBERTY" (October 31, 1765: 2). The same sort of pageantry, with or without references to Wilkes, characterized Charleston's displays of opposition to royal policy from that time to the outbreak of the war with the mother country.

Celebrations and declarations of support, for that matter, also had more of a festival air than we are accustomed to in our sober twentieth century. When the news of the Stamp Act's repeal reached Charleston in May of 1765, reports the South Carolina *Gazette,* the companies of artillery and light infantry

> appeared under Arms, and went through their Exercise, Firing &c.... In the Evening the Town was handsomely illuminated, and the Day closed with Loyalty and Mirth, echoing with loyal Toasts to his Majesty King George the Third ... the great Patriot, Mr. Pitt, ... and our other worthy friends in England [May 6, 1766: 2; elipses in original].

These were the rituals of public celebration: illuminations, toasts, marches, displays of colors. Essentially the same displays, for example, appeared in Charleston on the king's birthday, at least when the king was favored there. Charlestonians used the same symbols, actions, and occasions for celebration and execration, for support and opposition. They were, in short, a general set of means for stating political positions.

Here we touch on some characteristics of eighteenth-century popular collective action which are fascinating to follow in detail but which I mention here only in passing. Popular collective action employed a vocabulary of words, symbols, and gestures which was rich, varied, expressive, and purposeful, yet broader than any particular application. It was a vocabulary held in common, available for a variety of needs. People drew on much the same vocabulary, with appropriate changes of emphasis, to express favor and disfavor. Often a negative performance had a positive twin, and vice versa; in the case of the widespread cacophonous mocking ceremonies variously called Rough Music, Skimmington, and Shivaree, for instance, people commonly had at their disposal a parallel approving ceremony in the form of the serenade. The moral reprobate received Rough Music, while the moral hero (including, sometimes, the reprobate who had made amends) received a serenade.

There was, moreover, a good deal of continuity between the displays of sentiment which were authorized, or even promoted, by the authorities and those which ordinary people undertook despite—or even in opposition to—the authorities. That continuity was a matter not only of vocabulary but also of basic form and content. The most direct continuity lay in the fact that authorized public gatherings such as scheduled markets, holiday celebrations, and hangings so regularly provided the occasions on which ordinary people gave collective voice to their grievances, hopes, and demands. In addition to that continuity, popular collective action often *consisted* of a crowd's performance of a routine which was normally the function of the authorities—indeed, which ordinary people thought the authorities themselves had failed to perform. That was the secret of the so-called food riot, in which the pivotal actions were the forced inventory of grain in private hands, the seizure of excess grain for placement in a public store, the blockage of grain scheduled to be shipped out of the locality, and the forced sale of food to the local poor at a price below the prevailing market—all measures the authorities took in times of high prices and short supply. But it was also the essence of a number of actions which the American colonists took in the course of the struggles leading up to the revolution: the substitution of people's courts for the royal equivalent, the tearing down of stamp distributors' premises, the ceremonious destruction of tea. Hanging and burning in effigy fell into the same category, for they were legal punishments commonly visited upon miscreants who were convicted in absentia.

The final continuity casts a new light on those I have already mentioned. It lies in the fact that so much popular collective action addressed itself directly to the local authorities, and in a style one might call aggressive supplication: aggressive, in that the postulants clearly conveyed the threat to take the law into their own hands but supplication, nonetheless, in that the people involved are prepared to cease and disband if only the authority in question will play the proper patron. The standard sequence occurred in the May 1768 confrontation of the coal-heavers with Sir John Fielding, who "persuaded them to part with their flag, to silence their drums, and to discharge their fidlers" on his proposal to arrange talks with the coal-masters. What lies behind this sequence is general reliance on elite patronage to pursue an interest. The distance between a politics of deference and a politics of direct action was much less than our twentieth-century experience would lead us to expect. The deference was contingent on the proper performance of the authorities, and the alternative was not far away: It was direct action against, or instead of, the authorities. Mutiny, the characteristic rebellion of patron-client structures, was a general form of eighteenth-century revolt.

All these forms of collective action and of rebellion rested on a series of crucial assumptions: that ordinary people grouped into more or less corporate bodies—communities, gilds, religious groupings, and the like—which exercised collective rights; that the law protected those rights; that the authorities had an obligation to respect and enforce the law; that the chosen spokesmen of a corporate body had the right and obligation to make public statements of their grievances and demands. During the eighteenth century, as C. B. Macpherson has long insisted, the extension of the theory and practice of capitalist property relations (of possessive individualism, to use Macpherson's phrase) was undermining the premises of such a corporate system. The rapidly growing number of landless wage-laborers, for example, caused increasing damage to the principle that they were essentially servants, dependents of farms or shops whose masters represented them and whose collective interest was their own. The demand for popular sovereignty threatened a fundamental alteration of the system. But in the meantime the available forms of collective action assumed the system's existence.

Most of these observations apply to eighteenth-century Anglo-American social life in general, and not only to that of Anglo-American cities. What was special about the cities? Because of its relatively great differentiation by trade, neighborhood, creed, and place of origin, the eighteenth-century city served as the repository of a popular culture solidly premised on the rights and vigor of corporate communities. Yet, at the same time, it served as the spawning-ground for principles and practices which would come to dominate the lives of ordinary people during the nineteenth century. This dual character applied over a wide geographic range—not just London or Charleston but also Milan, Madrid, and a great many other western cities as well. It also applied over a wide range of day-to-day experience: marketing practices, industrial production, popular entertainment, and much more.

We have already had several illustrations of the first side of this dualism. Seen under a good historical lens, Ben Franklin's "mob" differentiates into specific interests. In the London of the 1760s, those interests appear in the form of trades: sailors, coal-heavers, and so on. I now have to qualify something I said earlier: Careful eighteenth-century observers generally made a distinction between a mob and a crowd representing some recognizable interest. A mob, by and large, was a dangerous crowd which, if it could not easily be identified with an established popular interest such as a trade, was the more dangerous for that fact. When the interest was recognizable, the observer commonly said something like "the coal-heavers," "a numerous body of watermen," or "a congregation of Protestant Dissenters." The crucial question was which interests had the right to voice demands and complaints within the city.

We have also seen innovation at work in the Wilkite movement and in the American conflicts which began with the Stamp Act crisis. They were two important elements in a much longer and broader set of changes. Through such organizations as the Sons of Liberty and the Society of Supporters of the Bill of Rights, they expanded the role in popular collective action of voluntary special-interest associations built outside existing corporate structures. In a process too complex to trace here, the urban activists of the later eighteenth century were helping to create a set of organizational forms and performances which would become the standard collective-action repertoire of the nineteenth century: The emergence of the demonstration, the development of the electoral campaign, the spread of the strike, the creation of the social movement all depend to an important degree on struggles and changes which were already visible in major western cities toward the end of the eighteenth century.

Looking only at London and Charleston, one might think these were uniquely Anglo-American developments. The Anglo-American experience *was* special in some regards. The Common Law tradition appears to have made the establishment of a single precedent for a particular organizational form or action peculiarly advantageous to the interest that could claim that precedent. The ability to choose between appealing to Parliament or to the king gave an organized interest room for maneuver which was not available, for example, to its counterpart in Berlin at that time. There are lines of imitation, collaboration, and even causation which run from the British financial arrangements for the Seven Years War and its aftermath to the fiscal conflicts of the 1760s to the struggles (in Britain and America alike) around the American Revolution and thence to the French Revolution of 1789. Nevertheless, the changes in popular collective action we have been tracing transcended the Anglo-American experience and by no means resulted uniquely from that experience. Ultimately, we will have to search for their origins in the expansion of capitalism and the concentration of power in the national state. Those processes loomed large in the British and American experiences, but they occurred widely elsewhere as well.

PREREVOLUTIONARY PARIS

Let us abandon this perilously abstract discussion by hustling across the English Channel and back to concrete cases. A glance or two at eighteenth-century Paris will put the Anglo-American experience into perspective. Our faithful year 1768 was not as turbulent in Paris as in Charleston or London. Yet it did not lack events: During the year the Marquis de Sade was finally incarcerated for his perverse treatment of a woman he proposed to hire as a governess but immediately put to other uses; Queen Marie of France died; the executioner at the Place de Grève set a new record by hanging seven criminals on the same day; the Parlement of Paris confirmed the conviction of a husband and wife for neglect of their child (who died of their ill-treatment) and sentenced the husband to three days in the stocks plus life in the galleys, the wife to perpetual banishment; and the visit of the king of Denmark to Paris, toward the end of the year, set off a round of dazzling balls and banquets.

These news items from 1768 all appear in the journal of Siméon-Prosper Hardy, the bookseller whose day-to-day chronicle of Parisian events, now deposited in the Bibliothèque Nationale (B.N., Manuscrits francais 6680 to 6687) is among our richest sources of both the everyday and the extraordinary events of 1764 to 1789. The relatively forgettable events of 1768 played themselves against the backdrop of rising food prices and increasing misery. In the Paris region, toward the end of the year grain prices reached their highest levels since the crisis of 1740. During the next two decades, only the subsistence crises of 1775 and 1789—two of the weightiest in the entire French experience—would surpass the peak of 1768 (Dupâquier et al., 1968).

Five years earlier, the king had broken with the past by declaring "free trade" in grain to replace the old regime's extensive controls over the movement and sale of cereals. Now a wide debate was raised over the wisdom of free trade. In November 1768, that debate dominated the agenda of an extraordinary "police assembly"—a meeting of high officials responsible for the policing of Paris, in the broad sense of providing for the city's security and welfare. One of the memoranda prepared for the assembly reported:

> The King had made a declaration giving all his subjects freedom to trade in grain, and that declaration of 1763 was registered by the Parlement. The 1767 harvest was spare in all provinces of the kingdom, and the freedom to export meant that much grain and flour left the country, with the result that grain prices rose little by little this year. So much so that in the provinces a pound of bread cost five sous, and in Paris four sous three deniers. There were popular uprisings in several big cities, and the King had to send troops in. Finally the King, moved by pity for his people, arranged

to bring foreign grain into various ports, for distribution in the provinces—all the more useful because the 1768 harvest was not abundant everywhere, and because it had rained continually everywhere, the grain would not be very durable. The officials of Paris extended every effort to deal with the discontent of the poor [AN (Archives Nationales) K 1022].

To the extent that they could do so without attracting royal displeasure, officials reinstated standard controls and interventions.

The measures did not come soon enough to forestall popular indignation. From Brittany and Normandy came news of major food riots. In Paris itself, no major streetfighting or attacks on presumed hoarders occurred; for that, Parisians would have to wait for the enormous food riots of 1775. Nevertheless, some of the standard signs of an old-regime subsistence crisis appeared in the capital. Let us look at only two of the relevant entries in Hardy's journal. The first is for September 14:

Since the king was hunting in the plain of Boulogne with the prince of Soubise and many other lords, the residents of Saint-Cloud and Boulogne, who had prepared memorials on the dearness of bread with the plan of throwing themselves at the king's feet and presenting them, were only able to give them to the chief officers of the guard. . . . The previous day, twelve women of Meudon had kneeled on the Bellevue road, and one of them had shown the king a piece of bread as black as ink [B.N. Fr. 6680].

Meanwhile, people in the city were murmuring as "seditious posters" appeared everywhere. On the seventeenth of November, Hardy reported that

at the Quinze-Vingts gate, rue St. Honoré, across from the rue de Richelieu, where the duc de Choiseul [Minister and Secretary of State] lives, people found a badly-drawn poster showing the king holding a cup and asking alms of the duke, whom the hangman was marching up to the gibbet. They say that they also found a poster stuck up in a church, over the holy-water font, saying PRAY TO GOD FOR THE KING WHO IS DEAF, BLIND AND MUTE [B.N. Fr. 6680].

As it happens, prices began to ease in December, and the threats of "sedition" declined. Yet the scattered and relatively gentle threats of 1768 tell us something about the character or routine contention in eighteenth-century Paris. The strategy of aggressive supplication, which we have already detected in London and Charleston, lies behind the many warnings of direct popular action to secure food at prices poor people can afford to pay: If the king's ministers will do their duty, runs the message, we won't have to do anything unruly. In the process, the popular critics of royal policy maintain the myth of the beneficent king surrounded by corrupt or incompetent ministers. The use of the staged tableau, the obvious visual symbols and forms of popular retribution borrowed directly from official procedures characterized French collective action just as well as that of Britain and America.

To see the dramatization of demands and complaints more clearly, we have only to approach the Revolution of 1789. On Friday, August 29, 1788, Hardy set down this account in his journal:

> Toward seven o'clock at night, the Foot Watch and the Horse Watch having been ordered not to appear in the Palace Quarter, and the rowdy youngsters, backed by the populace, who had planned to come declare a sort of open war on the watch, were emboldened by their absence; the youngsters began to gather on Pont Neuf and at Place Dauphine, in the interior of which people had to close all the shops and illuminate all the facades of all the houses along with those of the rue du Harlay. Toward nine o'clock the populace of the faubourg St. Antoine and the faubourg St. Marcel came to swell the number of the local smart alecks. The disorder grew and grew; instead of sticking to lighting firecrackers, which were already bothersome enough to the inhabitants, they then lit a big fire in the middle of the Place Dauphine. They fed the fire with anything they could find in the vicinity, such as the sentinel's watch-house from the Pont Neuf near the statue of the bronze horse, and the stands of orange and lemon merchants in the same place, which were made of simple planks, the grills of poultry merchants from the Quai de la Vallée, all at the risk of burning the nearby houses. On that fire they burned the effigy of Monseigneur de Lamoignon, the current French Minister of Justice (*Garde des Sceaux*), after having him do public penance for his wrongdoing [B.N. Fr. 6687].

Later, the crowd destroyed the Pont Neuf guardhouse, chased away the Watch, then seized and burned their uniforms and arms before going off to attack guardhouses elsewhere in the city. Before the night ended, a large crowd confronted the Paris Guard in the Place de Grève, and seven or eight people were killed (Rudé, 1959: 32).

Aspects of the gathering of the Place Dauphine are similar to the events we have surveyed in London and Charleston: The illumination, the bonfire, the burning effigy were international symbols. Yet the crowd spoke with a French accent; it shot off petards and used the nearby statue of Henri IV as a reminder of the French people's ancient liberties. The "public penance" imposed on Lamoignon's dummy mimicked the *amende honorable* which was a frequent element of a sentence for a serious crime: Before going to the gibbet, a convicted criminal often had to appear in a public place barefoot and clad in a simple gown, wearing a sign summarizing his offense, carrying a lighted candle, and confessing publicly what he had done.

The participants had more specific reasons for being in the Place than the "rowdy youngsters" Hardy described. The Place Dauphine backed onto the royal courts of justice, and the nucleus of the "youngsters" consisted of law clerks from nearby offices. It is uncertain, despite Hardy's assertions, how many of the participants actually came from the working-class quarters of St. Antoine and St. Marcel. In any case, crowds at the Place Dauphine had for several days been cheering the recall of the popular Finance Minister Necker and acting out a ceremonious trial of his predecessor, the Cardinal Lomenie de Brienne.

At the mock trial of August 27 the effigy of Brienne appeared in glorious episcopal robes. Hardy reported:

> After having carried the mannequin to the equestrian statue of Henri IV, and after having pushed him down on his knees before the statue, they carted him all round the square, then after reading him his death sentence, and making him ask forgiveness of God, the King, the Judiciary, and the Nation, they lifted him into the air at the end of a pole so that everyone could see him better, and finally threw him onto an already-lighted pyre [B.N. Fr. 6687].

In this instance as well, the public apology caricatured a standard feature of the royal punishment for serious crimes. The ringleaders also read a mock decree against Lamoignon, who was responsible for the implementation of a sweeping judicial reorganization; that *soi-disant* reform would, in Jean Egret's words, "wipe out the political role of French *parlements*" (1962: 246).

The Paris Guard finally managed to disperse most of the crowd, but their troubles had not ended. Trooper George Bernard and ten of his men formed a chain across the entrance to the Place Dauphine. "Toward midnight," he reported, several groups of young people tried to break the chain and enter the Place Dauphine. Having kept our composure and calmly asked them to withdraw, we were assailed with a volley of stones, which redoubled when the second detachment, from the rue de Harlay, partly mounted and partly on foot, crossed the place in order to chase out the rest of the people. The chevalier de Sorbonne was hit with a piece of plank from one of the little orange-merchants' stands which the rioters had broken up in order to throw the pieces at the Guard [B.N., Collection Joly de Fleury 1103].

Later that night, several run-ins between troops and youngsters around the royal courthouse produced serious injuries. On the twenty-eighth the guard had stationed itself at the two entrances to the Place Dauphine and turned away nonresidents, while the mounted guard battled the crowds assembled on nearby streets. According to Hardy, three members of the watch were killed that night, and many on both sides were injured. The following night the watch stayed away from the Place Dauphine, and the bonfire which consumed the effigy of Lamoignon blazed at the center of the square.

Over the following month, the pattern repeated itself, with variations, as Parisians celebrated the dismissal of Lamoignon and the return of the exiled Parlement to Paris. (The Parlement did not return the compliment; its first official action after resuming its sessions was to ban unauthorized gatherings and the throwing of firecrackers.) The repeated demonstrations of popular support led Restif de la Bretonne to ask,

is it flattering to receive homage from the same mouth which can, at a whim, belch obscenities? Thus the Parlement realized that it was dangerous to receive the fiery expression of joy from the hands of twelve- to fourteen-year-olds, of apprentice goldsmiths and clock-makers, of Savoyards, Auvergnats and coal-heavers. These last three are the most dangerous kind of troublemaker because of their natural crudeness and because they have no fear of the disasters fire might cause, given their poverty and the distance from their own hovels out in the *faubourgs* or in the impenetrable streets of the popular quarters. I admit that I have trembled every time I have seen the lower levels of the people excited, and I have trembled because I know them, because I know their hate for everything comfortable; it is an eternal and violent hate which asks no more than a chance to move into action. . . . It is of the greatest importance to repress their gatherings, not to leave their disorders unpunished. If just once that ferocious beast thought it could dare, it would overturn everything. I fear it so much that I would not dare to write this, or to have it printed, if it could read. But it can't read, that rabble of which I am now speaking; it will never be able to read, so long as it is the rabble [Restif, 1930: 194].

Sound familiar? Like Ben Franklin twenty years earlier, Restif de la Bretonne was baffled and frightened by the early phases of an unprecedented popular mobilization. One might consider Restif to be remarkably prescient, since the massive, decisive actions of the Parisian crowd at the Bastille and elsewhere were less than a year away. Yet what that usually acute observer failed to see, or chose not to see, was the conventionality and ritualism of these Parisian "disorders." The novelty was not in their form, but in their context.

One of the more surprising things about Hardy's invaluable journal is how little the detail of popular collective action in Paris changed with the advent of the revolution itself. The pace, intensity, and effectiveness of popular collective action increased dramatically in 1789, but the form and content of contentious gatherings changed rather little. Food riots, torchlit processions, mocking rituals, and the public representation of corporate interests continued to characterize the contentious gatherings of the time. The context, however, had altered so much that crowd actions could reach a scale and have an impact that had been inconceivable during more than a century of growing state power. Among other things, the crowd had allies and supporters in the middle class who now dared to voice their support as never before.

As the revolution moved on, the forms of popular collective action in Paris changed significantly. Although France lacked a single figure the likes of the incomparable Wilkes, it did produce many effective political entrepreneurs, part of whose work was to stimulate, organize, or use popular mobilization. From 1789 to 1792, the creation of clubs, militias, committees, and public forums far surpassed anything the French had seen before. The revolutionary leaders themselves went in for top-down mobilization to a degree that the British Wilkites and Radicals never dreamed of—or at least never had the opportunity to attempt. The locally organized National Guard and similar quasi-military units played a central role in the mobilization. The repeated processions of the early revolution and the great ceremonies typified by the Federation Festivals of 1790 and 1791 synthesized old-regime pageanty with the revolutionary representation of a nation under arms and on guard against counterrevolution. In a characteristically different manner, the French were also creating new forms of popular collective action based on special-purpose associations and breaking with the corporate structures of the old regime. Parisians, like Londoners, were creating the repertoire which would become the dominant means for the pursuit of shared interest in the following century.

CONCLUSION

A few well-chosen colorful incidents cannot prove so grand a thesis. Rather, they can appear to prove almost any thesis one chooses, just so long as the selection of events is astute. That is the weakness of the "posthole history" Richard Sennett recommends to us and with which he hopes to substantiate his own thesis of the fall of public man from the urban heights of the eighteenth century. My own efforts to deal with the problems of this paper in a truly systematic manner show me, alas, a complex, recalcitrant, and sometimes tedious reality. (The Appendix suggests some of the technical difficulties involved in being systematic about that reality.) In the long run, we have to substitute careful, continuous wall-building for the driving of an occasional posthole. By my own arguments, that means undertaking a close analysis of the day-to-day life and fine structure of the city in order to locate the full web of collective action in that city.

We end, then, with two working hypotheses and a research agenda. The first working hypothesis is simply a useful commonplace. The character of collective action in the eighteenth-century western city reflected the character of the city itself: The city was segregated into small subcommunities, organized politically as an interlocking set of corporate interests and patron-client networks, accustomed to doing much of its business (and pleasure) in the street, and peopled largely by poor, illiterate workers. Such a city produced a web of collective action which capitalized on authorized public gatherings such as markets, hangings, and ceremonies; which used street theater, ritualized mockery, and garish symbolism generously; and which frequently consisted of a crowd undertaking actions which, in the view of ordinary people, the authorities themselves should have performed. The borrowing of authoritative forms of action frequently extended to the ritual details: burning in effigy, displaying the head of an executed traitor, posting of decrees, and so on. With the growth of the nineteenth-century industrial city and the concomitant reorganization of urban politics, these distinctive features of eighteenth-century popular collective action faded away.

The second working hypothesis is that, in those cities of the late eighteenth century, new forms of action were emerging which would become in the following century the dominant repertoire of collective action through most western countries, in cities and villages alike. Urban activists such as John Wilkes were busy inventing the voluntary special-purpose association as a means of pursuing their interests. In the process they were fashioning the demonstration, the mass meeting, and similar devices in order to display and deploy their power.

I conclude with a reminder of the opportunities for research. The materials of eighteenth-century popular collective action are rich and abundant. Because so many of them come from the pens of the police or the notebooks of elite observers such as Franklin or Restif de la Bretonne, they require careful control. Their study necessarily draws us to closely examine the political and social structures which produced them. They provide an extraordinary opening for retrospective ethnography; for the synthesis of literary, cultural, political, and social analysis; for the creation of an eighteenth-century history which involves ordinary people as striving, calculating human beings rather than as passive victims or faceless mobs.

APPENDIX:
A NOTE ON METHODS AND SOURCES

Although this chapter does not present any systematic evidence, its ideas and materials draw on several systematic studies concerning Boston, Charleston, London, and Paris. In general, my procedure in these and related studies has been to (1) work out a standard definition for a type of event involving collective action; (2) search a delimited set of sources for all mentions of that type of event; (3) prepare a uniform record for each event mentioned in the sources which—after collation of multiple mentions and close scrutiny of the information available concerning the events—appear to fit the definition; (4) search for additional information about those events in archival materials and published historical works; (5) add that information to the records, but *avoid* adding new events discovered in the course of the further search; and (6) compare the characteristics of the catalogued events according to period, place, participants, issues, and so on. In the larger inquiries of this kind—for example, in the analysis of strikes in France from 1830 to 1968—I have ordinarily organized a research team and worked out a routine of machine-assisted coding and analysis. In a number of the smaller inquiries, I have either done all the work myself or worked by hand with one or two collaborators.

The studies of Boston, Charleston, London, and Paris have involved a deliberately fabricated category of event called a "contentious gathering." A contentious gathering is an occasion on which a number of people gather in a publicly accessible place and visibly make claims which would, if realized, bear on the interest of some other person(s). As a practical matter, I include events in which at least ten people appear to have assembled and adopt a series of concrete rules for identifying publicly accessible places, claims, and so forth. The rules capture just about every event a historian or contemporary observer would call a "riot," a "disorder," a "disturbance," a "protest," or something of the sort. However, they also bring in a number of parades, processions, ceremonies, festivals, rallies, organized meetings, and other gatherings in the course of which people made claims. Thus, John Bohstedt enumerates an average of 35 "riots" per year in England as a whole over the period from 1790 through 1810; John Stevenson identifies an average of 7 "disturbances" per year in London from 1790 through 1821; while in 1828 and 1829 (the only years for which we have more or less definitive totals) we have descriptions of 555 and 573 "contentious gatherings," respectively, for England, with 217 and 214 of them coming from Middlesex (that is, essentially, London) alone (Bohstedt, 1972: 52; Stevenson, 1979: 306; Schweitzer et al., 1980: 79-80). Although we may later discover that "riots" and "disturbances" became more frequent between 1810 or 1821 and 1828, surely the bulk of the difference in numbers is due to the breadth of our definition.

The small studies of Boston and Charleston were explorations, undertaken mainly to put the more extensive work on France and Britain into international perspective. They dealt with 11 years scattered over the period from 1755 to 1784. For events in Boston, I consulted the *Boston Gazette, Gentleman's Magazine,* and the *Annual Register* in order to construct the catalog, then searched the papers of the Colonial Office (Public Record Office, London) and a variety of published works for supplementary information. In the case of Charleston, the basic enumeration came from the South Carolina *Gazette, Gentleman's Magazine,* and the *Annual Register,* with supplementary information from the Colonial Office papers, the South Carolina State Archives (Columbia, S.C.), and historical publications. (For reports of those two studies, see Tilly, 1977, 1979.)

The work on London consists of two overlapping inquiries, both more extensive than the explorations of Boston and Charleston. The first is a detailed analysis of contention in Great Britain—that is, England, Scotland, and Wales—from 1828 through 1834. In this case, a good-sized research group identified all contentious gatherings mentioned in seven publications: the *Morning Chronicle,* the *Times* of London, *Mirror of Parliament, Hansard's Parliamentary Debates, Votes and Proceedings* of Parliament, the *Annual Register,* and *Gentleman's Magazine.* For more information on the events, we examined long runs of the Home Office's correspondence (Public Record Office, London) and explored several other archival series. Once the event dossiers were assembled, we prepared and analyzed machine-readable descriptions of the events, coupled with systematic information about the areas in which they occurred. (More details on materials and procedures appear in Schweitzer, 1980; Tilly and Schweitzer, 1980; Tilly, 1978a, 1980a.)

A companion inquiry, begun only recently, focuses on London but stretches out the time period to 1755-1834. Within that period, we selected ten pairs of adjacent years, then cataloged every contentious gathering mentioned in the *Annual Register, Gentleman's Magazine,* and either the London *Chronicle* (for the early years) or the *Times* (later). Machine-readable descriptions were again made of the events, but this time we coupled them with very detailed observations on changing land use, population characteristics, and economic activity in the individual parishes and wards of Middlesex, Surrey, Sussex, and Kent.

The study of Paris is less single-minded and disciplined than the investigation of London. It is actually a composite of pieces from a series of inquiries into changing forms of collective action in France from 1600 to the 1970s. I have concentrated my effort on five cities and their regions: Angers and Anjou, Dijon and Burgundy, Lille and Flanders, Toulouse and Languedoc, Paris and the Ile de France. No uniform set of sources covers the four centuries in question, and my documentation has many gaps. But where I can locate long and relatively homogeneous series of documents containing frequent reports on contentious gatherings and their contexts, I have attempted to go through the entire series carefully, transcribing the material on gatherings and transcribing or summarizing the complementary information as well. Among seventeenth-century sources, for instance, I have compiled reports from all issues of the *Mercure françois,* the *Mercure galant,* the *Gazette de France,* and the *Muze historique*; have labored through the main series of correspondence of the *contrôleurs généraux* with the intendants and other officials of the seven *généralites* having jurisdiction in the five regions (series G^7, Archives Nationales, Paris); have drawn the relevant information from a number of monographs and published collections of documents such as Liublinskaya's and Mousnier's editions of correspondence of Chancelier Séguier; and have drawn abundant but less continuous material from other series of the Archives Nationales, from the documentary collections of the Bibliothèque Nationale (Paris), from the municipal archives of Angers, Dijon, Lille, and Toulouse, from the departmental archives of the five regions, from the Archives Historiques de l'Armée (Vincennes), and from a wide variety of published articles and monographs. Obviously, in these circumstances it is harder to specify and verify the nature of the "sample" of contentious gatherings than in the cases of Boston, Charleston, and London. On the other hand, the evidence in these varied sources is rich and ample. The material on Paris resists quantification but invites close analysis of contexts and connections.

3

Revolution and the
Rural Community in the
Eastern Netherlands

WAYNE TE BRAKE

RURAL REVOLUTION IN
THE EIGHTEENTH CENTURY

The political historiography of the Dutch Republic has always been oriented to the cities of the western maritime provinces which stood at the center of Europe's burgeoning commercial economy in the seventeenth and eighteenth centuries. Though this concentration on urban politics reflects obvious demographic and constitutional circumstances that distinguished the United Provinces from other European polities, it rests implicitly on a polarization of town and country that needs to be reexamined. The work of economic and social historians who have undertaken

AUTHOR'S NOTE: The research for this article was made possible by a Fulbright-Hays Doctoral Dissertation Research Fellowship from the U.S. Office of Education. Jojada Verrips and Kitty Verrips-Roukens kindly read and commented on an earlier version of this paper; though I did not heed all of their advice, their criticism helped me to sharpen the argument at crucial points.

systematic investigation of the Dutch countryside indicates not simply a close integration of town and country but a dynamic and shifting relationship that is itself problematic and worthy of careful study (Slicher van Bath, 1957; Van der Woude, 1972; Faber, 1972; De Vries, 1974). Thus, to polarize town and country and simply to assume the domination of the former over the latter is both to impoverish and to distort our understanding of political and social processes in this perennially important region of Europe (Tilly, 1974).[1]

The Dutch Patriot Revolution of 1787 clearly illustrates this problem. Like political conflicts more generally in the Dutch Republic, the Patriot Revolution, which nearly succeeded in destroying the Dutch *ancien régime,* is usually seen as an urban-centered affair.[2] To be sure, urban problems and urban politicians predominated in the long crescendo which led from the beginning of the Fourth English War in 1780[3] to Patriot revolution and Organist counterrevolution in 1787. At first the businessmen, lawyers, students, and professors who acted as spokesmen for the dissident Patriot movement directed their fiercest attacks at the Prince of Orange, blaming him and his advisers for the disastrous military and economic consequences of Dutch involvement in the American Revolutionary War; but as their movement gained momentum, the Patriots' leaders ever more insistently attacked the insularity and corruption of the powerful urban oligarchies and demanded fundamental reform of the municipal magistracies. Beginning with the city of Utrecht in 1786, the revolutionary Patriots unseated the "aristocrats," whom they had come to identify as their chief enemies, and wrote new constitutions for municipal government in dozens of cities and towns throughout the republic.[4] By the fall of 1787, when Prussian military intervention in support of Organist counterrevolution cut the process short, by virtue of their municipal revolutions the Patriots had actually come to power in three of the seven Dutch provinces and divided power in two more.[5] In sum, the familiar eighteenth-century refrain of political rejuvenation through democratic representation was sung mainly in the cities and towns of the loosely confederated republic; never, to my knowledge, did the revolutionary Patriots make any concrete proposals to extend democratic representation to the countryside as well as the towns.

So what had revolution to do with rural communities? Apparently a good deal more than the traditional wisdom would lead us to expect. Looking at the small eastern province of Overijssel, one is struck by the extent to which the Patriots found political allies outside the walls of the three cities and the many chartered towns that were judicially and administratively distinct from the countryside. Of the 25 revolutionary militias that were organized to defend Overijssel from "tyranny," at least 11 were located in the villages and hamlets of the *platteland* (countryside).[6] It is easily possible that between 25 and 30 percent of the Patriot militiamen were countrymen (GAZ OA A-75).[7] How can we account for all this political activity? What were the roots of Patriot mobilization in the countryside? What did rustics—peasants and rural craftsmen for the most part—have to gain through alliance with the revolutionary Patriots in the cities? Because documentation for the countryside is so sparse, it is unlikely that we will ever be able to answer these questions completely. Nevertheless, the relatively well-documented example of revolutionary activity in the village of Bathmen suggests some interesting hypotheses. There, a striking degree of mobilization for political action during the 1780s alerts us to a more subtle development that was gradually transforming the agrarian landscape and undermining the rural community in the eastern Netherlands. But before we can proceed to this larger problem, we must first look closely at Bathmen itself and the conflicts that emerged there during the Patriot Revolution.

Bathmen lay some ten kilometers to the east of the city of Deventer in the *drostampt* (region) of Salland. With a population of 408, the village of Bathmen was the only significant settlement in the entire *schoutampt* (administrative district) of Bathmen, which had a total population of 1112. An assortment of artisans and tradesmen (blacksmiths, tailors, weavers, shoemakers, bakers) and a few governmental and religious officials lived in the village, but the overwhelming majority of the district's inhabitants (73 percent of the heads of households) worked primarily in agriculture. Alongside the *boeren*—independent peasants or yeomen—there were a large number of land-poor cotters as well as some landless laborers called *daghuurders*.[8] In sharp contrast to other agrarian communities in the eastern Netherlands, where the locally resident landed nobility might cast a broad shadow over the social landscape, no titled aristocrats resided in Bathmen (RAO SA 5321; Slicher van Bath, 1957).

As part of the *platteland,* the people of Bathmen stood outside the mainstream of Dutch political life. Sovereignty over the countryside in Overijssel was claimed by the provincial Estates in which power was more or less balanced between the *Ridderschap,* the body of the nobility, and the delgates of the three so-called *hoofdsteden*—Deventer, Kampen, and Zwolle, the principal cities of the province. Locally, preservation of law and order and administration of justice were entrusted to the *schout* (sheriff) and his assistant, who were subordinate to the regional *drost* and were appointed by and ultimately responsible to the provincial Estates. Still, the people of the platteland retained considerable autonomy in matters of local importance, such as the calling of ministers; maintenance of dikes, waterways, and bridges; and the disposition of communal resources. The institutions to which these functions were attached varied from place to place, but in Bathmen (and more generally in the central and eastern parts of the province) the focal point of communal life was the *Mark* corporation. These rural communes, which were characteristic of the areas of predominantly arable agriculture in the eastern Netherlands, were administered by corporations of designated landowners (*geërfden*). Since their inception in the middle ages, the Mark corporations had accrued a wide range of local functions, but their primary concern was the management and protection of communal property (Formsma, 1948; "Marckenboeck," 1892; Slicher van Bath, 1946; De Graaf, 1946).

Although the people of Bathmen had no direct or sustained involvement with the outside political world, they were clearly politicized and active during the 1780s. In 1787 local leaders reported to the provincial association of Patriot militias that their unit had no less than 150 men under arms (GAZ DA A-75). This means that more than half of the adult males in the entire district had joined the militia, which probably makes Bathmen the most highly mobilized community in all of Overijssel. Unfortunately, we do not have a complete list of the membership or a record of the group's activities. We do know, however, that the Patriots in Bathmen were actively involved in the provincial association of militias and that, in 1787, 30 Patriots from Bathmen volunteered for service in the Patriots' provincial army (GAZ OA A-75). The ages of these volunteers ranged from 18 to 51, the average age being 32. Of the 20 men I could identify in the census of 1795, most were from the immediate neighborhood of the village, and among them agricultural workers predominated: two were boeren, six cotters, and four daghuurders. In addition, there were three tailors, a baker, a blacksmith, a carpenter, and an innkeeper. The captain was no less than the schout's assistant, the second-ranking officer in the district. All in all, if the volunteers are representative of the whole militia, we might conclude that the Patriots were a reasonable sample of the entire community, as Table 3.1 shows.

For our purposes, however, the most interesting background characteristic of the Patriot militiamen is not immediately obvious. Judicial records indicate that three-fifths of the members whom we could identify had, just a few years earlier, been prosecuted and fined for participating in a violent demonstration and in particular for damaging property belonging to E. H.

TABLE 3.1   Occupational Profiles in Bathmen and Loo

Occupation	*Census 1795*		*Land Invaders** 1783*		*Volunteers** 1787*	
	Number	*Percent*	*Number*	*Percent*	*Number*	*Percent*
Agriculture						
Boer	28	23	9	21	2	10
Cotter	52	43	17	40	6	30
Day laborer	8	7	1	2	4	20
Subtotal	88	73	27	63	12	60
Manufacturing						
Smith	2	*	1	2	1	5
Wooden Shoemaker	2	*	1	2	1	5
Weaver	3	2	1	2	–	–
Cooper	1	*	–	–	–	–
Shoemaker	3	2	2	5	–	–
Carpenter	6	5	4	9	1	5
Tailor	5	4	4	9	3	15
Subtotal	24	20	14	33	6	30
Service						
Merchant	1	*	–	–	–	–
Innkeeper	1	*	1	2	1	5
Hospes	3	2	1	2	–	–
Schout	1	*	–	–	–	–
Assistant Schout	1	*	–	–	1	5
Minister	1	*	–	–	–	–
Coster	1	*	–	–	–	–
Subtotal	9	7	2	5	2	10
Total	121	100	43	101	20	100

*Less than 2 percent.
**Land invaders and volunteers who could be identified in the census of 1795.

Putman and C. W. Sloet (RAO RB [Rechterlijkarchief Bathmen] 27). Though the evidence is not conclusive because the sample is so small, it is here, I think, that we find our best indication of the origins of the revolutionary Patriot movement in Bathmen. As far as I have been able to reconstruct the development, the militia had its roots in a protracted struggle for control over land, the most vital resource in this agrarian community.

Controversy and conflict first emerged in Bathmen in the fall of 1779–that is, before the beginning of the Fourth English War and the crisis that ensued.[9] At its annual meeting in October, the Mark of Bathmen and Loo, comprising the northern, more populous half of the district, voted to allow private enclosure of communal wasteland (*woest*). Upon the payment of a nominal fee, the encloser would gain exclusive title to the new land. As the Dutch word *aangraving* suggests, however, the process of enclosure in the Netherlands usually entailed reclamation as well; to dig a drainage ditch (the Dutch verb is *graven*) around a plot of communal land was to signify its appropriation for private use.[10] Since the resolution to allow enclosure was sponsored by E. H. Putman, it is not surprising that he, along with C. W. Sloet, immediately undertook the first enclosures. Hiring a number of local laborers, they dug ditches, built fences and dikes, seeded grain, and planted trees on wasteland adjoining their existing farmsteads. To complete the project, Putman and Sloet even had houses moved onto their new land ("Marckenboeck," 1892: 99).

Meanwhile, the decision to allow enclosure, originally adopted with little apparent discussion, seems to have awakened deep concern among some members of the Mark corporation. At its meeting in the fall of 1780, the Mark discussed and finally approved a supplementary resolution that was proposed by the Abbess of ter Hunnepe, who was the hereditary chair of the Mark ("Marckenboeck," 1892: 92-94). Among other things, the resolution stipulated that no enclosures must be allowed to compromise the general interests of the Mark and that, therefore, all enclosures would have to be inspected and approved by the Mark. Accordingly, the Mark was scheduled to hear the report on the formal inspection and consider approval of the first enclosures at its meeting in December 1781. That enclosures had by this time become a hot issue is indicated by a sizable jump (from 17 to 27) in the number of landowners represented at the meeting. In any case, the report was favorable, and the first enclosures were formally approved.

Final approval of these first enclosures seems to have exploded latent tensions into open conflict, for within six months the locus of the controversy had shifted from the meeting hall to the streets. On May 28, 1782, a large group of men and women gathered at the home of Jan Westerhuis in the village of Bathmen. Together they marched the short distance from Bathmen to the neighborhood of Loo where they methodically broke down dikes, filled in drainage ditches, ruined crops, and uprooted trees planted on the new land of Putman and Sloet. Less than two weeks later, on June 10, the scene was reenacted; this time the group reportedly carried banners and were accompanied by a drummer. Since the local authorities were apparently slow to act, Putman eventually appealed to the drost of Salland and through him to the provincial Estates. In a letter dated October 23, 1782, Putman complained bitterly of continued abuse and alleged that five residents of Bathmen just a few days earlier had threatened to destroy the cotter's house on his new land if it were not removed within 14 days ("Marckenboeck," 1892: 99-100; RAO SA 106). Alarmed by such lawlessness, the Estates immediately passed a resolution solemnly urging the people of Bathmen to seek a "legal" resolution to their grievances and warning that all acts of violence would be prosecuted. Accordingly, in the spring and summer of 1783, more than 100 people were charged and assessed stiff fines for their involvement in these incidents.[11]

ENCLOSURES AND LAND INVASIONS

To connect the land invasions in Bathmen with opposition to the decisions regarding enclosure of commons land, as the prosecutors in Bathmen did, is also, by extension, to place these events squarely into the mainstream of European economic and social history. The history of eighteenth-century enclosures in England and France teaches us, however, that enclosure did not necessarily lead to dissension and conflict, much less to violent resistance. Thus, our problem is to discover why enclosures evoked such a bitter reaction in Bathmen.[12] In my estimation, two features of the drama—the cast of characters and the physical setting— deserve special attention and point toward an explanation of the violence and its significance for our understanding of Dutch history during this period. Let us begin with the actors.

In broadest outline, the struggle over land enclosures in Bathmen pitted a broad coalition of local people against wealthy investors from outside the community. Since reclamation and enclosure in the Netherlands entailed considerable investment in labor and materials, it should not be surprising to find that neither Putman nor Sloet was a simple peasant. Rather, both men were rentiers from nearby Deventer, and as Burgemeesters, both were influential members of Deventer's patrician oligarchy.[13] If we look, furthermore, at the enfranchised landowners who attended or were represented by proxy at the important Mark meetings in 1780 and 1781,[14] we find that Putman and Sloet were typical of nearly half of the active members of the Mark corporation. Of the 27 voters named in the minutes of these meetings, 12 can be identified as residents of Deventer. Nine were either currently in municipal office themselves or, as in the case of the widow of Burgemeester Jordens, members of prominent patrician families; two more would become municipal officers in 1787.[15] In the census of 1795, four of these people listed their occupations as rentier and two as merchant (RAO SA 5347). Only the brothers Brinkhuis (Arnoldus, Jan, and Willem), who were bakers, held no political offices, and collectively owned a single farmstead in Bathmen, were exceptions to the overwhelmingly patrician character of the landowners from Deventer.

Compared with this clearly identifiable block of investors from Deventer, the remaining members of the Mark corporation seem a rather heterogeneous lot. In the first place, only seven can be positively identified as residents of Bathmen, though an additional six are likely to have been local residents as well (RAO SA 5321). From the village itself, there were several landowners who were not peasants: a miller, a carpenter, an innkeeper and a *hospes* (landlord). Remarkably, then, I can identify only four boeren and two cotters among the members who attended the Mark meetings; and even if we assume that the remaining three local landowners were peasants, only a minority (at most one-third) of the people who took part in the important decisions on enclosure were peasant proprietors.

Though we do not know how the actual voting went in the crucial meetings of the Mark, some evidence suggests that the assembly was narrowly divided between locals and outsiders (RAO RB 27). In 1780, when the Mark upheld the enclosure decision in principle but voted to require a formal approval procedure that would take into account the general interests of the Mark, the residents of Deventer outnumbered the residents of Bathmen nine to seven. That despite this resolution the local landowners nevertheless perceived their interests to be threatened is indicated by the fact that their number increased from seven to twelve at the meeting when the first enclosures were to be considered for approval. What is more, most of the local members designated lawyer J. B. Auffenmorth from nearby Goor as their proxy and spokesman. At the same time, however, the number of voters from Deventer increased to twelve. The outcome, then, appears to have been determined by two landowners, widows whose residences I cannot identify, who had designated E. H. Putman, the victorious encloser, as their proxy.

Regardless of whether this scenario of the inner dynamics of the Mark corporation is correct, the subsequent land invasions were clearly undertaken by a broad coalition of Bathmen residents against the two patricians from Deventer. Of the 103 persons accused of participating in the land invasions, I have been able to identify the occupations of 43, all of whom were residents of the Mark of Bathmen and Loo (RAO SA 5321). As one might expect, the bulk of the protesters—nearly two-thirds—were peasants:

seventeen (40 percent of the entire group) were cotters, another nine (21 percent) were boeren, while only one was a daghuurder. In addition, there was an assortment of artisans (14, or 33 percent), a hospes, and an innkeeper (see Table 3.1). All in all, this group, compared with the occupational profile of the community in 1795, seems to have been a fairly representative cross-section of the local population. In any case, it is not surprising to find six of the enfranchised members of the Mark among the protesters, including hospes Jan Westerhuis and innkeeper Willem Bessem, who were identified as the leaders of the demonstration.

The broad pattern of local mobilization, then, seems clear: A small but determined minority of the members of the Mark, having lost the battle for control of the commons within the Mark corporation, sought and found a broad base of support within the local community as they took matters into their own hands. But since the actors themselves are largely mute in the surviving records, we can only speculate about what Putman and Sloet, the targets of their violence, represented in their minds. Was it simply because they were outsiders that they aroused the fear and hostility of the people of Bathmen? Or was it because only the relatively wealthy patricians from Deventer could afford the capital investment required to take advantage of the reclamation/enclosure possibilities within the Mark? While both of these elements may have entered into the conflict, a closer analysis of the agricultural context in which the land invasions occurred is necessary to understand the bitterness and determination of the protesters.

While it is generally true of European society that "wasteland" rarely went unused or was wasted, the peasant ecology of the region around Bathmen imparted to the woest a special significance that was radically different from the more common pattern of short-fallow grain farming in Europe.[16] In the eastern Netherlands and the neighboring areas of western Germany, the peasants traditionally practiced a variation on the infield-outfield system by which they kept certain favored plots of land in continuous cultivation of rye by means of careful turf-manuring (Slicher van Bath, 1963: 59, 258-259).[17] Typically, the arable humus was stripped or cut from untilled lands and mixed with animal dung to provide fertilizer for the favored plots under continuous cultivation. In the absence of artificial fertilizers or large quantities of manure, this system was perhaps well-suited to the extremely variable soil conditions of the region ("Bodem," 1965: blad 10, sheet 3). It is nevertheless true that continuous cultivation of rye in this manner necessitated extensive areas of untilled land—the woest or outfield—and involved a great deal of work in transporting the turf from one field to another.[18] Of course, the ratio of arable land to turf land required to maintain the productivity of the soil varied with the quality of the soil. Poor soils needed up to ten years to regenerate humus and produced poorer fertilizer, requiring as many as 100 wagon loads per hectare. With better soil conditions, humus might be restored in seven years and require only 40 loads of fertilizer per hectare of arable land. As a rule of thumb, one needed approximately 20 times more turf land than arable land (Slicher van Bath, 1957: 414-415; 1963: 258).

In communities like Bathmen, then, the woest was used not only for the more familiar purposes of grazing cattle and gathering fuel or building materials but most importantly for turf-manuring; it was an essential resource that had to be carefully conserved and protected. Population growth especially threatened the ecology of continuous rye cultivation by creating pressures to expand the arable land at the expense of the woest.[19] In the thirteenth century, a period of general population expansion, the mark corporations of the eastern Netherlands were created, according to Slicher van Bath (1946), largely to protect uncultivated lands from the encroachment of outsiders; and the large stretches of woest that survived for the next five centuries bear eloquent testimony to the fact that the marken were generally successful in this task. During the seventeenth and eighteenth centuries, however, it was not pressure from outside but the steady growth of the community itself that threatened to undermine the ecology of continuous rye cultivation in Bathmen. Land-tax records indicate that by the beginning of the seventeenth century, 9.2 percent of the total land area in the district of Bathmen was used for arable agriculture. Because the remaining land was used for other purposes besides turf-digging, the possibilities for further expansion of the arable were severely limited (Slicher van Bath, 1957: 422).[20] Nevertheless, during the next two centuries, slow but steady population growth greatly increased the pressure on available land resources in Bathmen. Slicher van Bath (1957: 453-454) estimates that between 1675 and 1764 the population of Bathmen more than doubled; and census data indicate that between 1748 and 1795 Bathmen continued to grow, though at a slower rate (RAO SA 2193, 5321). Since there were no significant cottage industries in Bathmen, the excess population had to be absorbed into the agricultural economy.

Not surprisingly, the people of Bathmen attempted to relieve the pressure of two centuries of population growth by increasing the amount of land under cultivation at the expense of communal wastelands. Slicher van Bath (1957: 438) calculates that between 1682 and 1749 alone (the only period for which land reclamation figures are available), arable land in Bathmen was increased by nearly 50 percent, which was the highest figure for all of Overijssel. With few exceptions, the additional arable acreage was acquired by means of small-scale encroachments on the commons. For the most part, the reclamations of the seventeenth and eighteenth centuries added small pieces of arable land to existing plots. Slicher van Bath (1957: 441) describes the development: "In many cases, the reclamation was paired with the division of the homestead from which the reclamation proceeded. Thus, the reclamation led not to increased welfare for a single family, but to a more desperate existence for two families." The consequences can be seen as well in the shifting profile of the agrarian population. In 1603, farmsteads in Bathmen on the average were quite small (2.87 hectares), and there was a sizable number of cotters (52) alongside the more substantial and independent boeren (60). By 1795, the number of boeren had declined by 17 percent, while the number of land-poor peasants, the cotters, had increased by nearly 70 percent. At the same time, Bathmen's population growth gave rise to a sizable number of landless laborers, or daghuurders. In 1795, these rural proletarians, who had no land and only their labor to sell, amounted to 14 percent of the heads of households who depended on agriculture for their livelihoods (Slicher van Bath, 1957: 442, 453-454).[21]

By the last quarter of the eighteenth century, the cumulative effects of two centuries of population growth and land reclamation were surely threatening the traditional economic and social fabric of this small agrarian community. Still, there is no evidence to indicate that Bathmen's development had reached a stage of acute crisis, the sheer hopelessness of which could account for the agitation and turmoil of the 1780s. By comparison with other agricultural districts in Salland and Twente, for example, only a relatively low proportion of Bathmen's population was indigent and in need of public charity (RAO SA 2694).[22] In any case, as we have just seen, reclamation and enclosure of commons land was not new to Bathmen.

SHARPENING CONFLICT

What was new and apparently intolerable to the people of Bathmen in the 1780s was the scale and character of the undertaking. Slicher van Bath describes the earlier enclosures as largely informal and extralegal; they were piecemeal efforts by local peasants to shore up their increasingly difficult economic position. The Mark's resolution in 1779, however, gave legal sanction to an apparently open-ended process of reclamation and enclosure—a process that ultimately threatened not only the viability of the community's agricultural system[23] but the raison d'etre of the Mark corporation itself. For to enclose the commons was ultimately to foreclose on the future of the community's most important institution. To be sure, the supplemental resolution of 1780 placed limits on the process by tying approval of actual enclosures to the "interests of the Mark." But by 1781 it was clear that the "interests of the Mark" could be interpreted rather loosely. The corporation approved, apparently by a close vote, two enclosures that involved significant investments by outsiders who certainly had no personal stake in the future of Bathmen's communal life. In addition, the enclosures created entirely new farmsteads complete with houses, and thus clearly departed from the older, piecemeal pattern of enclosure. Finally, the fact that trees were planted on at least some of the enclosed land indicates that the outsiders were diversifying their investments and altering the pattern of local agriculture. Rather than leasing all of the new land to local peasants, Putman and Sloet were diverting some of the woest to long-term investment in highly profitable forest products. Thus, enclosure of this kind both threatened the precarious balance between arable and turf land and removed some of the land from the traditional food production system altogether.[24]

As the pieces of the story come together, the land invasions of 1782 seem almost a natural and predictable outcome of earlier developments in Bathmen. Through enclosure of part of the woest, outsiders—capitalist investors from the city—threatened to undermine both the ecological and the institutional foundations of the rural community and thereby provoked a violent, defensive reaction from the local population. But how natural and predictable was the next step in the progression—the alliance between the protesters in Bathmen and the broader Patriot movement in Overijssel? In the short run, the connection seems obvious enough. At the same time the people of Bathmen were protesting the enclosure of their commons land, their neighbors in Deventer were beginning to mobilize one of the first and strongest Patriot movements in the entire republic; and in their first big petition drive in October 1782, the Patriots of Deventer picked up on the conflicts in Bathmen. While calling for a general redress of constitutional abuses, the petition cited "the events in Bathmen" alongside the Fourth English War as one of the reasons for their grave concern about the political health of the republic (Gemeentearchief Deventer Republick II, 133). Very soon thereafter, Burgemeester E. H. Putman, an outspoken Orangist, emerged as the principal target of the Patriots' attack on their local government; and in February 1783, the Patriots scored what they considered a significant victory when they forced Putman's unprecedented removal from the Magistracy (Te Brake, 1977: 46-47). At this level, then, the alliance appears to have been based on an obvious and certainly reasonable principle: The enemies of my enemies are my friends. Their enmity thus sealed, the contest between the Patriots and Putman continued until Putman emerged at the head of the Orangists' counterrevolutionary regime in Deventer in September 1787. By extension, then, the aftershocks of the Orangist counterrevolution were to be felt in Bathmen, too. In 1788, the local authorities revived their case against a select group of land rioters in 1782, chief among whom were several leaders of the local Patriot militia and their relatives (RAO RB 27).

Viewed from the perspective of ideology and goals, however, the alliance between the Patriots of Bathmen and Deventer seems more ironic than natural. At bottom, the people of Bathmen appear to have been defending the integrity of their corporative agrarian community against the subversion of outsiders. In the absence of direct testimony from the actors themselves, one might argue that implicit in their actions was a demand for popular sovereignty within the Mark—an assertion, however inarticulate, of the right of the general populace to veto the decisions of the members of the exclusive corporation. Still, one suspects, again in the absence of demands to the contrary, that the people of Bathmen were perfectly willing to continue to allow a small group of landowners to preside over the "interests of the Mark" as long as these were not equated with the narrow, private interests of the landowners themselves.

An amusing letter written to the editor of a local political journal in 1785 illustrates the problem we encounter here ("Blaadje," 1785: 63-64). The author, who identified himself as a simple peasant, confessed to being confused by some of the words Patriot writers were using. He wanted to be sure that his friend, the local sexton, had given him the right definitions. The "Angelmanen" ("Englishmen"), according to the sexton, were the counselors of the Prince of Orange who advised him to side with the English. The "Paterjotten" ("Patriots"), by contrast, were those who opposed the "Angelmanen" and said the Prince was not always right. More significantly, the sexton simply could not remember what the word "Demikraten" ("Democrats") might mean. Still, he reported confidently that "Arikraten" ("Aristocrats") were "the City people who wear big, square buckles on their shoes"; in Holland, even people who wore wigs were called "Arikraten," although some of them did not have buckles on their shoes.

It is possible—perhaps likely—that this letter was not authentic and that the Patriotic Dutch boer was being mocked for his apparent simplicity.

But it is also possible that the Patriots in the countryside tended to distrust "city people" and to lump all those who wore buckles and wigs—doubtless including both Putman and a number of good Patriots—into the category of "aristocrats" who were, after all, among the chief enemies of the Patriot movement. In either case, the letter highlights a central difficulty in the Patriot coalition in Overijssel: The rhetoric of participatory democracy and individual rights which infused the writings of the urban Patriots was not easily translated to the rural political setting where the vocabulary of communal rights and corporate interests was likely to have greater currency. As it happened, the old-regime corporatism that defined and protected the rural commune would soon come under direct attack from both the Patriots and their ideological and political heirs, the Batavians of 1795.[25] The constitutionalist lawyers who came to dominate the Patriot movement in Deventer, for example, turned against the corporatist demands of the local gilds in 1786 and, as a result, provoked a decisive and ultimately fatal split within the Patriot movement there (Te Brake, 1977). By 1798, the first constitution of the Batavian Republic, by creating a centralized, unitary state, undermined the independence of both provincial and local institutions and specifically abolished the gilds on grounds that such "private jurisdictions" violated the principles of unity and indivisibility (Schama, 1977: 259-260). Finally, by royal decree of Louis Bonaparte in 1810, the marken were enjoined to divide their common lands among the enfranchised landholders. Thus, the customary rights and corporate interests that were defended by the early Patriots in Bathmen were eventually casualties of the revolutionary upheaval that swept away the Dutch old regime.

WHY LOCAL CONFLICTS MATTER

To look to the eventual dissolution of the marken in Overijssel is also to beg the obvious question of the broader significance of the conflicts in Bathmen. To be sure, one cannot state firm conclusions on the basis of a single case study; more and different kinds of research must be done both for other communities in Overijssel and for other provinces in the republic. Still, some broad observations seem to follow from the fragmentary evidence at hand.

The first has to do with the revolutionary politics of the 1780s. As I suggested at the outset, Bathmen was only one of a number of rural communities that produced active Patriot militias in the 1780s. In at least two other cases, local conflicts involved friction between large landowners and a broad spectrum of the local populace. At Windesheim, a small village near Zwolle, judicial records indicate that members of the Patriot militia attacked the local heer, who, in contrast to the patricians in Bathmen, was an absentee noble landlord living in Friesland (GAZ OA A-74). At Wolde, a mark in the eastern region of Twente, Patriots attacked local landowners—specifically, three noble families whose extensive holdings (two-thirds of the arable land) allowed them to control the affairs of the Mark—when the landowners refused to let the local Patriot militia sell *aangegraven* (newly enclosed lands) in order to buy arms for the militia. The Patriots charged, in particular, that the landowners regularly used the aangegraven land for their own private benefit (RAO SA 911). At Vriesenveen, however, the pattern appears to have been different. There, two rival factions divided the community, each group claiming to represent the "true" Patriot cause (GAZ OA A-75). These three rather disparate cases suggest, then, that while conflicts over land were not unique to Bathmen, they are also not likely to be universally the backdrop against which Patriot mobilization occurred in the countryside. At the very least, however, one thing seems certain: the Patriots in the countryside were fighting their own battles; their struggles were not simply hollow imitations of the urban originals. Unless we take these conflicts seriously and study them in their own terms, we are not likely to understand either the breadth of the political discontent that underwrote the Patriot Revolution or the depth of the crisis that affected Dutch society at the end of the old regime.

A second point to emphasize is the importance of the enclosure of commons land in the eastern Netherlands. At the end of the eighteenth century, many areas of the eastern Netherlands, but especially Overijssel, were characterized by large stretches of *woeste grond,* the sort of land that was essential to the ecology of continuous rye cultivation. By the middle of the nineteenth century, however, most of this land had been brought under cultivation, both as new meadowland and as arable acreage. According to Slicher van Bath (1957), the process began in Overijssel sometime in the second half of the eighteenth century and accelerated rapidly during and after the revolutionary period; between 1811 and 1833 alone, more than one-third of the woest was reclaimed, enclosed, and diverted to other agricultural uses. In the immediate vicinity of Bathmen—the area Slicher van Bath calls the *Sallandse akkerbouwgebied*—cultivated land expressed as a percentage of the total land area jumped from just under 7 percent in 1749 to more than 30 percent in 1833. This scale of reclamation entailed nothing short of an agricultural revolution, for in the process the ecology of continuous rye cultivation was destroyed. Technologically, the key to the transformation was the increasing cultivation of fodder crops which allowed for larger herds of cattle, greater quantities of manure for fertilizer, and less dependence on turf fertilization and the woest. The result was the development, by the latter part of the nineteenth century, of the modern agricultural system in which arable acreage exists mainly to support livestock raising (Slicher van Bath, 1957: 484-503).[26]

The transformation of agrarian society indicated by these figures on land reclamation was neither simple nor unimportant, but the way in which it was achieved remains obscure and largely unnoticed in the historical literature (Van Stuijvenberg, 1957: 185-186). Slicher van Bath (1957: 484-486) suggests in passing that the increasing tempo of land reclamation must be attributed to economic factors rather than official pronouncements, such as royal decrees calling for the division of commons land. Still, he is not able to specify the intermediate steps by which economic stimuli—particularly rising agricultural prices and the decline in the rural textile industry—were translated into reclamation and enclosure of the woest *in spite of* the Mark corporations which were intended to protect it. In Bathmen, we can see the beginnings of the process vividly and in surprising detail. There reclamation and enclosure of the woest were predicated on a pattern of urban (even more specifically, patrician) investment in arable land; it was at the insistence of these investors that the Mark corporation legally sanctioned, by a close vote, large-scale reclamation and enclosure of the woest. If this analysis is correct, it is not implausible to suggest that Bathmen was typical of a broader development in Overijssel. The infusion of urban capital into the countryside was, indeed, a common and striking phenomenon in eighteenth-century Overijssel (Slicher van Bath, 1957; Faber, 1965: 86). Furthermore, published excerpts from Overijssel *markeboeken* indicate a fairly common pattern of dissension over enclosure of the woest. The combination of the two, as we have seen in Bathmen, could be explosive.

A final point has to do with the explosion and the threat to the rural community that occasioned it. The rural commune, the mark, was ultimately one of the casualties of the revolutionary era—an era which, in Overijssel at least, produced two revolutions simultaneously. Agricultural revolution, which entailed the transformation of the woest, undermined the raison d'etre of the mark, while political revolution, which eventually created the unitary Dutch state, undermined the mark's local autonomy and thus hastened the process of agricultural transformation. The experience of Bathmen in the 1780s illustrates how these two revolutionary movements were related, though not necessarily in ways we might expect, given the final outcome. Though we know that in the long run the agricultural revolution brought a new economic prosperity to Overijssel, we must recognize that in the short run it entailed real costs for the rural commune and the people who inhabited it. Thus, in the early years of the revolutionary era when the lines of political demarcation were not yet distinct, those who perceived the threat to the rural commune and resisted the agricultural transformation could be found momentarily in the political revolutionary vanguard.

NOTES

1. Though Tilly's discussion is clearly oriented toward Asian problems, the theoretical issues he considers, following the lead of Antonio Gramsci, are certainly relevant to this discussion of revolution in the Dutch countryside. See also Elias (1974).

2. The standard works on the Dutch Patriot Revolution are Colenbrander, (1897-1899), Geyl (1947), De Wit (1974). In English, the best and most recent survey of the entire revolutionary period is Schama (1977). See also Palmer (1959).

3. The Fourth English War is the Dutch term for their involvement in the American Revolutionary War on the side of the French and the American colonies. From the beginning, the war went badly for the Dutch: The English seized Dutch colonies in the West Indies and successfully blockaded Dutch shipping to Amsterdam.

4. Ironically, these municipal revolutions have attracted very little archival research. For the most part, historians have tried to analyze "national" developments using a voluminous pamphlet literature to follow debates and controversies. For the pivotal case of Utrecht, see Vijlbrief (1950), and Van Hulzen (1966). On municipal revolution in the province of Overijssel, see Te Brake (1977).

5. The Patriots controlled the provincial Estates of Holland, Overijssel, and Groningen; the Orangists controlled Zeeland and Gelderland. There were rival Estates, both claiming sovereignty, in Utrecht and Friesland.

6. I refer here only to the militias that sent delegates to the provincial association of Patriot militias. See GAZ OA [Gemeentearchief Zwolle, Oud Archief] A-75. For the locations of these militias see the map in Te Brake (1977: 70). There may have been as many as five or six more militias in the countryside that were not represented in the provincial association.

7. In July 1787, 19 of the 25 militias reported a total of 2874 men under arms. Unfortunately, all of the militias that failed to report their membership figures were from the countryside. But if the figures we have for rural militias are typical, we could estimate that there were somewhere between 900 and 1000 Patriot militiamen in the countryside, with a total of nearly 3500 in the entire province.

8. These figures are based on the occupational census of 1795, RAO [Rijksarchief in Overijssel, Zwolle] SA [Staten Archief] 5321. On the difference between *boeren* and *cotters*, see Slicher van Bath (1957). Unfortunately, we have no direct evidence concerning property ownership in Bathmen, but, judging from participation in the most important communal institution (the *Mark*), in which membership was based on ownership of property, we can estimate that less than one-third of the

landowners were peasants. Slicher van Bath (1957: 635-637) suggests that peasant proprietorship may have been increasing in the seventeenth and eighteenth centuries, but there is no evidence to suggest this for Bathmen in particular.

9. Unless otherwise noted, the following narrative account is based on eyewitness accounts, excerpts from official documents, and other materials in RAO RB 27.

10. I use the word "enclosure" with some hesitation because of the peculiar connotations it has in English history. Dutch writers often refer to this simply as *ontginning*—that is, "reclamation"—though I think this disguises two important features of the process of *aangraving*. In the first place, communal property was being appropriated for private use. Second, as we shall see later, the land being enclosed was not unused, as the term "reclamation" suggests; it was simply being diverted to new uses. Thus, it should be noted that "enclosure" is used here to refer to a peculiarly Dutch process that usually involved reclamation of the land in question.

11. These are the trial records that comprise the bulk of RAO RB 27.

12. I do not, of course, wish to suggest that the process was entirely nonviolent in England and France; it clearly provoked violent action in many cases. The important problem in the long run is to determine under what conditions those who were opposed to enclosures actually organized protests to protect their interests.

13. This identification, as well as the others below, was a serendipitous spin-off from my dissertation research on the city of Deventer where Putman was a prominent figure in the conflicts leading to the Patriot Revolution of 1787. See Te Brake (1977: 46-47 and passim).

14. The names of those present at these meetings can be found in excerpts from the Markeboek included in RAO RB 27. It should be noted that not all those who were enfranchised by their ownership of property attended all the meetings.

15. The complete lists of the names of all the magistrates and town councillors of Deventer can be found in Dumbar (1732-1788) and Kronenberg (1921). See also Te Brake (1977: 100-102, 186 n.16).

16. Wolf (1966) lists five basic paleotechnic ecotypes and discusses at length what he calls Eurasian grain farming (short-term fallowing). Slicher van Bath (1963: 244) gives a far more specific list of the various tillage systems found in Europe in the seventeenth and eighteenth centuries. On the common uses of wasteland, see Slicher van Bath (1963: 72-74). The most useful classification of tillage systems is presented in Boserup (1965). Based on the intensity of land utilization, Boserup's classification runs from forest fallowing to multicropping and has the clear advantage of taking into consideration the entire village territory (including the so-called waste) instead of riveting our attention solely on the fields under cultivation.

17. For a more detailed analysis, see Slicher van Bath (1957: 410-418). The English word "turf," meaning a piece of earth or sod, should not be confused with the Dutch word "turf," meaning peat.

18. On the relationship between intensity of land utilization and work, see Boserup (1965).

19. On the importance of population growth in bringing about agricultural change, see Boserup (1965; her arguments are persuasively anti-Malthusian).

20. See especially Slicher van Bath's conclusion about Bathmen: "*ontginningsmogelijkheden ontbraken hier*" (Reclamation possibilities did not exist here).

21. Thus, there were 55 boeren, 88 cotters, and 24 daghuurders in 1795. It is especially the growing number of daghuurders throughout the province that leads

Slicher van Bath to describe rural Overijssel as a *"Samenleving onder spanning"* (a society under tension).

22. Bathmen (9 percent) compares favorably with Ommen en den Ham (38 percent) and Borne (32 percent). Slicher van Bath (1957: 452) calculates that 25.1 percent of the population was indigent in the entire *Sallandse akkerbouwgebied*–that is, the central part of the province, which was characterized by arable agriculture as opposed to pastoral agriculture.

23. See Slicher van Bath (1957: 415): "The call to division of the communal lands must certainly have sounded like encouragement of suicide to the boeren, in that further reclamation would corrode the very foundation of their operation."

24. Here, again, it is important to emphasize that the woest was always used, not wasted, and that is was essential to the ecology of continuous rye cultivation. Too often, the planting of trees on heath land (*heide velden*) is seen simply as reclamation, implying that the land was previously unused.

25. Though the Patriots were defeated in 1787 by foreign intervention, Dutch revolutionary sympathies did not die. At the beginning of 1795, in advance of the French revolutionary armies, the Dutch undid the Orangist restoration of 1787 and established the Batavian Republic based on the principles of liberty, equality, and fraternity. French sponsorship of the Batavian Revolution under the Directory eventually gave way to the creation of a client kingdom (ruled by Napoleon's brother) and direct annexation under the Napoleonic Empire. For this reason, the entire period of Dutch history from 1795 to 1813 is often known as the "French time."

26. It is possible that with the disappearance of continuous rye cultivation some of the woest actually fell into disuse for the first time in centuries. The matter warrants further investigation using nineteenth-century sources.

4

Contentious Gatherings in
Lancashire, England, 1750-1893

FRANK MUNGER

FACES OF CONFLICT
IN LANCASHIRE

Consider two events which occurred in the early decades of the nine-teenth century in Lancashire, England. At a weekend market in Man-chester in June 1800, a group of women, presumably regular patrons, engaged in a familiar form of dispute over the price of potatoes. The Manchester *Mercury* reported the event on June 17:

> In consequence of the high price of old potatoes on Saturday night a number of women attempted to seize them from the vendors in the market and to dispose of them at their own price. Jn. Leaf, Esq., magistrate, took great pains to convince them that taking the farmers' property by force would only tend to increase the price of it, as they consequently would not bring it for sale. A number of special constables were assembled, by whose exertions a regular sale of potatoes were made at a reduced price but such was the ferocity of some of the women whose aim was evidently to create a riot that they abused the more orderly who had purchased potatoes seized and threw them about. Such are the principles upon which mobbing

is generally conducted and it is observed that those who are least entitled to relief are the most violent.

The disturbance at the Manchester potato market possessed the familiar features of the classic "food riot," perhaps the most characteristic form of contentious gathering in rural England in the eighteenth century. The role played by the special constables, who were ordinary citizens sworn in temporarily to aid the Justice of the Peace, was itself not unusual. Perhaps the extraordinary occurrence was the women's continued violence after they had succeeded in restoring the normal market price. The paper moralizes about this aspect of the event, accepting the forced sale without comment.

Not so long afterward, on August 16, 1819, quite another type of event occurred less than a mile from the site of the Manchester potato market. On this occasion, huge numbers of the working class were involved, perhaps as many as 100,000, who gathered to make clearly drawn demands of the government of England: repeal of the Corn Laws, enactment of a minimum wage, and, most importantly, parliamentary reform. In form, the gathering at St. Peter's Fields was intended to represent a controlled demonstration of power. The masses of participants practiced marching in orderly array for weeks in advance to demonstrate self-discipline and the peaceful tenor of the demands. As a result of preliminary sparring with local authorities over the legality of such a meeting, leaders had consulted an attorney to make certain they were acting within the law. Notwithstanding the advice they received, and the absence of any violence on the part of participants, on this occasion a peaceful meeting met with massive, bloody repression. That the bloodshed at "Peterloo" was the result of ineptness is not as important as the fact that after the massacre the English Ministry and parliamentary elites united in legal and moral defense of the repression which took place there.

There is a representative diversity in these two events. They are typical of the commodity riots, strikes, demonstrations, parades, assemblies to draft parliamentary petitions, public meetings to boycott butter, and many other gatherings in which common people massed to assert a claim against the holders of economic or political resources. Yet they contrast sharply as well. The number of participants, objectives, duration, and means of action are different. Important questions flow from these differences. What determined the objectives, form, timing, and size of each gathering?

The potato market scuffle and mass meeting at St. Peter's Fields present an interesting puzzle in the response of authorities. Why did collective theft meet with leniency while a peaceful meeting to petition Parliament met bloody repression?

It would be a serious mistake to characterize these gatherings by their sensational and violent aspects. To focus on popular "protest" merely because it is public, sometimes accompanied by violence (often by authorities), and because the participants were members of a class which otherwise was invisible in public life is to characterize such gatherings implicitly as having a nature separate from other forms of social action. These attitudes color and limit much current work on popular gatherings.[1] Even as these studies describe struggles by close-knit groups in the populace over many years of contention for control of food, money, land, or political power, they accept the characterization "disturbance" and often "riot" used by authorities.[2] The effect is to remove "protest" from everyday social action and view it as a breach in an otherwise peaceful social landscape.

The forced sale of potatoes and the meeting of August 1819 bear three important relationships to working-class life in general. First, both events reflect contention for power. Underlying each was a conflict between holders of economic or political resources and members of English society who were making a claim to a greater share of these. The behavior of participants reflected these interests. The gatherings were not simply a form of reaction to transitory hardship, nor were they irrational outbursts. As social action, they represented rational and effective means of mobilizing to make specific claims. For a class with no institutionalized access to political power and few economic resources, collective action through gatherings in public places represented one major means of making a claim.

Second, both events reflect the interplay of local and national politics. During the eighteenth century, food supply to nonproducing areas such as London and other cities had become a major domestic political concern. The government increasingly opposed enforcement of laws interfering with the flow of food from the countryside to these markets in times of shortage. In 1800, England's food supply had reached critical lows after a bad harvest. In that year a royal proclamation cautioned against doing the very thing the special constables at Ashton-under-Lyne were doing—interfering with the free market. The commodity riot soon disappeared from the repertoire of collective action in Lancashire; the last was seen in 1812. By contrast, meetings of the type at St. Peter's Fields appeared for the first time after 1800. The political focus of the great gathering was characteristic of the growing importance of explicitly political objectives in nineteenth-century collective action.

Third, the events are linked to the ability of participants to act in concert. Those involved in the forced sale at the potato market were there because the market brought them together at the same time and place. We can imagine the frequent, routine contact at local markets among participants. It is likely that many of them knew each other. They knew the customary prices and probably the seller as well. Moreover, in Lancashire, as elsewhere in England, a pattern of direct action to maintain customary prices was familiar. This was by no means the first forced sale, although the direct assistance of authorities was unusual. The very fact of sale indicated an underlying shared knowledge of the normal price, presumptions of right and wrong, and confidence in community support. That the meeting at St. Peter's Fields was interwoven with the daily routines of working-class life and collective action is equally easy to see. The degree of advance preparation was striking. The march to the grounds was orderly and by significant groupings—family and community. In both events the line between routine and exceptional collective action is blurred to nonexistent. With this blurring we also lose the distinction between violent and nonviolent as separate and distinct modes of collective action.

In this study we refer to these forms of social action as *contentious gatherings* in order to stress the links just made. Contentious gatherings are viewed as the product of two kinds of processes: (1) processes which brought the working class[3] into conflict over control of land, food, taxes, wages, political power, and other resources, and (2) processes by which particular participants were mobilized for given objectives at a particular time and place. As a formal matter, a contentious gathering is taken to be 20 or more persons gathered in public in a single place to make a claim against another person or group. The definition was used to extract accounts of contentious gatherings from four sources of information about Lancashire in the late eighteenth and early nineteenth century.[4] The resulting collection of events, supplemented individually by whatever information was available from archival and secondary sources, constitutes a continuous profile of gatherings in the county. We will look first at the impact of economic development in Lancashire between 1793 and 1830 on contentious gatherings. Some common arguments relating contentious gatherings to economic hardship are examined and rejected. Contentious gatherings are conceived instead as indicators of contention for power. This conceptualization sees contentious gatherings closely tied to changes in economic and political structures accompanying the rise of industrial capitalism. The remainder of the chapter examines the main effects of this transformation on contentious gatherings.

In the mid-eighteenth century, Lancashire was still predominantly an agricultural region with few established crafts or incorporated towns and a slowly growing cottage textile industry. The lack of structure in the towns and trades made them attractive for new industry, since the masters and owners who wished to expand and change the organization of production had few legal constraints to consider and little resistance from organized trades.[5] In 1750, the manufacturing of cottons, fustians, linens, and woollens, as well as articles made from silk, was mainly outwork but was already moving toward concentration of ownership of materials: looms, jennys, cotton, and twist.[6] Small loomshops represented the extent of centralization of weaving. As continental markets opened to the inexpensive textiles of Lancashire, it became profitable to apply a series of cost-cutting modifications in the tools of the trade developed over a long period of slow technological innovation. In weaving, the fly shuttle was introduced in the 1730s, and weaving by power was contemplated as early as the 1780s (but not firmly established until the early 1820s). In spinning a workable model of the jenny was available about 1764. Carding was done by machine as early as 1770. The water frame for spinning was employed at factories in one Lancashire site in 1769 and in two other nearby locations in 1774 and 1778. In the early 1780s Crompton developed the spinning mule, the basic piece of machinery in spinning factories for the next half-century.[7]

Table 4.1 shows the introduction of machinery toward the end of the eighteenth and early decades of the nineteenth century. The introduction of machinery in the late eighteenth century made spinning more efficient and "twist" cheap, but weaving remained basically a cottage industry in small loomshops and attics around Manchester, Bolton, Bury in the south, and Preston and Blackburn in the north of the county. High wages in weaving drew migrants. In 1788 there were approximately 108,000 weavers in England, Scotland, and Wales, most of them in Lancashire.[8] By 1820, the number of handloom weavers had risen to nearly a quarter of a million, even though the trade had long since ceased to pay a living wage.

Growing competition from the continent, the closing of continental ports after the onset of war with France, and declining profit margins in a highly competitive industry produced a series of cyclical slumps which depressed handloom weavers' wages. These slumps also affected the economic well-being of every other trade in Lancashire. The boom-slump

TABLE 4.1   Introduction of Machinery in Great Britain
Textile Manufacturing, 1788-1845

Year	Weaving		Spinning (Number of Spindles)		
	Handlooms	Powerlooms	Jenny	Waterframe	Mule
1788	108,000[a]	*	*	*	*
1789	*	*	400,000[e]	310,000[e]	700,000[e]
1801	164,000[a]	*	*	*	*
1811	204,000[a]	*	155,880[f]	310,516[f]	4,209,570[f]
1813	212,000[a]	2,400[c]	*	*	*
1819	240,000[a]	14,500	*	*	*
1829-31	225,000[b]	80,000[b]	*	*	*
1835	*	108,210[d]	*	*	*
1844-46	60,000[b]	225,000[b]	*	*	*

a. Wood (1910: 125).
b. Ellison (1886).
c. England only. Usher (1929: 302).
d. Factory Returns (1835).
e. Colquhoun (1788: 4).
f. Daniels (1930: 108-111).
* Missing data

pattern in England's textile manufacturing districts was apparent in 1780 and well established by 1815.[9] The source of the most serious slumps lay not only in the low prices of goods manufactured abroad but in overproduction as well. Crises were often deepened, and sometimes triggered, by contraction of the home market during agricultural crises when food was in short supply and prices were high.

The rapid increase in numbers of working-class contentious gatherings in the late eighteenth century in Lancashire and elsewhere in England coincides with the hardships of the Industrial Revolution created by the cycle of boom and depression accentuated by the war with France (1793-1815) and the closing of both continental and American ports for much of this period. It has seemed natural for generations of economic and social historians to argue that such periods of economic distress, and their effects on the hardest hit—the unskilled proletariat—produced social unrest displayed visibly in upheaval.[10] Factors generating such periods of economic crisis were closely tied to rapid economic development, and thus contentious gatherings are viewed as reactions against the temporary effects of "take-off" during the Industrial Revolution.

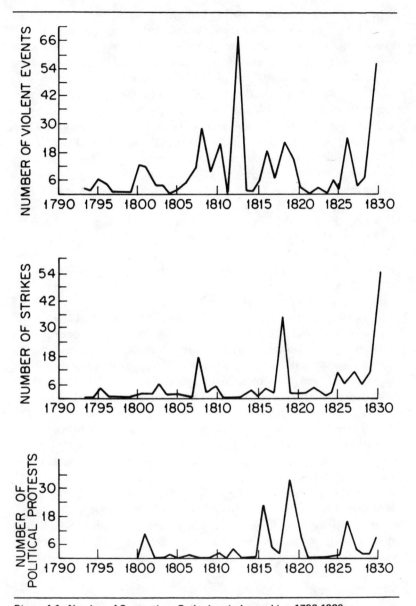

Figure 4.1   Number of Contentious Gatherings in Lancashire, 1793-1830

If such an explanation works, Lancashire should be a good testing ground. Figure 4.1 shows trends in three forms of contentious gatherings in Lancashire between 1793 and 1830.[11] If accumulated stress as a result of economic hardship, or any other process, acted as the main determinant of contentious gatherings, the pattern should be the same for all three types of gatherings—collective violence, strikes, and political gatherings. The patterns are quite different, however. Violence peaks in years of food shortage (1800, 1812), Luddism (1812), and in some years in which widespread strikes occurred (1808, 1810, 1818, and 1830). Political contentious gatherings follow quite a different pattern not clearly related to hardship or other stresses. Strikes, on the other hand, sometimes peak during business slumps (1818, 1830), sometimes during booms (1810, 1825).

We are likely to be misled if we rely on visual comparisons. A more sophisticated analysis is possible using regression analysis. Oatmeal prices,[12] the Gayer-Rostow index of social tension based on food prices and the trade cycle,[13] and increments in numbers of machine operatives in England as a whole[14] are three measures of stress due to hardship, unemployment, and the displacement of workers by machinery. Table 4.2 reinforces the visual impression that stress alone was not a cause of contentious gatherings, since each type of contentious gathering follows a different pattern. However, the table suggests that the timing of particular types of contentious gathering was not random, but rather was keyed to specific issues and opportunities for action. Strikes most clearly deviate from the predicted "stress" pattern. Strikes rise as industrial differentiation falls, as oatmeal prices fall, and as the Gayer-Rostow Index falls. This suggests that a *boom* period is the best predicator of strikes. None of these correlations is significant, suggesting that more than one factor was at work; but the pattern of action when workers were needed most by owners of factories is consistent.

Violent contentious gatherings display the clearest positive correlation with measures of stress. Prices strongly predict collective violence, but, contrary to the stress hypothesis, there is no correlation with industrial displacement.[15] The apparent inconsistency of these correlations disappears if we think of prices as a measure of issue salience rather than a measure of stress alone. While violence occurred during strikes and other forms of contentious gatherings, the most common contentious gathering in which objects were seized or persons attacked was the food riot, the concerted effort to control food distribution. Not surprisingly, price increases were a precise indicator of the timing of these events.[16] Trade slumps and industrial displacement, independently of price rises, were not.

TABLE 4.2   Standardized Regression of Measures of
             Collective Action on Measures of Stress

Dependent Variable	Oatmeal Prices	Prices/ Trade Cycle	Factory Operatives	Time	N	R^2	D-W[a]
Panel 1							
Strikes	-.10			.44*	29	.24	1.77
Violence	.60*			.49*	29	.37	2.15
Political	.22			.21	31	.06	1.83
Panel 2							
Strikes		-.32		.41*	24	.17	2.25
Violence		.46*		.17	24	.22	1.26
Political		.34*		.02	26	.12	1.90
Panel 3							
Strikes			-.14	.45*	23	.21	1.90
Violence			-.11	.08	23	.01	2.18
Politcial			-.23	.11	24	.06	1.89

Starred (*) coefficients are more than twice their standard error.
a. Durbin-Watson statistic.
b. All dependent variables have been transformed to reduce the effects of outliers in the distributions. The actual variables are *ln* number of strikes), *ln* (number of violent events), and *sqrt* (number of political contentious gatherings). Independent variables are raw scores.

Political gatherings follow yet another pattern, this one less clearly linked either to stress or to obvious issues and opportunities for action. Political gatherings are only weakly correlated with price rises or rapid industrial development, but there is a clear statistical relationship between political gatherings and periods when prices rose and the trade cycle was in a slump. This pattern, like the others, provides little support for stress theories, since it provides no explanation for the failure of other indicators of stress to predict the timing of political contentious gatherings.

CAPITALISM AND
CONTENTION FOR POWER

The obvious importance of the characteristics of particular contenders and the failure of generalized stress to predict the timing of contentious gatherings force our attention back to the effects of capitalism on the lives of Lancashire's working class. The main direct effects on Lancashire's population were to reduce the majority of workers to propertyless wage-earners and to reorganize the patterns of routine community interaction. Each transformation produced contention for local control of important resources. Capitalism also accelerated nationalization of the economy. Hence, local contention for control of key resources in the capitalist economy was inevitably nationalized. The long-run patterns of contentious gatherings were necessarily affected by the manner in which local contention for power became incorporated in contention for national political power.

The primary effect of capitalism was the creation of a propertyless class dependent on wages for a living. While Christopher Hill estimates that for most of the seventeenth century, full-time wage laborers were a minority of the population, the proportion increased rapidly in the eighteenth century.[17] By 1780, Lancashire's industrial work force alone, a large proportion of which neither owned materials or tools nor controlled the sale or distribution of products, already comprised a minimum of 30 percent of the population.[18] The Industrial Revolution reduced some crafts to proletarian status as the changing means of production and shifting ownership divested them of control of apprenticeship, materials of work, and ultimately even the tools of their trade. Other occupations, such as machine operators, were proletarian by definition. Thus, proletarianization proceeded at an uneven pace through the work force.

These effects of industrial capitalism were accompanied by demographic change resulting from population growth and the centralization of the control of work. These demographic changes affected the growth of communities, the patterns of social interaction among members of the working class, the flow of goods to markets, access to factories, and contact with authorities. Capitalism brought increasing involvement of national political power. Proletarianization was accomplished only with the aid of Parliament and the common law courts, which removed restrictions on entry into trades, refused to set wages under the Statute of Artificers, made combinations of workers illegal, and otherwise played a partisan role.[19] A propertied middle class, ranging from wealthier tradespeople, to merchants, to industrialists of all magnitudes, grew as a result of the economic transformation. After 1780 this middle class became an active political force pressing Parliament and the ministry for more favorable economic policies on one hand and an extension of the franchise on the other. As employers of, and sellers to, the working class and as the political opposition to the enfranchised elite, this middle class became an important link between local and national contention for power.

PROLETARIANIZATION OF
THE WORK FORCE

Proletarianization of the work force created issues for collective action. The issues included not only diminished economic security created by loss of direct control over work materials, working times and places, and the direct pressure on family roles,[20] but also the very *right* to control conditions of work. Refusal of employers to respect apprenticeship restrictions and traditional work organization provoked collective action ranging from lawsuits to enforced apprenticeship restrictions, strikes, and destruction of machinery.[21] Machine-breaking was a means of contesting the transfer of control over work—in particular, the pace of work and the economic return from work. Instances of machine-breaking to enforce restrictions on the organization of work occurred in the late seventeenth century when weavers destroyed "dutch" looms in London. By 1727 smashing stocking frames was made a capital offense.[22] In Lancashire in 1753 a mob wrecked the house of John Kay in protest against the introduction of his invention, the fly shuttle. In 1768, Hargreaves' spinning jennies were destroyed at Blackburn, and in 1779 spinners and their families attacked Arkwright's mill at Birkacre, destroying all jennies with more than 24 spindles.[23] A significant amount of public opinion supported the objectives of the spinners in the latter case. In 1812, however, Luddism was crushed by military force, as was the attempted destruction of powerloom factories near Blackburn in 1826.

Gradually, workers were forced by employers, with the firm backing of authorities, to concede control of the means of production. Machine-breaking became a relatively minor tactic of workers. Factory workers, unlike the artisanal trades, were left with one point of leverage: control of labor supply. Hence, factory-based production, both because it provided a central site and because labor was the only resource under workers' control, made union discipline and picketing the key to success. Union discipline provided one-half of the leverage from picketing; the threat of violence constituted the other half. Labor violence was directed less and less at machines and more and more at fellow workers. The inability of factory workers to hold back the use of private property for profit in order to improve the conditions of work or to exercise more control over recruitment of workers led to a noticeable quickening of the pace of strikes among the industrial trades after 1800. The frequent strikes by mule spinners were an effort to bargain for wages in the absence of legal means for such negotiation.

Proletarianization proceeded unevenly in the work force in Lancashire with the consequence that different trades mobilized for contention at different times and for different objectives. The skilled trades and traditional crafts—tailors, bootmakers, watchmakers, chandlers, saddlers, ropemakers, silk weavers and others—did a burgeoning business with the wealthy middle class and were not threatened with loss of control over the means of production until late in the Industrial Revolution. When they struck, it was for higher prices for their products, not increased wages. Occasionally, members of the skilled trades were indicted for combining to enforce apprenticeship restrictions, but for the most part these artisans seem to have been successful in maintaining the organization of their trades throughout this period.

A second group of skilled trades was much closely tied to the changing means of producing textiles. Some crafts—calico printers, feltmakers, paper makers, and foundry workers—were established in the county for the first time as a result of the rise of textile production. Their control of apprenticeship was unchallenged until industrialization directly affected the specialized processes they controlled. For example, in the period between 1810 and 1825, calico printing was virtually absorbed into the large spinning companies; as a result, calico printers (and related crafts) lost all leverage over employers.[24] Similarly, in the 1820s, employers of felt hatmakers grew large enough to finance a battle with the Lancashire feltmakers' organization and win.[25] Once employers' economic resources greatly surpassed those of the employees' combinations in these trades, employees were quickly reduced to proletarian status after a brief period of contention. Thereafter, combining was more difficult, and wage rates became the main issue in contention with employers.

Mule spinning was a skilled trade which owed its existence to the invention of machinery. Factory owners employed a few master mule spinners as independent contractors and permitted them to hire the other employees needed to run the machinery. Thus, while mule spinners did not own materials or tools of their trade, they retained considerable leverage over wages and work organization. Mule spinners retained this leverage until simplified machinery was introduced in the 1830s which could be run by unskilled employees. By contrast, handloom weavers were slowly destroyed by the expansion of the textile industry. The weavers were easily reduced to proletarian status, since looms could be rented cheaply and broadloom weaving was easily learned. Temporarily high

TABLE 4.3   Percentage Contentious Gatherings by Trade
by Type of Gathering in Selected Years[a]

| Gathering Type | Trade | | |
	Weavers	Spinners	Artisans
Meetings	15.1 (13)	8.7 (6)	5.3 (1)
Meeting + Petition	3.4 (3)	0 (0)	0 (0)
Demonstrations	9.3 (8)	13.0 (9)	5.3 (1)
Strikes	45.3 (39)	46.4 (32)	57.9 (11)
Violence	26.7 (23)	31.9 (22)	31.6 (6)
Total	99.8 (86)	100.0 (69)	100.1 (19)

a. 1800, 1801, 1805, 1806, 1808, 1810, 1812, 1818, 1830. Numbers are shown in parentheses.

wages during the boom at the end of the eighteenth century drew masses of migrants, first from the agricultural proletariat in Lancashire, then workers from other counties, and finally impoverished Irish. The large number of weavers quickly drove wages down, and in the first half of the nineteenth century handloom weavers gradually became poorer and were driven into other trades. Powerloom weaving developed after 1820 and quickly reduced handloom weavers to marginal economic status.

Comparison of the contentious gatherings of the traditional crafts, spinners, and weavers reveals the impact of the various routes to proletarianization taken by different trades in contending for power by each. While the number of gatherings in which each group participated increased over time, the patterns as well as the objectives were quite different. There were fewer contentious gatherings involving the skilled trades; Table 4.3 shows these were mainly strikes. Moreover, 75 percent of the strikes by artisans were clustered in years of prosperity (1810) or mild upswings following a trade depression (1818). Comparing weavers' and spinners' strikes with increments in an index of industrial production shows that spinners tended to strike during boom periods (r^2 = .45) while weavers' strikes followed no pattern (r^2 = .004). Both of these trades engaged in a wider variety of contentious gatherings than did the skilled crafts. The differing patterns are explained in part by the kind of control over work each attempted to maintain. The skilled crafts were concerned primarily with self-discipline, apprenticeship, and the organization of the craft. As long as this control was maintained, they were not in regular contention for power with employers. Spinners had similar leverage over the supply of labor, but to assert their leverage they had to withhold their labor from employers; hence their frequent strikes. Weavers struck seldom but struck many employers at once, mainly in response to wage cuts. They frequently engaged in other forms of contentious gatherings, including drafting petitions to Parliament for a minimum wage. Lacking the leverage of the spinners, they attempted many other forms of contention to solve the problem of economic dependence in other ways. Spinners, too, began to broaden their forms of contention in the late 1820s as their economic position slipped.

CENTRALIZATION AND URBANIZATION

Underlying the different patterns of contention by spinners and weavers we can see another aspect of the impact of industrial capitalism. Spinners had the advantage of a centralized work place; weavers did not. Mule spinners were skilled, few in number, and, until factory management advanced considerably, they were independent managers of the machinery under their direction with full authority to hire and pay subordinates. Handloom weavers had a most difficult job of organizing. Weaving was mechanized late and, through most of the period, was highly decentralized. The "taking home" day on which worked-up material was carried to the employer's warehouse and new twist dispensed facilitated informal association among the weavers who walked together and perhaps drank together afterward. But organizing all the weavers of a single large employer to resist wage reductions required substantially more effort than organizing the mule spinners at a single factory. Because of the decentralization of work sites, weavers could not mobilize on an effective scale for any length of time. In 1799, a weavers' committee at Bolton mounted a petition drive to see parliamentary aid for handloom weavers. The organization which resulted was short-lived and unsuccessful. It was revived in 1807, 1811, 1818, and 1826, each a period of short-term, countywide collective action by weavers. By contrast, the spinners' union was more successful, mounting large-scale strikes in Lancashire in 1810, 1818, and 1830, drawing financial support from nonstriking workers at great distances.

The strikes by the mule spinners, handloom weavers, and skilled trades in 1818 illustrate the way in which union organization affected the form contention took. The skilled trades conducted peaceful demonstrations in support of their strikes and won higher wages quickly. Both spinners' and weavers' strikes were accompanied by considerable violence, which was provoked by the inability of either trade to control the labor supply of employers in any other way. Spinners periodically were able to control the labor supply in small strikes for a limited period of time through union discipline alone; many victories were won in this manner between 1800 and 1825. Weavers, lacking a union of such strength, traditionally attempted to control the supply of labor by collecting the shuttles of all weavers in the region. In 1818, striking weavers attempted to intercept nonstrikers on their way into town for more twist, a strategy which failed.[26] Spinners also turned to violence in 1818 in order to control strike-breaking workers. Since they had the advantage of a centralized work location, they succeeded in their strike, while the weavers failed. In both instances violence was preceded by demonstrations to mobilize community support for the strike; only after this failed to achieve their ends did weavers begin attacking scab workers in earnest.

Just as the capacity to defend working conditions depended in part on the capacity to form a union and the existence of a centralized work site at which to control the supply of labor, centralization of production, distribution, and association among members of the working class affected many other contenders. For some, increasing concentration aided mobilization. For others, urbanization worked against the grain of preexisting association to nullify or weaken efforts to mobilize. For example, the proximity of markets to working-class communities, as well as the cohesiveness of those communities, had an important effect on whether a food riot occurred. As open air markets disappeared in larger towns, commodity riots also declined.

The southeastern quarter of the county (Salford Hundred) was the most densely populated, the most highly industrialized, and the most urban. The center of growth was Manchester, an unincorporated town presided over by an ancient court leet and a parish vestry. In 1717, Manchester's population was about 20,000. By 1780 15-20 waterframe spinning factories were already located there. In 1801, the population had grown to 90,000; within two decades, Manchester had overtaken Liverpool to become the largest city in the county. The villages around Manchester in the southeastern and east-central portion of the county experienced similar growth. Factories were established in some of these, but many were essentially working-class villages, sites of outwork, local commerce, and little else. Bury, a village of less than 2,000 in 1750, grew to more than 7,000 in 1801 as one of several centers of calico manufacture and printing

TABLE 4.4   Percent Contentious Gatherings by Type by Location

Gathering Type	Market	Location Industrial Site/Rural	Other Rural	Industrial Site/Urban[a]	Other Urban	All Locations
All Meetings	18.5	1.4	56.5	–	31.1	19.5
Demonstrations	7.4	3.5	13.0	9.9	21.3	11.4
Strikes	–	50.9	–	53.5	–	25.6
Violence	74.0	43.9	30.4	36.6	47.5	43.5
Total	99.9	99.7	99.9	100.0	99.9	100.0
N=	(27)	(57)	(46)	(71)	(61)	(262)

a. Urban = More than five persons per acre.

established by the Peels. Bolton, with less than 5,000 inhabitants as late as 1773, increased to over 12,500 in 1801.

The density of the settled population alone provided opportunities for association. As the working-class villages of the region swelled, the parish organization which traditionally held communities together groaned under the weight of the increased population. Poor law administration and policing were heavy burdens for parishes. Yet associational life among the working classes reached new highs of vitality. Friendly societies multiplied.[27] Chapels increased in membership.[28] Communication with large numbers of workers all over the region became possible through messages tacked along roadways and the distribution of handbills in the towns. With the advent of steam power after 1810, spinning factories began to move into a few large centers of production and out of the countryside and sources of water power. The concentration of work as well as marketing in a few large towns such as Manchester, Bolton, and Stockport meant that the large towns increasingly became the center of networks linking working-class communities, a point of contact between trades, and a place where, unlike many of the working-class villages, workers, gentry, and middle class lived and worked in close contact. Even justices of the peace tended to move into the towns to be closer to their tasks after 1800.

The form and location of contentious gatherings were influenced by urbanization. Contentious gatherings in Lancashire, as far as we can tell from biased sources, were always more urban than rural from 1750 on. Even rural participants of the eighteenth century chose the towns as sites at which to contest control over resources such as food or jobs because towns were the loci at which control was exercised. Moreover, even for eighteenth-century participants, the largest towns of the county had symbolic meaning. If not the residence of the most important gentry, towns were where the gentry who were leaders of business and commerce and county officials performed many of their official functions. They were the site of the most important public buildings, the host for visiting dignitaries and the centers for celebrations which drew large crowds from the countryside. With industrialization, there was a short-lived movement of some types of contentious gatherings to the countryside, following the first factories. Yet, while more contentious gatherings took place outside the chief cities—Manchester, Boston, and Liverpool—in each successive decade of the nineteenth century, they also occurred more frequently in areas of high population density.

The increasing urbanization and heterogeneity of participants interested in a common issue meant that communities were displaced as collective actors by formal associations, such as the "combination," the committee to petition Parliament, the town meeting, or the social or political club. Table 4.5 shows that the proportion of actors organized formally in associations increases steadily. Many associations were also built upon community networks. For example, an association was formed at Preston in 1815 to boycott butter. This form of consumer protest by buyers at a customary market replaced the food riot once the open market disappeared and collective action could not be effectively mounted against the many shopkeepers who controlled commodity prices in towns. The political Hampden Clubs, which formed throughout southeastern Lancashire in the following year, also recruited members through friends and community acquaintances. Associations were effective in an urban setting: They could be a base for mobilizing participants who did not contact each other routinely in any other context. They could command a range of resources which permitted selection of a variety of strategies. By contrast, without other organizations, members of a community in which the food riot was a customary form of protest might or might not choose to protest in time of need. But as a community it was highly unlikely to respond to food shortages with a petition to Parliament or other organization-based form of collective action.

The heterogeneity and density of the city provided an audience which could be mobilized through diffuse public appeal. The development of the demonstration as a new type of contentious gathering in Lancashire in the early nineteenth century showed an awareness of the new opportunities for mobilizing support. In form, the demonstration was similar in appear-

TABLE 4.5 Types of Working-Class Collective Groups of Actors[a] in Contentious Gatherings in Lancashire, Selected Time Periods

Actor Type	Time Period						
	1800-1801	1805-1806	1808/1810	1812	1818	1830	All Periods
Formal Associations							
Combinations	4	3	48	3	38	77	173
Political Societies	0	0	0	1	0	3	4
Petition Committees	8	2	1	1	2	3	17
Town Meetings[b]	0	3	3	0	6	3	15
Others	1	0	2	54	3	22	82
Total Associations	13(16.7)	8(25.0)	54(29.3)	59(40.4)	49(26.8)	108(31.7)	291(30.2)
Other Actors							
Employees of One Employer	3	0	6	6	15	75	105
Workers from One Town	1	1	43	7	49	30	131
Employees of Sev. Employers	4	3	8	1	14	41	71
Employees from Sev. Towns	0	0	5	0	15	4	24
Crowd: Political	16	2	22	17	20	17	94
Users of a Common Market	5	0	0	11	2	0	18
Other Crowds, Assemblies	36	18	46	45	19	66	230
Total Other	65(83.3)	24(75.0)	130(70.7)	87(59.6)	134(73.2)	233(68.3)	673(69.8)
Total All Types	78(100)	32(100)	184(100)	146(100)	183(100)	341(100)	964(100)

a. Friendly societies have been omitted.
b. Announced and chaired by local authorities.

ance to the parade or celebration in which members of a community organized by some traditional grouping—family, lodge, trade—march in affirmation of community sentiment. The contentious demonstration—first for poor relief in 1816, and later for strike support in 1818 and political mobilization in 1819—also conveyed the message that the participants believed they represented a position on a given issue which should have the moral support of the community. The peacefulness and discipline of the form furthered the image of rectitude. Like public meetings to discuss issues or to petition Parliament, demonstrations were an urban strategy for mobilization and collective action where population density placed potential demonstrators within easy traveling distance.

NATIONAL POLITICS AND
CONTENTION FOR POWER

Between the French Revolution and the first Reform Act, working-class contentious gatherings were directed at new objectives. Parliament became a focus of claims made through contentious gatherings. First, there was an increase in the number of petitions to Parliament for action. Many of these petitions sought to preserve conditions which were disappearing as a result of industrialization, a living wage, and restoration of control over work and family through Factory Acts.[29] In conjunction with the middle class, working-class petitions also voiced opposition to policies which had a negative effect on the economy of Lancashire. Second, throughout this period, a significant proportion of contentious gatherings sought political change in a more fundamental sense. The primacy of issues related to economic rights rather than political rights is apparent even in working-class movements for parliamentary reform between 1800 and 1830, but the goal of achieving political power grows steadily in importance beginning with the decade following the French Revolution.

If we take a broader view of contentious gatherings for a moment, stretching our field of vision to include the span between 1600 and 1850, the interplay between national political contention and local contentious gatherings is striking. Major episodes of national political reorganization produce their local sympathizers, opponents, or opportunists. The Reformation, the Jacobite uprisings of 1715 and 1745, and the first Reform Act in 1830-1832 are all periods marked by widespread contention, violence, and large numbers of gatherings. Other, less massive effects of shifting political alignments are also clear. The increasing flow of food from the

TABLE 4.6 Objectives of Contentious Gatherings in Selected Time Periods

Objectives[a]	1800-01	1805-06	1808/10	1812	1818	1830
Destruction of machines/cloth	0	0	8	16	6	2
Seize control of shuttles, cloth	2	2	10	33	3	7
Attack fellow workers	4	2	20	12	15	36
Change wages	4	7	108	3	98	135
Total Work-Related	10(20.0)	11(40.7)	146(76.4)	64(63.4)	122(77.2)	180(65.4)
Oppose local government action	1	0	1	4	2	0
Seek parliamentary action	4	1	6	7	21	30
Seek political change, other	10	1	12	3	9	33
Total Political	15(30.0)	2(7.4)	19(9.9)	14(13.9)	32(20.2)	63(22.9)
Seize or control food supply	13	0	2	18	0	0
Rescue (from authorities)	1	0	5	0	0	4
Religious conflict	0	0	0	3	0	2
Brawls, fights, fairs, "rough music"	1	0	4	1	1	7
Diffuse, mixed, confused, uncertain	10	14	15	1	3	19
Total Other	25(50.0)	14(51.8)	26(13.6)	23(22.8)	4(2.5)	32(11.6)
All Objectives	50(100.0)	27(100.0)	191(99.9)	101(100.1)	158(99.9)	275(99.9)

a. Longest-range objective is given priority. Missing data (118 cases) and actors defending themselves from direct, physical attack (189 cases) have been omitted.

countryside to the national capital and to other growing urban centers involved the government in the protection of the food supply in times of shortage. Efforts to produce military recruits during the war with France triggered both press gang and militia riots. Moreover, both enclosure and the free market in labor were policies promoted actively by a government with an increasing stake in a capitalist economy. Each policy had its visible impact on local contention for power. Nevertheless, the common people, for the most part prior to 1789, were not contenders for national political power. The French Revolution provided a powerful example; its ideology was a stimulus to the growth of working-class political awareness.[30] Two different kinds of political upheaval in England following 1789 accelerated the nationalization of local contention for power. The first was the massive repression of working-class collective action following the onset of war with France in 1793. The second, and ultimately more important, was the slow rise to political power of the middle class, which forced expansion of the franchise in the first Reform Act in 1832.

REPRESSION:
POLITICAL REACTION AND AFTER

In 1789, the French Revolution shook the English establishment, and in 1793 England declared war on France. For the next 26 years, partially as a result of the continental blockade and later loss of cotton supplies from America, the textile industry suffered cyclical slumps which affected the working classes of Lancashire more than any other group in England. Wages in the industry were already declining under the impact of continental competition before the declaration of war. War brought economic insecurity, worker conflict with employers—who were themselves gaining increasing political and economic voice nationally—and political reaction. The political reaction of the war years colored the English establishment's view of working-class collective action. The ideology of 1789 was indeed widespread among the working classes, and several national organizations committed to these principles and to political change were established by artisans.[31] Between 1793 and 1820 more than 60 acts directed at repression of working-class collective action were passed by Parliament.[32] By 1799, virtually every form of working-class association or collective action was illegal or licensable by the justices of the peace.[33] Much of this statutory baggage expired unused, to be revived again during the Luddite machine-breaking period of 1812 and again in 1817-1819 during the buildup of working-class interest in parliamentary reform. But as a measure of elite suspicion of popular unrest, the legislation is important.

Political reaction, combined with the ideology of political economy, resulted in the deepest penetration of governmental regulation into working-class lives since the Statute of Artificers of the sixteenth century. The enactments during the Industrial Revolution preserved the authority of the employer, property owner, and justice of the peace over the working class but forbade members of the working class to engage in collective resistance. At a stroke, all grievances against private and community authority became sustained conflicts over political power, although consciousness of the change developed slowly and unevenly among the working class.

Justices of the peace were responsible for enforcement of the new laws. Tory justices perceived the Jacobin presence among the working class more often than did Whig justices.[34] The former were more likely to engage in an active dialogue with the Home Office about the likelihood of rebellion. This is clear from the widely cited Home Office Papers, the correspondence beween the Home Office and county officials. The Manchester Division of the Lancashire Quarter Sessions was Tory. In the late 1790s, justices of this division began to employ spies, with the encouragement of the Home Office. In many instances the spies were members of the local militia companies which the justices commanded as county gentry. Although their credibility was often questionable, spies in Lancashire became an important conduit of information about working-class issues, whether increased wages or revolution. Spies gave the system of repression preventive as well as reactive capacity. Justices could seek out suspected centers of discontent and take action before or as collective action occurred. Hence, intensified interaction with local authorities reinforced the point that political power could not be separated from other forms of power sought by working-class groups.

No theme runs more consistently through the history of collective action in Lancashire than the impact of repression on contentious gatherings. The great waves of protest in Lancashire in 1800, 1808, 1812, 1816-1819, 1826, 1829-1830 were all terminated by massive repression. The police of pre-1830 England were deceptively tolerant of many forms of contentious gatherings. The justices of the peace mobilized sufficient force for repression very slowly. The more advance notice and the more public the form of gathering, the more effective they could be. During the buildup of a great strike wave or political movement, the military could be called in and the fragile working-class organization underlying the mass mobilization destroyed without the appearance of great bloodshed.

Two examples will illustrate how contentious gatherings in Lancashire were channeled by repression. The first concerns the changing targets of violent contention. Collective violence, in the absence of an effective local police force, had a history of success. Violence against property was a common strategy for protest directed against major community resource holders such as suppliers of food. As protest and protesters urbanized and as authorities themselves mobilized to protect increasingly valuable industrial resources located in towns, massive violence became more costly. Machine-breaking in 1779, 1792, and 1812 in Lancashire was a relatively "cheap" means of contention. However, in 1826, machine-breaking took eight participants' lives. In 1830, collective violence followed quite a different pattern: it was carried out by small groups of striking spinners. Violence took the form of threats and harassment of fellow workers. This constituted a substrategy accompanying the main form of collective action, such as a picket line or a demonstration during a strike.

The second illustration concerns the movement for parliamentary reform among the working class in Lancashire between 1816 and 1819. The channeling effect of repression on the forms of contentious gatherings in these years is difficult to prove by direct evidence, but the sequence of events is suggestive. In 1816, many towns in southern Lancashire formed secret Hampden Clubs on the model of the London society of that name formed to consider parliamentary reform. The leaders of these clubs were largely artisans, and their agenda, according to spies' reports, was discussion of vague plans for political change and occasionally revolution.[35] If the courses of action they chose indicates anything about their intent, the Hampden Clubs were perfectly respectable. The action they promoted in 1817 was a march to London with a petition for parliamentary reform for the Prince Regent. The authorities were prepared for much more, and viewed the march as proof of the interpretation which the conservative Home Secretary Sidmouth and the rabid Lancashire Justices of the Peace had conveyed to Parliament's Committees of Secrecy. The march was disbanded by authorities and the participants arrested. The leaders were imprisoned for up to a year without benefit of the writ of habeas corpus.

Having thus failed to mobilize in secret, after an interlude in 1818 in which many trades struck successfully for higher wages, the working class evolved a new form of mobilization for parliamentary reform. Public debating societies were formed, once again led by members of the skilled trades, who had led the Hampden Clubs and had struck successfully in the previous year. These societies were carefully tailored to the requirements of the Seditious Meetings Act, which the events of 1816-1817 had evoked

TABLE 4.7   Active Justices of the Peace in 1800 and 1816
Compared with Number of Contentious Gatherings
and Percentage Repressed by Administrative Subdivision

| | *ADMINISTRATIVE SUBDIVISION* | | | | |
	Amounderness, Lonsdale, Blackburn	*West Derby*	*Bolton*	*Ashton-under-Lyne*	*Manchester*
Active JPs 1800[a]	6	4	2	0	4
Active JPs 1816[a]	9	11	4	1	7
Gatherings[b]	43	25	37	52	124
Percentage Repressed	16.3	32.0	54.1	23.1	48.3

[a]A small number of active justices of the peace are not included because their residences are unkown. None of these lived in the vicinity of Ashton-under-Lyne.
[b]Gatherings in 1800, 1801, 1805, 1806, 1808, 1810, 1812, 1818.

from Parliament. The authorities, unable to suppress these union societies, issued warnings against attending their public rallies, the largest of which was planned for August 1819. So careful were authorities that the Home Office cautioned against preemptive action, although the legality of this large meeting might have been questioned under the Seditious Meetings Act. So careful were participants that they sought legal advice before meeting and set the agenda for the meeting on this basis. The tragic outcome of the meeting at St. Peter's Fields in Manchester on August 16, 1819 is well-known. Eleven died and over 400 others were sabered or trampled in a shocking display of inept policing. Important here is the degree to which authorities and targets of repression "jockied" for position along the boundary between a legal gathering and one which could be repressed with impunity. After "Peterloo," the working-class movement for reform was at an end for a decade. Repression thus could be selective: relatively lenient toward most political and nonpolitical collective action but nonetheless effective in suppressing the most effective efforts of the working class toward collective contention for power.

Conversely, contentious gatherings and working-class collective action flourished where repression was least likely to occur. As a crude measure of the likelihood of repression we may use the location of residences of justices of the peace in Lancashire. There was likely to be a ready response to contentious gatherings where justices of the peace lived or held petty sessions. Because of the broad authority of the justices of the peace, constables, special constables, militia, and regular army troops could be summoned more quickly, perhaps led by the justice himself. Comparing this measure of the capacity for repression with the rate of repression and the number of contentious gatherings, we find that Ashton-under-Lyne, which had the fewest active justices of the peace between 1800 and 1816, had both the lowest rate of repression among the industrialized districts of Lancashire (this excludes Amounderness-Lonsdale-Blackburn) and the second largest total number of contentious gatherings.[36] A recent intensive study of collective action by the working class in this part of Lancashire confirms both the level of contentious activity and the significance of the low capability of authorities to maintain social control.[37]

GROWTH OF THE NATIONAL POLITY, THE STRUCTURE OF POWER, AND WORKING-CLASS MOVEMENTS

The rising hostility of authorities toward working-class collective action of all types was a response to the fear of upheaval following the French Revolution. That fear was fed by the increasing interest of the working class in political ideology.[38] Since the hostility was triggered by fears of revolution, it is not surprising to find that in periods when the fear of revolution was particularly high, repression of political contentious gatherings was also high. Table 4.8 shows that in 1800-1801 and 1812 the rate of arrest of participants opposing the policies or form of government climbed irrespective of the violence or size of the contentious gathering. Significantly, both periods are precisely those in which the suspicions of Parliament concerning the revolutionary designs of the working class were at their height. The level of suspicion is reflected in the creation of Parliamentary Committees of Secrecy to examine the evidence of revolutionary plots, increased support for repression of contentious gatherings by justices of the peace, and new laws adding or increasing penalties for participation in contentious gatherings.

The contrasting relationship between working-class opposition to government and arrest rates in 1808-1810 (and the absence of a correlation in 1818—another year of Committees of Secrecy and fears of revolution) reflects another significant factor in the nationalization of politics: pressure from contenders other than the working class. The year 1808 marked a period of mounting opposition by the middle class to the commercial policies of the ministry. The middle class of Lancashire opposed the

TABLE 4.8   Standardized Regression of Arrests[a] (per event) on
Number of Participants,[a] Level of Violence, and
Level of Hostility to Authorities by Year

Years	Number of Participants	Level of Violence[b]	Opposition to Gov't[c]	N	R^2
1800-01	-.35*	.49*	.34*	79	.35
1805-06	-.40*	.78*	-.14	29	.37
1808/10	.21*	.42*	-.20*	132	.25
1812	.01	.26*	.42*	76	.21
1818	.09	.57*	-.01	63	.34
1830	.05	.40*	.02	175	.16
All Years	.04	.43*	.03	554	.18

Starred (*) coefficients are more than twice their standard error.
a. The square root of arrests and participants were used instead of raw scores to correct for skewed distributions.
b. Violence is measured as a three-level, ordinal variable: 0 = no violence; 1 = threats, minor property damage, punching, isolated fist fight; 2 = more violence than 1.
c. Opposition to government means manifest hostility to authorities (beyond resistence to arrest or other form of direct repression), or objective involving a substantial change in the policies or form of government. Hostility was entered as a dummy variable, present or not present.

Orders in Council closing the continental ports and the Corn Laws which made food expensive for workers in the textile industry. At the close of the eighteenth century, this political opposition was important: Justices of the peace enjoyed unchallenged control over the appointment and super- vision of constables in the unincorporated areas of Lancashire. Their legal powers were enhanced by social prestige and by the lack of viable alterna- tive governmental institutions. Nevertheless, justices of the peace were dependent on community-generated resources. It is at the points of poten- tial conflict over resources between justices and the community that middle-class members of the community began to make their presence felt. Jurors, taxpayers, potential recruits for the militia, and special constables were drawn from among the propertied owners of the county, large and small. Manorial, township, parish, and county officials of some types were elected by middle-class taxpayers and property owners. What might loosely be referred to, following Dicey, as the growth in importance of "public opinion" in the early nineteenth century in England actually

TABLE 4.9   Standardized Regression of Measures
of Collective Action on Measures of Issue
Salience, Opportunity, and Economic Hardship

Dependent Variable	Trade Cycle[a]	Oatmeal Prices[b]	Change in Production[c]	Middle Class Opposition[d]	Strikes	Time	N	R^2
Strikes	.12	-.08	.24	.52*		.25	29	.40
Political Assemblies	-.33	.23	.17	.37*		-.05	29	.34
Violence	-.01	.37*	-.20	.33		.30	29	.47
Violence			.21	.02	.45*	.18	38	.37

Starred (*) coefficients are more than twice their standard error.
a. Gayer Trade Cycle Index (Gayer et al., 1953: 355). Dependent variables transformed as described in Table 4.2; independent variables entered as raw scores.
b. Average oatmeal prices for the county of Lancaster.
c. W.G. Hoffman Index of Industrial Production (Mitchell and Deane, 1971: 271).
d. See text and note 39.

describes the increasing mobilization of many of the groups which could challenge control of resources by the traditional landed elites in one or more of these ways. The influence of these groups affected the use of repression. Some members of commercial groups challenged the justices' views of the scope of political liberties and of the legitimacy of particular modes of repression.

The mobilization of the middle class not only rivaled the power of the landed elites in Lancashire after 1750, thus affecting repressive policy; it also provided resources for some forms of working-class contention. Table 4.9 shows the striking relationship between working-class contentious gatherings and mobilization for political opposition to government by the middle class.[39] The influence of middle-class mobilization was so pronounced that the measures of economic change predict neither strikes nor political contentious gatherings when middle-class mobilization is also a predictor. Middle-class mobilization itself was stimulated in part by the business cycle, and thus was negatively correlated with measures of industrial growth.[40] As we would expect, collective violence was not strongly affected by middle-class mobilization; but because violence occurred during strikes as well as commodity shortages, there was a weak positive correlation.

The relationship between working-class political contentious gatherings and middle-class mobilization for political opposition explains both the timing of contentious gatherings and the fragility of working-class political contention by comparison with the more robust trade union movement. The difference lies in the direct links that existed between working-class political contention and middle-class opposition to government. The increasing level of commercial or middle-class mobilization for contention over the income tax of 1806, ending the war with France, the Orders in Council, and peaceful reform of Parliament made mobilization by the working classes around similar issues easier; at the same time, working-class demands seemed less extreme. Members of the middle class provided leadership, financial assistance, intervention in Parliament, protection from repression, and other forms of direct material support. The availability of these resources contributed to timing of waves of political contentious gatherings. Alliances on these issues between middle-class members of Lancashire communities and members of the working class occurred when they suited middle-class needs. Coalitions were formed around a narrow range of issues: the preservation of civil and political liberties, taxes, some types of factory legislation, and limited political reform. In each of these cases, parliamentary policy was the ultimate issue: the monarchy or the underpinnings of private property were not in question. Acceptance of these priorities meant that working-class political action was often deflected, by virtue of the initial coalition itself, from the targets which might have benefited working-class contenders most.

Thus, the way working-class mobilization for political change was joined with non-working-class political movements mattered a great deal. Regardless of the proportion of the working class which may have accepted more radical objectives, leaders of the most effective efforts to mobilize working-class support for political change were tied very strongly to middle-class platforms and ultimately to middle-class support for change. The available data suggest that there were well-established patterns of political leadership among the working class which made it difficult to build movements for political change of any size without taking advantage of one of three factors: links among towns provided by members of skilled trades, the focusing effect of orators, or the leadership of informed members of the elite.[41] Each of these forms of leadership ultimately led to incorporation of relatively conservative programs of change with working-class political mobilization.[42] The working-class expression of more basic political reform never crystallized into a larger movement before Chartism and the emergence of different patterns of leadership.

The capacity of the middle class to suppress working-class contention for power in other ways grew as well. The position shopkeepers, merchants, and industrial managers were achieving as a class was based on the control of property accumulated at the expense of the working-class members of the community. Hence, the commercial and industrial middle class was often at odds with the working class over questions of wages, prices, or working conditions and in accord with landed elites who wanted to preserve the fundamental institutions of property. The cohesion among the commercial elites of southwestern Lancashire and their accumulation of economic resources contributed to effective channeling of working-class collective action after 1820. Increased private resources and cohesion among factory owners enabled them to suppress or channel working-class collective action even without a strong police force. Increased employer resources reduced the effectiveness of strikes by permitting lockouts and permanent replacement of strikers. Increased cohesion forced more traditional, paternalistic employers and smaller employers to follow this pattern of retaliation. The appearance of the first company unions around 1820 is further evidence of the increased relative strength of employers.

Middle-class cohesion facilitated political control in Manchester, where the middle class won control of the vestry and the Improvement Commission in the 1820s. Although the power of the justices of the peace was declining, there were no mobilized groups to undermine middle-class control of the town with whom working-class dissidents could form an alliance. Moreover, in the wake of their victory, the middle-class leadership of the town promoted projects which benefited workers and drew many of their leaders into elite-controlled institutions or parties. Workers who could vote in 1832 were integrated into the existing structure of elite political factions and struggles. Workers drawn to the cause of parliamentary reform were invited to join the Political Union formed for the working classes under elite leadership in 1830. (Many of the more militant working-class reformers refused.) Working-class members of dissenting chapels were drawn into the parliamentary struggles for an end to the slave trade and for parliamentary reform through petition drives organized by middle-class institutions in 1829-1834.

In sum, the middle class, as political contenders in England in the early nineteenth century, played a divided role with respect to working-class political mobilization. The increase in repressive measures by the authorities in large part was an effect of the transfer of control of town governments to improvement-minded, organization-oriented members of the commercial establishment. Moreover, as the middle class gained in political power, it commanded more and more influence over the allocation of resources for repression; it was the elites' propensity for repression which governed the reaction of authorities in Lancashire in 1830. At the same time, the middle class tended to create a penumbra of protection for working-class political mobilization in the wake of their own political mobilization. Thus, on the one hand the middle class, as owners of the means of production and supporters of the government they increasingly influenced, were repressors of the working class. On the other hand, as contenders for an increased share of political power, they implicitly encouraged the working class to engage in some collective contention. This contention, in turn, sometimes brought middle-class support and sometimes treated the middle class as opponents. The short-term success of working-class economic and political mobilization and the long-term failure of working-class economic and political contention for power between 1789 and 1832 can be explained in part by the bifurcated influence of the middle class. Similarly, the fact that class alliances were made between the middle and working class only over political issues helps explain the unbroken chain of trade union militance in contrast to the sporadic appearance of political militance within the working class. Both, of course, drew from a common experience and underlying objectives.

CONCLUSION: CONTENTIOUS GATHERINGS AND FUTURE RESEARCH ON POLITICAL PROCESS

I have argued that contention for power in England determined the issues, grievances, and claims of the working class between 1750 and 1830. Long-term economic change and the restructuring of the polity which followed meant that workers gradually lost control of the means of production, that communities lost control of the distribution of goods in the market, and that control of the use of public space by authorities increased. To the extent that these changes have been one-directional and are still occurring, protest "modernized" during the Industrial Revolution. The English polity entered an era in which the use of public and private authority was similar to patterns familiar in contemporary society.

There remain important questions about basic political processes which the study of contentious gatherings can help answer. First, what governs success of a contender in the long run? Second, what are the long-term effects of different reward/repression capacities of authorities? Third, how do new contenders succeed or fail in becoming incorporated into the structure of routine contention for political power? Finally, how are claims made by protesters defined and legitimated, and what part do legal and political ideologies play in contention over claims which are made as a matter of "right?"

This chapter has examined a small part of the process by which long-term claims were generated, put forward, manipulated by authorities, and (in a few cases) resolved in England. In the period 1750 to 1830, working-class contentious gatherings were "politicized," in the sense that control of political resources became a long-term objective. This objective became imperative by the nature of conflicts with employers and others on whom the working class was dependent. For the working class, achieving effective voice among private and public power-holders became a continuous concern. For authorities, concern about working-class contention for power fluctuated, but the response to working-class contention for power was a major factor in political process in nineteenth-century England.

NOTES

1. The "standard" view that protest is the direct result of stress, dislocation, or some similar dissatisfaction experienced by individuals appears in at least three variants. The first argues that economic hardship produces violence and other forms of protest. While seldom propounded without considerable qualification among sociologists, such a theory is the basis for a number of classic statements by contemporary economists and social historians (Darvall, 1934; Rostow, 1948). A second strand of theory argues that protest is a function of the discrepancy between individuals' expectations and achievements—i.e., relative deprivation (Gurr, 1969). A third associates social movements, violence, panics, and a wide variety of other forms of collective behavior with stresses created by breakdown of normal social organization. In particular, rapid economic development is said to be associated with the emergence of all forms of protest: The more rapid the development, the more "regressive" (violent) the protest (Smelser, 1959).

2. See for example Shelton (1973), Stevenson and Quinault (1975), and Stevenson (1979).

3. It is important to recognize that participants in most "popular" contentious gatherings were members of the working class. By "class" I mean a relationship. Class membership is determined by relationships to others, mainly by control over rela-

tions of production. The participants in contentious gatherings in Lancashire in the late eighteenth and early nineteenth centuries were overwhelmingly proletarian; that is, they did not own the means of production on which their living depended. Marginal cases of class membership notwithstanding, I will argue that proletarianization, and thus membership in the working class, was the major force shaping contention for power reflected in contentious gatherings in Industrial Revolution Lancashire.

It is also important that other contenders on the scene had class positions. A middle class made up of merchants, shopkeepers, owners of factories, owners of loomshops, wealthier artisans, and tradesmen rose rapidly in political power in the wake of the successful entry of the wealthiest industrialists into the enfranchised elite. This group, owners of property and the means of production, but not uniformly employers of labor, played a critical role in mediating contention for power. It was a group slowly being integrated into the political structure and fully aware of the importance of national political power.

4. The newspapers were the Manchester *Mercury,* 1800-1830, the Lancaster *Gazette,* 1801-1830, and the Blackburn *Mail,* 1800-1820. The fourth source was the Home Office Papers. The principal bias of the newspapers of the early nineteenth century was their (not surprising) tendency to report a greater proportion of the events which occurred near the city in which the newspaper was published. The Manchester *Mercury* was published for many years by a person who was also the postmaster of Manchester. In addition to being ideally situated to receive reports of news in Manchester and London, he occasionally employed stringers in a few other towns in the county of Lancaster. It is easy to understand why the *Mercury's* coverage of events in southeastern Lancashire towns is fairly reliable but not so reliable for events in other parts of the county. By contrast, reports of disturbances contained in the Home Office Papers reflect the geographic distribution of justices of the peace in the towns and countryside of the county. The Home Office Papers have less bias toward reporting events in towns in the early nineteenth century, but neglect events in quarters of the county where no active justices resided, such as Oldham. Combining these sources to form a "sample" of events produces a more representative group of popular gatherings than a single source used alone.

The definition given in the text was interpreted broadly. A claim was taken to be evidenced by an announced shared focus, direct action, or symbolic action by a group. Information about selected events was coded and placed in a computer for analysis. Two "samples" of events are used in this study. The first represents annual data about three types of contentious gatherings between 1793 and 1890: strikes, political contentious gatherings, and collective violence. The three might overlap, of course. A second sample containing detailed information about events in nine years was analyzed to provide greater definition to the findings. The nine years are 1800, 1801, 1805, 1806, 1808, 1810, 1812, 1818, and 1830.

5. It is likely that wages could be kept low because the proletariat was rural and partially self-supporting through farming their own plots of land or part-time farm labor for wages.

6. For one account of this process which stresses its importance in subsequent struggles between workers in the textile industry of Lancashire and their employers see Bythell (1969), especially Chapter One.

7. See in particular Hill (1969), Mantoux (1962), Clapham (1929), Chapman (1904), and Moffitt (1964).

8. This figure, like the others cited in Table 4.1, is an approximation which is impossible to verify directly. It appears in only one source (Wood, 1910), but has gained respectability through frequent citation. Much more helpful would be estimates of the proportion of the work force engaged in textile manufacture, or, specifically, handloom weaving. A census of looms in the Parish of Manchester in 1751 reported in Wadsworth and Mann (1931) permits estimation of the proportion of the work force engaged in weaving even at that early date—between 25 and 30 percent. The proportion cannot have declined between 1751 and the end of the century.

9. See Hobsbawm (1964: 130ff) for a fuller explanation.

10. Lancashire and its history of machine-breaking, strikes, and political movements are known to a large audience as characteristic of the economic discontinuities of the Industrial Revolution. Hence, it has been a favored proving ground for the theories reviewed in note 1, supra.

11. Violence is defined as an attempt to seize control of or to destroy property or as an assault on persons. A political contentious gathering is a gathering at which a principal objective is opposition to a major governmental policy, the ministry, or the form of government (which includes discussion of parliamentary reform).

12. An oatmeal price index was constructed from reports of prices (in pence) per load which appeared weekly in the Lancaster *Gazette*.

13. This is an Index of Social Tension created by W. W. Rostow. Rostow built his index from one created by A. D. Gayer (Gayer et al., 1953: 355) to reflect the trade cycle. Gayer's index is an interval index running from one (low point in the trade cycle) to five (high point in the trade cycle), and depends in significant part on nonquantitative data on levels of unemployment. Rostow (1948) employed the trade cycle index in combination with food prices to measure social tension. He reduced price levels for England as a whole to a one-to-five scale and added it to the trade cycle index in such a manner that a ten indicated lowest trade and highest prices while a one indicated a boom period with low prices. The ratio of the two indices which I have used in this analysis accomplished the same purpose.

14. The index of factory operatives was compiled by G. W. Wood from factory inspectors' reports and covers the period 1806-1830 (Mitchell and Deane, 1971).

15. The correlation between collective violence and the Gayer-Rostow Social Tension Index is an effect of the strong correlation between collective violence and food prices. There is no correlation between collective violence and the trade cycle.

16. Hobsbawm (1964: 131) provides a chart of the months in which food riots occurred in the eighteenth century compiled from the reports in *Gentlemen's Magazine* mentioned in Wearmouth (1945).

17. See Hill (1969: 171ff) for a fuller description of the composition of the laboring population in the seventeenth century.

18. Foster (1974: 19) offers this estimate based on his own intensive research using primary sources in Lancashire. The estimate is supported by Wadsworth and Mann (1931), who set the proportion at between 25 and 30 percent in 1751.

19. See Hill (1969: 174) on the repeal of portions of the Statute of Artificers in the seventeenth century. Kelsall (1938) provides a detailed picture of wage rating by Justices of the Peace and the reasons for its discontinuance.

20. These issues are stressed by Smelser (1959) to the exclusion of others which, in my opinion, were more important in shaping collective action.

21. Wadsworth and Mann (1931: 361-376) provide a detailed account of the alternative strategies employed by weavers at mid-century in Lancashire to maintain an effective combination and to retain effective control of apprenticeship.

22. Hill (1969: 265-266) and Darvall (1934) provide illustrations of machine-breaking in the seventeenth, eighteenth, and nineteenth centuries.

23. See Hammond and Hammond (1970: 54-55) and Wadsworth and Mann (1931: 375).

24. See "Report of the Select Committee to Consider Means of Lessening Evils Due to Fluctuation in Employment in the Manufacturing Districts," *Parliamentary Papers* (1830, X, 221).

25. Giles (1959) gives a history of the rise and fall of the feltmakers in Lancashire.

26. Smelser (1959) explains the violence which accompanied weavers' strikes by the buildup of strain from the displacement of handloom weaving in the economy and the disintegration of the communities and families of handloom weavers. The latter events are placed 20 years before the historical fact, in my opinion, and there are more persuasive reasons for the violence, as I try to show.

27. See Lipson (1915: Vol. 3, 392).

28. The increase is discussed generally in Wearmouth (1945). For a more detailed account of a single town (Oldham) see Foster (1974: 27-29 and passim).

29. Smelser's discussion of the opposition among the working class to the various Factory Acts, some of which proposed a *reduction* in the number of hours children could work, is particularly illuminating (1959: 265ff).

30. Thompson argues that "[i]n the years between 1780 and 1832 most English working people came to feel an identity of interests as between themselves, and as against their rulers and employers" (1964: 11). Of fundamental importance to his explanation of the growth of this awareness is the interaction between collective action and discovering what and who mattered in contention for power.

31. Among these were the London Corresponding Society, and, still more important when viewed from Lancashire, the United Englishmen, which achieved a large membership in Manchester and nearby towns by the end of the century.

32. As impressive a measure of the political reaction of English elites as this may seem, surprisingly little use seems to have been made of most of this legislative baggage. Clearly, much of it was passed *after* the events which stimulated parliamentary interest. Many of the acts merely altered penalties for behavior which was already criminal, and hence they altered the behavior of judges at trial more than the behavior of justices of the peace who arrested those brought to trial or the behavior of participants in events subject to the new laws. The bulk of the repressive legislation between 1799 and 1820 was of this type. But if the laws which purported to create new crimes or increased the penalties for old ones added little to the firepower of the government, procedural changes which altered the politically inspired checks and balances of the English legal system put substantial numbers of

citizens in jail and kept them there. Foremost among these were the acts suspending the writ of habeas corpus in 1794 and 1817, the authorization of ex officio warrants in political libel cases, and acts creating petty sessions or out-of-court jurisdiction over combinations and meetings outside the controlling power of juries.

33. Meetings to discuss political or religious grievances were licensable under the Seditious Meetings Acts (36 Geo. III, c.7 [1796]; 47 Geo. III, c.19 [1817]); all combinations of workers were made illegal by legislation in 1799, amended in 1800 (39 & 40 Geo. III, c.106). Federated political organizations were outlawed by the Seditious Organization Act, which named the London Corresponding Society and the United Englishmen specifically (39 Geo. III, c.79 [1799]. Finally, even friendly societies were required to register with the Clerk of the Peace of the Quarter Sessions to achieve legal recognition, a procedure which made their accounts available for auditing (33 Geo. III, c.54 [1793]).

34. Thompson notes (1964) that the very different pictures of working-class militance and unrest in Industrial Revolution Lancashire and Yorkshire are due in part to the predominance of a Tory magistracy in Lancashire and a Whig Lord Lieutenant and magistracy in the West Riding. Similar differences created checkered reporting of "seditious" and "revolutionary" tendencies in various parts of Lancashire.

35. It has been said that the Hampden Clubs were made up largely of starving weavers (Smelser, 1959; Thompson, 1964). However, it is clear that the club's leadership was made up largely of members of skilled trades and that weavers constituted a minority (44 percent) of those arrested among the Blanketeers. This revised view accords well with the argument that groups with the best base for mobilizing participants are more likely to be involved in collective action.

36. Our focus has been mainly on the manufacturing districts of Lancashire, hence the interesting comparison between Ashton-under-Lyne, Bolton, and Manchester. It is quite clear that the rate of repression was lower still and the rate of contentious gathering relatively high in the northeast, nonindustrial, part of the county. While more justices of the peace had residences in this quarter of the county than in others, they resided at some distance from the towns where contentious gatherings were most likely to take place—Preston, Blackburn, and Ulverstone. Further, the population and the residences of the justices were widely dispersed, with few natural centers of action.

37. Foster (1974) provides a meticulously documented case study of Oldham, Lancashire, demonstrating the subtle effects of economic forces on ruling class formation and on the effectiveness of social control of working-class contention.

38. Thompson (1964) documents the rise in political awareness.

39. The index of middle-class mobilization was constructed by coding accounts of middle-class collective action in Lancashire each year. Collective action here meant any action (public or private) in which a group of five members of the middle class made a claim against other persons or institutions. The practical effect of broadening the meaning of collective action was to permit counting petitions where no public meeting had taken place. (The code categories "scale" by definition.)

Code Value	Interpretation	Coding Criteria
0	No mobilization	No collective action by middle classes.
1	Low mobilization	1-3 petitions for local or national political reform or for fundamental policy change (opposition to the war with France, the Orders in Council or the Corn Laws, etc.)
2	Intermediate mobilization	4 or more petitions for local or national political reform or for fundamental policy change.
3	High mobilization	Evidence of actors continuing agitation for local or national political reform or for fundamental policy change, regardless of the number of petitions. Example: founding a newspaper or forming a political party for the above objectives.

The index of changes in industrial production is W. G. Hoffman's index which appears in Mitchell and Deane (1971: 271). The Gayer Trade Cycle Index, supra, note 13, and the Hoffman Index of Industrial Production are used instead of the measures used in Table 4.2 because of their greater validity, in my view. The Index of Social Tension merely combined food prices and the Trade Cycle Index. The Index of Operatives captures only one of the ways in which increased or decreased production created stress due to differentiation and industrial change.

40. The coefficients of regression are:

Middle class mob. = .1 (Time) –.27 (Trade Cycle)**

**$P > .10$, N=38, R^2=.08, D-W=1.01

41. Political leadership was linked to the specific organization of English working-class political societies or groups. The London Corresponding Society or societies of Constitutional Information which arose during the 1790s are typical of the loosely federated collections of partisans, with more tightly organized cells of friends in each town who communicated with groups in other towns. In Lancashire, the United Englishmen appear to have been organized along the lines of Methodist sects, into cells of 20 or so, according to one spy report. Contact was maintained among cells, but there is little evidence of effective continuing leadership or collective action. The rapidity with which the United Englishmen, and other working-class political societies, were declared illegal and the fact that they were never tacitly tolerated by justices of the peace, as many combinations were, also contributed to the short life of these societies and the leadership they might have provided.

42. The suggestion I make is not that working-class leaders were more conservative than has been suggested by others, but rather that even the most radical were
either coopted in the manner explained, infra, or silenced by harassment or arrest, or
simply left without an effective organization for political action and forced out of
the political arena, perhaps back into the trade union movement.

5

Industrial Capitalism, Conflict, and Working-Class Contention in Lancashire, 1842

BRIAN R. BROWN

THE "LANDMARK" YEAR

George Rudé (1964: 187-190) interprets 1842, especially in relation to events in Lancashire, as "an important landmark in British labor history." Based on the Plug Plot disturbances of the late summer, Rude perceives a basic transformation in the modes of working-class collective action. He largely attributes the transformation to the convergence of the politically organized Chartist agitation with a developing *industrial* labor movement. This chapter develops a more rigorously framed analysis and interpretation of the dynamics of Lancashire working-class contention during this "landmark" year. The central argument proposes that the shape and dynamics

AUTHOR'S NOTE: Charles Tilly offered encouragement, guidance, and criticism throughout the study. Youssef Cohen disagreed persistently enough to make things much clearer, and Lynn Lees made helpful comments on an earlier version. Linda helped in too many ways to be acknowledged here. Finally, the Sociology Department of the University of Michigan provided essential financial support.

of Lancashire Chartism and the political mass strike of 1842 were the result of a set of patterned political interactions specifically grounded in the class relations of liberal-industrial capitalism.

While our point of departure is this historically based problem, our mode of proceeding follows from recent developments in the sociology of collective action. With significant debts to historians like Rudé, the sociological study of collective action has broken away from the sociopsychological assumptions of collective behaviorists and settled into a more convincing political-sociological framework. The arguments here are developed within this emerging political sociology of collective action. Class structures and relations, organizations, political processes, and interactions are the dominant elements in the analysis.

This chapter has three interconnected sections. First, we identify the social origins of Chartist contention through an empirical confrontation between two theoretically and historically distinct interpretations of its bases. We then move to a consideration of how the 1842 character of the relevant social relations created opportunities and advantages for Chartist political mobilization. The final section focuses on the interrelationships between the dynamics of Chartist contention during 1842 and the August-September mass strike. Throughout, the argument emphasizes how the ebb and flow of Lancashire's working-class "movement" was shaped by the *intra-* and *inter*actions of workers, working-class activists, dominant classes, and state authorities. Most ambitiously, then, this study is intended as an empirical mapping of the concatenation of structural conditions, social relations, and political processes central to the historical logic of working-class formation.

The main body of information for this study consists of a systematic enumeration of worker collective action in 1842 Lancashire. The basic source for the enumeration was the *Northern Star*—the most complete record of worker activity for this time. This extensive enumeration allows us to overcome a basic weakness in previous studies of Chartism and the strike of 1842 (Mather, 1974; Foster, 1974). Though quantitatively rigorous in other respects, these studies have relied on essentially illustrative and impressionistic evidence in their discussions of the patterns of working-class action. Consequently, their discussions of the relationships among social conditions, political processes, and worker collective contention are primarily "a combination of the suggestive hypothesis and the apt anecdotal illustration" (Hobsbawm, 1971: 27). Before we can realistically move beyond this level of discussion about these relationships, it is essential that we more rigorously establish what the spatial and temporal patterns of worker action were. Our strategy of enumeration is designed to accomplish this task.

Our procedure was to enumerate all events reported in the *Northern Star* (NS) that met two basic criteria. To be included, the event had to involve presumably at least ten people *and* there had to be some indication of worker presence in the event. The last criterion was considered met unless the report in the *Star* expressly indicated that the participants in the event were other than workers; for example, rate-payers only, shop-keepers, "millocrats," etc. The *Star* was especially intent on identifying collective gatherings which did not involve workers, since their exclusion from the collective and political life of the country was its major concern. In the absence of precise figures on the number of participants in an event, the numeric criterion was fulfilled whenever the report indicated partici-pants above a "few" or "several" by employing terms like "numerous," "well attended," "respectably attended," and so on.

The final enumeration consisted of 791 events of collective action over the 51-week period from December 25, 1841, to December 16, 1842. These events were then divided into two basic categories: noncontentious collective gatherings and contentious collective actions. For reasons which will become apparent as we proceed, the choice was made not to restrict the enumeration to only those events in which the participants voiced some claim, demand, or grievance. The *class organization* category con-tains all those events in which such claims were not expressly involved. It represents occasions on which ten or more people, workers included, met for celebrations, discussions, associational concerns, lectures, debates, and so on. It includes events such as the meetings of trade unions and benefit societies, dinners and soirees to celebrate Henry Hunt's birthday, lectures by Chartist "missionaries," and organized debates on the present condi-tions of the country. "Class organization" seemed an appropriate designa-tion, since these types of events provide us with a relatively good surface "indicator" of everyday working-class associational life and activity.

Collective contention events are those which included workers and met the criterion for "contentious gatherings" suggested by Charles Tilly (1978a: 276); that is, all those "occasions in which ten or more persons outside the government gather in the same place and make a visible claim which, if realized, would effect the interests of some specific person(s) or group(s) outside their own numbers." For the purposes of this study, these contentious gatherings were subdivided into two groups: Chartist conten-tions and non-Chartist contentions. The Chartist category included all contentious gatherings in which the visible claim made was for the enactment of the People's Charter into law. Obviously, non-Chartist contentions were all those not involving a demand for the People's Charter. The entire enumeration was aggregated in terms of the parish in which the event occurred; the parish totals were then converted into the rates of class organization and contention per 100,000 population in 1841. All the conversion involves, of course, is the standardization of the parishes in relation to their population differences, a necessary preliminary step in the analysis we are undertaking.

THE STRUCTURAL ORIGINS OF
CHARTIST CONTENTION

What were the social origins of Lancashire Chartist contention in 1842? Historians are still debating the basic issues and precise ramifications involved in this question. Their disputes tend to cluster around two conflicting overall interpretations. One line of argument locates the origins of Chartist contention in conflicts and tensions based in the transitional processes leading to urban-industrial society. An alternative interpretation of Chartism sees its origins in structural conflicts lying at the core of industrial capitalist society. Quite simply, the arguments revolve around the question of whether Chartist contention was a response to the destructuring processes of fundamental change or to the integral, structured conflicts of a fairly well-crystallized industrial capitalist order.[1] The sociologist of collective action experiences a sense of familiarity when confronted with this historiographical cleavage. It is, after all, a historically specific version of the endemic dispute between functionalist-inspired social change and Marxist-oriented social conflict theorists of collective action.[2]

Without pursuing an extensive review of either the historiography of Chartism or of theories of collective action, we must nevertheless probe a little more deeply into the contours of these basic alternative social interpretations of Chartism.[3] Let us begin by considering the logic of the "transitional" interpretation. Neil Smelser is without doubt its most self-conscious exponent. His central contention is that "social explosions" like Plug Plot and "political turmoil" like Chartist contention were "short-circuited" expressions of the "strains and tensions" that rapid urbanization and industrialization created for workers and their families. His argument focuses on the disruptive consequences of rapid sociostructural change.

In the late 1830's and 1840's, ... the spinners' and other factory operatives' involvement in social explosions was limited, particularly when compared with their activities in the early 1830's [i.e., their transitional period] and the excessive activities of other groups in 1837-42. One important reason for this is that the factory operatives were gradually approaching the completion of a sequence of differentiation whereby their family and community structure was entering the industrial era on a new basis. By contrast ... the weavers and related groups [i.e., those in their transition phase] were grasping for their very life [Smelser, 1959: 242].

Smelser's critical argument here (1959: 387) is that once the transition to the "industrial era" had been largely accomplished and workers were integrated into the modalities of urban-industrial life, "vigorous political turmoil," even in "years of unemployment and distress," was unlikely. In this view, Chartist contention was the consequence and expression of the matrix of social tensions specifically created by the processes of sociostructural change. That is, the crucial foundation of a population's propensity for radical collective contention was the extend of its involvement in social change. A negative corollary is that Chartist contention did not have its sociostructural roots in relatively persistent features of industrial capitalist society.

It seems to me that it is less embarrassing analytically to interpret cases of outright conflict between the classes as *distrubed reactions to specific structural pressures* rather than as the manifestations of a permanent state of war between them [Smelser, 1959: 394; italics added].

Actually, Smelser and some other transitionalists appear to go so far as to argue that radical contention is fundamentally about social change. Participation in political turmoil arises "among groups under pressure [i.e., from structural change], the aims of which are to safeguard or restore those elements of the division of labour which are directly under pressure" (p. 388).[4] Collective contention is not interpreted as the manifestation of relatively persistent conflicts between specifically related groups struggling over the distribution of social resources, rights, and obligations, but as struggles between groups and the processes of structural change themselves. It is rather an unmediated form of struggle between people and macrosocial processes of such a nature that, perhaps, only Don Quixote could fully comprehend it. This is, in any event, the way Smelser reinterprets worker contention during the industrial revolution in England.

The alternative interpretation of the social origins of Chartist contention was given classic shape by Engels in *The Condition of the Working Class in England:*

> The factory operatives, and especially those of the cotton district, form the nucleus of the labor movement. Lancashire, and especially Manchester, is the seat of the most powerful Unions, the central point of Chartism. . . . The more the factory system has taken possession of a branch of industry, the more the workingmen employed in it participate in the labor movement; the sharper the opposition between workingmen and capitalists, the clearer the proletarian consciousness in the workingmen. . . . In general, all the workers employed in manufacture are won for . . . resistance to capital and bourgeoisie, and all are united upon this point, that they, as workingmen, . . . form a separate class, with separate interests and principles, with a separate way of looking at things in contrast with that of all property-owners [1973: 276-277].

There is no mention of the peculiarly contentious consequences of transitional social change here. Engels points to the factory proletarians of industrial capitalism, their urban location, and the differentiation of class interests, class formation, polarization, and conflict as the foundations for Chartist contention. The factors he emphasizes are not indicative of a transition from one type of society to another—for example, from a preindustrial to an industrial society. Rather, they represent structural features of an established, functioning, industrial capitalist social order. Marx, also, at one point offers a challenge to the transitionalist thesis: "As soon as the working class, stunned at first by the noise and turmoil of the new system of production, had recovered its senses to some extent, it began to offer resistance" (1976: 390).

This "structural" interpretation of Chartism's social origins emphasizes a matrix of social relations and conflicts integrally structured by the social order of industrial capitalism.[5] The "completion" of a population's transition to the industrial era is not seen as signalling the end of an extraordinarily contentious phase but as marking the beginning of class conflicts and contentions arising from the social contradictions of industrial capitalism. Actually, industrial capitalism is seen to intensify contention by its crystallization of interclass conflicts, concentration of workers, and consequent expansion of the working class' capacity for organization and mobilization. Integration into industrial capitalist society is, for the structuralist, simultaneously integration into the contradictory structure of class relations implicit in it. In short, contrary to the transitional perspective which sees contention as a result of disequilibrating periods of sociostructural change, the structuralist emphasizes conflict, class formation, and mobilization.

Clearly, the structural and transitional accounts of Chartism's social origins propose distinct clusters of explanatory variables. Our empirical evaluation of these competing interpretations will involve a quantitative analysis of their respective abilities to account for the pattern of parish-level variations in the rate of Chartist contention per 100,000 of the 1841 population. By focusing on the Lancashire parishes in which some form of worker collective activity occurred, and investigating the correlation coefficients between the alternative explanatory variables advanced and the rates of Chartist contention, we will be able to establish the matrix of social relations which conditioned Lancashire's pattern of Chartist contention in 1842. Before we turn to the evidence, however, it is necessary to define quantitatively the explanatory variables in question.

The transitional argument would predict a positive relationship between an area's rates of urbanization, urban growth, and industrialization and its level of Chartist contention. In our analysis, *urbanization* is defined as the rate of change 1831-1841 in the proportion of parish population living in cities of 10,000 or more as of 1841. *Urban growth* is the 1831-1841 rate of change in the populations of those cities. Finally, *industrialization* refers to the ratio between the average annual rate of change in textile factory workers 1835-1838 and the average annual rate of population change 1831-1841. The structural interpretation argues for a positive relationship between Chartist contention and an area's level of urban-industrial development, proletarian concentration and, interactively, its degree of working-class organization. We define these independent variables as follows: *industrialism* is the proportion of the 1841 parish population employed as textile factory workers in 1837-1838; *urbanism* refers to the proportion of the 1841 parish population living in cities of 10,000 or more; and *proletarian concentration* is the number of textile factory workers 1837-1838 per 1,000 parish acres. Our indicator of the level of *working-class organization,* discussed earlier, refers to the 1842 rate of noncontentious worker collective activity per 100,000 population.[6]

The relevant data are presented in Table 5.1.[7] The contrast between the explanatory performances of the alternative interpretations could hardly be greater. While not one of the processes transitionalists see as

TABLE 5.1   Transitional versus Structural
Interpretations of Chartist Contention

	Chartist Contention	*Non-Chartist Contention*	*Class Organization*
Transitional Interpretation			
Urbanization			
Urban growth	-.23	+.11	+.12
Industrialization	-.13	-.02	-.39
Structural Interpretation			
Industrialism	+.52	+.61	+.64
Urbanism	+.07	+.38	+.28
Proletarian concentration	+.60	+.80	+.79
Class organization	+.50	+.68	
Non-Chartist contention	+.64		

positively influencing Chartist contention did so, all of the structuralist's explanations performed in the predicted positive manner. Moreover, the strength of the relationships between the structural variables and Chartist contention is, with the exception of urbanism, robust. The same cannot be said about the explanatory cluster central to the transitional interpretation. Its relationship to Chartist contention was, with one exception, so weak as to be irrelevant to its explanation. The exception is the negative correlation between industrialization and working-class organization. Rapid industrialization significantly depressed levels of class organization. Yet, the table shows a strong, positive impact of working-class organization on Chartist contention. In general, social change theories of contention argue that the disruptions of collective social routines which rapid change creates heighten levels of social anomie and therefore increase collective contention. In 1842 Lancashire, rapid industrialization does seem to have increased "social anomie"; this translated into not more but less Chartist contention.[8]

The only chink in the otherwise impressive armor of the structural interpretation is, perhaps somewhat surprisingly, urbanism. The usual argument is that urbanism facilitates collective action by reducing the costs of organization and mobilization. If urbanism is to play an important explanatory role in regard to any specific range of contention, the social

configuration of the urban environment must disproportionately concentrate the relevant actual or potential conflict groups. In the case of 1842
Lancashire Chartism, living in the city mattered less than working in the
factory. Urbanism actually performs much like the other "sociological"
variables of urbanization and urban growth; they were all relatively insig-
nificant in relation to Chartist contention. Factors and processes significant for characterizing societies per se, independently of their specific class
and group configurations, in our case are of little use for explaining
patterns of collective contention. Collective contention is grounded not in
unmediated relationships between people and macroprocesses and structures, but in the articulation of conflicts embedded in persistent webs of
structured social relations.

Consequently, the two most important sociostructural elements
accounting for variations in Chartist contention are class-related: proletarian concentration and capitalist industrialism. The social origins of
Chartist contention arose from within an industrial capitalist matrix of
social relations. Across the entire range of contentious and noncontentious
worker collective activity, proletarian concentration is the single best
predictor. Yet, when we "control" for level of class organization and
non-Chartist contention, the second-order partial correlation coefficient
between proletarian concentration and Chartist contention drops to +.16.[9]
This indicates that between the class structuration of industrial capitalism
and worker contention for the Charter there was an intervening process of
class organization and mobilization. The proportionate and spatial concentration of workers which industrial capitalism entailed facilitated their
active involement with one another—their formation as a class—and it was
from this basis that Chartism expanded. The inescapable conclusion is that
Chartist contention in 1842 Lancashire was primarily shaped by the active
crystallization of the economically determined class structure of industrial
capitalism. It was, to put a structural gloss on a remark of E. P. Thompson,
the expression of an industrial capitalist society no longer in the making
but already made.[10]

CLASS RELATIONS AND
POLITICAL MOBILIZATION IN 1842

While significant in their own right, these structural findings are obviously more in the nature of a prologue than a conclusion. Synchronic
structural analysis is useful primarily for identifying the field of structured
social relations within which collective contention arises. The class rela-

tions of industrial capitalism are not, however, historically invariant phenomena. Within constraints and the variability of historically specific conjunctures, they fluctuate between periods of varying degrees and combinations of interclass cooperation, competition, conflict, and confrontation. The relevant class formations also show historically varying levels of intraclass solidarity, interclass polarization, collective activation, and political articulation. For example, the relatively fixed structural map of Lancashire's industrial capitalist social order cannot account for the fluctuations in working-class contention that occurred during 1842 (See Figure 5.1). Nor can it help much in explaining why the 1842 levels appear so high relative to those of, for example,1843.[11] These questions about the specific ebb and flow of collective class contention require an investigation into the more historically contingent interactions that influence class formation, polarization, mobilization, and contention. In one way or another, the rest of our discussion will be concerned with these issues. In this section, we will look at how the nature of labor/capital relations in 1842 shaped the opportunities available to Chartists for the political mobilization and articulation of working-class interests.

Given what we already know, the place to begin is with a consideration of Lancashire's economic situation. To put it mildly, 1842 was not a good year for Lancashire's textile industry. It was in the grips of its deepest depression in ten years. R.C.O. Matthews argues that in previous downturns during the 1833-1842 period, entrepreneurs had suffered greater proportional earnings losses than the workers. Consequently, "many entrepreneurs faced the further deterioration in trade in 1841-1842 with their cash reserves already almost exhausted" (Matthews, 1954: 142). The dramatic rise in bankruptcies in 1842 is evidence enough of the textile manufacturers' dilemma. Two points about the structure of Lancashire's textile industry are important here. It was an extremely decentralized and, therefore, intensely competitive industry—a classic case of entrepreneurial laissez-faire capitalism. Moreover, "fixed costs did not bulk large in total costs in comparison to the costs of cotton and labour" (Farnie, 1979: 213). In fact, wage costs approached close to three-fourths of total costs in cotton weaving and one-half of them in spinning (Farnie, 1979: 296). Since raw material prices were determined on the world market, wages were the most "adjustable" element in total costs and were, therefore, an essential and basic medium of the industry's intense interfirm competition. Consequently, the extreme cash and profits squeeze employers confronted in 1842 was directly expressed in a massive offensive against wages. The extent of this can be seen in unemployment of 20 percent or more, short-time hours for about an equal number of workers, and wage rate reductions of 10 to 20 percent.

Clearly, by 1842, the conflict between the profits of capital and the wages of labor had reached an intense and open phase. The layoffs, slowdowns, and wage reductions imposed by earnings-threatened employers created basic contingencies of material life for the workers. These were not simply deprivations that the workers suffered; because they were the direct consequences of employers' actions, they involved an immediate personification of blame and responsibility. The overall situation in 1842 could be characterized as an "every-daying" of structural conflicts through their reduction to basic issues of material life. In short, Lancashire's workers were confronted with the immediate reality or prospect of immiseration. Theories of overt class conflict (Giddens, 1975; Mann, 1973; Miliband, 1977) suggest that this is precisely the type of situation that leads to increasing intraclass solidarity, polarizing interclass hostility, and expanding class action.

We are fortunate in having a reliable source that permits a glimpse into the workers' responses to this situation. W. Cooke Taylor traveled throughout Lancashire in 1842 speaking with various groups of workers. In Colne, he found Chartism that was developing with "fearful rapidity" among workers, who told him: "We used to think that something better would turn up, but we have waited so long that hope itself is worn out: we must do something for ourselves, because those above us will never do anything for us" (Taylor, [1842] 1968: 84). On the banks of the Irwell near Bolton, there were "many a wheel idle and many a chimney smokeless, consequently they [the workers] were determined Chartists" (Taylor, 1968: 155-156).

Taylor saw that in 1842 "a dangerous and increasing chasm between employers and the employed" was developing (p. 238). While expressing his own dislike of Chartist and other working-class activists, he nonetheless recognized that this expanding "chasm" was providing them with increased opportunities for agitation. The manufacturers "virtually abandoned their position, and thus threw all existing relations into confusion. The operatives, thus abandoned . . . were left free to follow any leaders that offered,—Unionists, Chartists, and political adventurers of every grade and description" (p. 282). Moreover, Chartism was developing not only among the unemployed but also among workers who still had some employment but were gripped by "a fearful looking forward to the

future" (p. 107). Their anticipation of disaster, of impending immiseration, made them even more tremulous than the unemployed.

> The falling feel more real misery than the fallen. . . . [They] are
> unable to enjoy their existing comforts because they feel them to be
> precarious, . . . and have hourly before their eyes examples of the
> sad result in which the deteriorating process must end [Taylor,
> 1968: 307].

Recast into the distancing language of conflict theory, Taylor proposed
a sort of "contagion model" of the development of Chartist commitments
among the workers. He saw them arising from within the vortex of class
experiences and relations created by the economic depression of 1842.
Caught in the midst of a downward-spiralling world, workers are increasingly coming together as a class and juxtaposing their interests to those of
their employers and rulers. This explosion of class polarization is the
backdrop against which Taylor interpreted the rapidly expanding success
of Chartist agitation. The agitators moved into, occupied, and cultivated
the expanding chasm between workers and employers. We have a fragment
of evidence which suggests the aptness of these arguments.

Among the over 500 instances of class organization events in our
enumeration, there were over 200 in which one or more speakers directly
advocated the People's Charter to their audiences. The speakers were very
often members of the National Charter Association and/or its paid "missionaries." Clearly, it makes sense to treat these gatherings as instances of
Chartist agitation whose obvious purpose was to create active support for
the Charter. If we measure the success of this agitation by the ratio of
Chartist contentions to agitational gatherings, then we can present some
evaluation of how economic circumstances may have influenced agitational success. When we compare 1841 "unemployment" information for
ten parishes to the agitational success ratio, we get the figures in Table 2.[12]
They suggest, and this is the strongest verb we can use, that where
unemployment was greater, there was also the most fertile soil for Chartist
agitation. Unemployment was more than twice as likely to lead to Chartist
contention in the group of parishes with greater unemployment. The fact
that this relationship holds in contradication to the levels of proletarian
concentration lends more credence to the findings. Unemployment was,
after all, only one of the contingencies Lancashire workers faced in 1842.

TABLE 5.2   Unemployment and the Success of Chartist Agitation

Percent Unemployed	Actual Range of Unemployment	Number of Parishes	Proletarian Concentration	Ratio of Contentions to Agitations
20 or greater	21-25%	6	240.1	.59
18 or less	10-18%	4	613.4	.25

Chartists were aware of the opportunities presented by the economic and class situation of 1842. In a *Northern Star* article, "A Few Words on Propagandism and Organization," Feargus O'Connor argued:

Our mission is with the sons of poverty and suffering; from them we must gain converts and disciples. Wherever oppression and tyranny exist on the part of the landlord, the master and the manufacturer, there should our missionary be, ... taking advantage of it to raise scorn and contempt in the minds of the people against the present accursed system. When man suffers from wrong and oppression his mind is doubly open to conviction of the divine principles of truth and justice [NS, May 28, 1842].

In 1842 the exertions and arguments of the Chartists—their rhetoric of class injury, division, and conflict—could strike a responsive chord in the everyday experiences of Lancashire's workers.

In a series of events in 1842 the class cleavages and consequent Chartist political opportunities were very much in evidence. The Chartists were not the only organized political group actively seeking worker support in 1842; the manufacturer-financed Anti-Corn Law League was also in the field. In relation to the workers, the league was pursuing the old-style strategy of mobilizing a working-class "tail" so as to frighten the land-holding "aristocractic head" into abolishing agricultural import duties. To the Chartists, this was little more than a cynical middle-class attempt to divert worker attention from the real problem of achieving political representation. They argued that the Corn Laws were just one more example of the evils of class legislation; that the extension of commerce the league saw as resulting from free trade would not benefit the workers; and that the cheaper food resulting from it actually meant that employers would reduce wages.[13]

The *Northern Star* reports a number of occasions when Chartists and Repealers directly confronted each other at public meetings. They would debate, argue, and fight out battles of resolutions, counterresolutions, and amendments in search of the exclusive support of the meetings. Most of the confrontations took place in February and March at meetings called on league initiative.[14] In February, Peel introduced his proposal for the establishment of a sliding scale on grain import duties, an idea anathema to the league, which demanded nothing short of a total repeal of the duties. It was in this context that the league stepped up the public agitation leading to confrontations with the Chartists, a clear case of an issue-oriented organization mobilizing in the wake of parliamentary action that could threaten its exclusive hold on the issue and its constituency. The league's mobilization and attempt to increase worker support led in turn to the competitive mobilization of the Chartist organization. This spiralling process of mobilization and countermobilization resulted in increased levels of collective contention with some Chartist gains (See Figure 5.1). In these cases, the sinews of worker contention in Lancashire led to the parliamentary center.

The class experiences and divisions of 1842 Lancashire were manifested in the Chartist/Anti-Corn Law League confrontations. A Manchester meeting illustrates how these larger realities entered into the shaping of collective events. Manchester shopkeepers, publicans, and traders called the meeting to consider possible remedies for the present distress. When the meeting finally got underway, thousands of people were assembled in Stephenson's Square. A Mr. Birch rose and spoke about the mutual interests of the working and middle classes, arguing that abolition of the corn laws, by extending commerce, would end the distress of the people. He then moved for a resolution for repeal of the Corn Laws. James Leach, Manchester Chartist and later acquaintance of Friedrich Engels, then spoke in support of a counterresolution for the Charter. He stressed that the workers were still in misery despite extended commerce, and countered Birch's resolution by saying:

> Birch had endeavored hard to convince you that your interests and the interests of the middle classes were the same. . . . Then I want to know what is the reason they will not give you the same rights as they enjoy, if your interests are identical? [NS, June 25].[15]

The meeting ended with the defeat of Birch's resolution and an overwhelming vote for the Charter.

The combination of a worsening economic situation and a political organization committed to working-class interests seriously reduced the scope for an old-style middle-class/working-class coalition.[16] The "tail" had developed a "head" of its own, and any further class alliances would not occur under exclusive middle-class hegemony. Nor did this competitive play of class political organizations arise entirely from the exigencies of the moment. The strategy of leaving no public space uncontested was a long-standing one for the National Charter Association. It was, in fact, enunciated at its founding in 1840:

> The Members of this Association shall also attend all public Political Meetings, and there, either by moving amendments, or by other means, enforce a discussion of our rights and claims, so that none may remain in ignorance of what we want, nor have an opportunity of propagating or perpetuating political ignorance or delusion [quoted in Thompson, 1962: 293].

A political generalization, rarely contradicted in practice, is that when the emergence of polarizing social formations occurs in a context of committed political organizations, the public arena, if it remains open, becomes a battleground where political commitments and actions are continuously forged. Lancashire in 1842 was not an exception to this rule.

We have come a long way from the historical rigidities of the structural to the pendulous world of political organizations struggling to achieve concrete interests and popular allegiances. Chartist contention in 1842 Lancashire was a consequence of structurally defined groups caught in a situationally accentuated conflict that found expression in and through consciously pursued politics. Each historical domain—structural, situational, and political—contributed its own characteristic pieces to the final mosaic of Lancashire working-class contention. Up to this point, we have been primarily concerned with establishing the character of those pieces. By turning to a discussion of the mass strike of August, we will be able to grasp more fully the nature of the material which bound them together.

THE POLITICAL MASS STRIKE OF 1842: THE DYNAMICS OF MOBILIZATION AND REPRESSION

Perhaps the historically most significant events of 1842 were the "Plug Plot" riots of the late summer. During August and September, Lancashire was the site of modern Europe's first political mass strike. However brief and unsuccessful their efforts, Lancashire workers combined in one series of actions the economic weapon of the strike and the political program of the People's Charter. They briefly succeeded in mobilizing their only remaining collective resource—their labor power—behind the demand for democratic rights. These so-called riots announced a major addition to the action repertoire of the modern working class. Largely unbeknown to themselves, the workers of Lancashire had created the reality of the general strike. These events concentrate and magnify many of the relations and dynamics we have been discussing. However, they also present a remarkable example of their opposite: demobilization through repression.

The mass strike of August and September commenced in earnest on August 5 in Staleybridge.[17] Its immediate cause was the announcement of a wage rate reduction at Bayley's cotton factory. At that, Bayley's workers stopped work, left the mill, and formed a procession. They marched through the nearby towns of Ashton, Hyde, and Oldham, where virtually all of the textile workers turned out and joined them. The strike had begun. Actually, it was not as spontaneous as it might appear. In late July, some employers in Ashton had threatened a wage reduction. This set off a series of workers' meetings in Ashton, Staleybridge, and Hyde in which it was decided that, if the reduction occurred, they would all go on strike. On August 4, the Ashton employers capitulated and withdrew their threatened reduction; but Bayley's of Staleybridge nevertheless implemented one the next day. The workers had therefore committed themselves to a defensive strike for "a fair day's wage for a fair day's work" when Bayley's made the fateful decision of August 5. The argument which clinched the demand for intertown solidarity was that, given the logic of the competitive market, a reduction in one town would soon become a reduction in them all. Thus, the immediate cause of the strike reflected the basic economic situation of the cotton industry in 1842.

By the ninth of August, the strike was general throughout Ashton, Staleybridge, Oldham, Duckenfield, and Hyde. On that day, almost 40,000 strikers met in Ashton and decided to march on Manchester and directly confront the manufacturers at the Cotton Exchange. More mills were turned out on the way to Manchester; but, upon arrival at the outskirts of the city, the police and military deftly maneuvered the crowd away from the exchange and to Granby Row Fields. After about an hour of speechmaking there, the strikers marched back to their home towns. Their presence in Manchester, however, initiated a series of strikes and turnouts which continued until September. The march on Manchester was not the only result of the August 9 meeting in Ashton. Six emissaries were elected to travel to north Lancashire and convince workers there of the need for solidarity in the strike. We can identify two of the emissaries, both members of the National Charter Association, in Preston on the 12th, where they addressed workers on the need to make the strike general. Strikes and turnouts, with bloody results, did occur in Preston on the 13th; but there is no evidence that the delegates from the south were directly involved (NS, August 20, September 17).

In any event, the *Northern Star* reports strikes and turnouts by the 12th of August at Bolton, Heywood, Rochdale, Bury, Burnley, Stockport, and Todmorden. By the 15th, they had spread into Chorley, Bacup, Wigan, and numerous other localities. The strike had by then become fairly general throughout Lancashire and northern Cheshire. Its mode of extension conformed in large part to the pattern of the Ashton area: A group of workers would strike, form a procession, and march about an area turning out other workers. Between the 10th and the 15th of August, the strike also took on an increasingly political character. Meetings of strikers added to their demand for "a fair day's wages" the demand that the People's Charter become the law of the land. Votes to this effect occurred in Ashton, Staleybridge, Wigan, Manchester, Hyde, Stockport, Oldham, Burnley, and Chorley. By August 15, the wage strike of the 5th had become a political mass strike.

Three points about the relation of the strike to prior developments in 1842 should be made before we turn to a closer analysis of its internal dynamics. The first observation of note is the position of the strike in relation to the overall pattern of worker organization and contention in 1842. Worker organization and contention were on the upsurge in May, June, and July, in terms of both instances and scale. Figure 5.1 presents the three-week swings in worker action for the year.[18] The May-June-July upward trend coincides with the meeting of the National Chartist Convention in London, the presentation of the National Petition demanding the Charter to Parliament, and Parliament's quick and decisive vote against giving the Petition consideration. It was, therefore, a period of political mobilization culminating in the direct presentation of Chartist demands to the ruling bodies of England and in their rejection. The increase of Chartist contention in June and July was an intense mobilization effort in the wake of this decisive political defeat. If the economic situation of 1842 accentuated class divisions at the level of material life, the political defeat of May could only have added salt to an already festering wound.

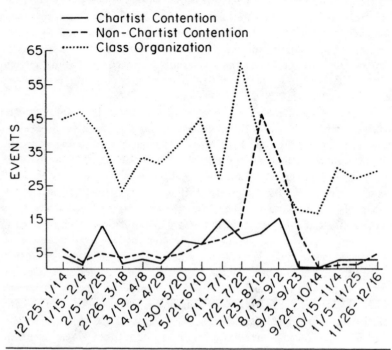

Figure 5.1 Three-Week Fluctuations in Working-Class Organization and Contention, 1842

The June and July expansions of class organization, non-Chartist, and Chartist contention were centered on the May political defeat. The class organizational gatherings were dominated by discussions of the people's present distress and the unjust system of class legislation which intensified it. The non-Chartist contentions primarily involved expressions of confidence in the Chartist leadership and thanks to T. S. Duncombe, M.P., for his support of the National Petition in the House of Commons. The Chartist contentions centered on the adoption of two measures proposed by the National Convention in response to defeat. Large public meetings sent forth a Memorial to the Queen calling for dismissal of the Peel ministry and the formation of one which would make the adoption of the Charter a cabinet measure. The second proposal was a Remonstrance to the House of Commons, the language of which directly expressed the cumulation of class grievances and wounds in 1842. After opening with a discussion of how the annual production of wealth in England was increasing while the condition of the working class was worsening, the Remonstrance went on to say that this was

> an anomaly not to be accounted for but in the monopoly of political powers, the unjust usurpation of authority, and the consequent bad government of the nation:

> That the great mass of the people are denied the right of representation in Parliament, and the present House of Commons, being elected by a limited class, legislates only for the interests of that class, to the utter ruin of the great majority of the people [NS, May 21].

Rhetoric such as this, during a period of intense political mobilization and economic misery, could not help but intensify class hostility and polarization.

The second important development in the May-July period was the recruitment of trade unions *as bodies* into the National Charter Association. This development involved a simple and, in 1842, compelling set of arguments, plus a process of linked recruitment. An example from the Manchester area provides the necessary outlines. In early May, Chartists addressed the carpenters and joiners of Manchester on the necessity of political power if the unions were to pursue their goals successfully. The carpenters and joiners then voted to join the NCA. The fustian cutters followed in late May; the mechanics, in early June; the smiths, on June 15; and the hammermen, in July. In the case of the fustian cutters and mechanics, delegates from the carpenters and joiners addressed their meetings in support of joining the NCA. At the meetings of the smiths and hammermen, delegates from both the mechanics and carpenters and joiners were present to advocate enrollment in the association. The period before August, then, was one during which trade unions were actively turning to the Chartists; and, as one joined, it endeavored to persuade and recruit others to do likewise. The political program of the Charter was creating a broad, interoccupational class solidarity around it (NS, May 28, June 4, June 15, July 16).[19]

The arguments advanced in support of joining the NCA were directly attunded to the economic situation of 1842. We have already discussed the structurally predictable pressures employers were putting on wages. The *Northern Star* reported wage reductions in Chorley, Colne, Crompton, Stockport, Blackburn, Manchester, and Wigan; and this is only a partial list. Moreover, it was, as we have seen, a wage reduction that set the immediate background for the August strike. The argument Chartists made to trade unionists and trade unionists made to each other echoed a May address of Blackburn's Chartists to the trade unions of that locality. The address argued that trade unions were established to protect the wages and conditions of labor, but that the present condition of workers demonstrated their failure in that task. The remedy was for unions to join the National Charter Association and "strike at the heart of the problem—class legislation" (NS, May 21). Delegates from the Manchester mechanics made essentially the same argument before the hammermen on July 12; saying that they

> had found that the trades' unions had not accomplished that for which they had been formed, namely the protection of the labour of the working man; and, therefore, they had come to the conclusion that nothing short of a participation in the making of the laws . . . would effectively protect their labour [NS, July 16].

The economic conditions of 1842 were a major element in the pre-August politicization of the trade unions. Not only workers but working-class organizations were being politicized and mobilized during the May-July period.

Our third point brings us back to the central dynamics of the strike wave of August and September. From considering the identifiable centers of diffusion for the strike (that is, those towns where strikes originated and from which workers formed into turnout "mobs" to extend it into other areas) one thing is apparent: They were places whose pre-August levels of working-class organization and contention were remarkably high. Ashton, Staleybridge, Rochdale, Bury, Stockport, Burnley, and Oldham had levels of worker action almost two times greater than the remaining active/contentious areas (See Table 5.3). The strike expanded outward from the most organized, mobilized, and politically contentious working-class areas to those which were less mobilized and contentious. The political mass strike of August and September represented an ecological example of the critical role a class-based activist core plays in mobilizing extensive class action. It was, for a while, very successful in mobilizing support; but, as we shall see, there was an even more organized, mobilized, and powerful opponent lurking on the horizon. Nevertheless, the three points we have made regarding the relationship of the strike to prior

TABLE 5.3   Comparison of Centers of Strike Diffusion and
Remaining Active/Contentious Areas in Terms of
Class Organization and Contention (per 100,000)

	Class Organization	Chartist Contention	Non-Chartist Contention
Towns of Strike Diffusion	66.9	9.0	8.5
Other Active/Contentious Areas	30.9	4.8	5.6

politicoeconomic developments dovetail with an observation of Rosa Luxemburg (1971: 48):

> With the spreading, clarifying and involution of the political struggle the economic struggle not merely does not recede, but extends, organizes and becomes involved in equal measure. Between the two there is the most complete reciprocal action.[20]

The time has come to look more closely at the internal dynamics of the strike itself. We will focus on them in relation to an actor which has, up to now, been conspicuously absent from the scene—the state. We will show how state-organized repression functioned to halt the strike's expansion and ultimately to produce the rapid demobilization of Lancashire's workers. The evidence represents a dramatic example of how repression can "short-circuit" the process of class mobilization and action. Before turning to the evidence, however, a few background remarks are essential. Earlier, we noted that the strike became increasingly political from the 10th to the 15th of August. Actually, the decisive moment linking the strike to the Charter occurred on August 12, when more than 200 delegates, representing 25 distinct trades and more than 20 localities, convened in Manchester and voted to strike for the People's Charter (NS, August 13).

That day also marked the end of the Home Office's nonrepressive stance toward the strike. With the possible exception of Manchester, Lancashire was a poorly policed county. If local authorities were to deal with large-scale disturbances, they had to rely on the military, whose domestic activities were controlled from the Home Office.[21] On August 13, at the Home Secretary's request, the Queen issued a proclamation offering a £50 reward for information leading to the apprehension and conviction of the "authors, abbettors, or perpetrators" of any act of turnout violence. It was also at this time that the Home Secretary forwarded instructions to the military commanders and magistrates of Lancashire to resist forcibly any further turnout actions so as to "protect Englishmen in the pursuit of their lawful occupations" (Public Record Office, London [HO] 41/17, August 15). The lines were drawn between the state-backed conception of individual liberty economically embodied in the notion of the "right to work" and the activist workers' efforts to enforce a collective solidarity in opposition to it. Consequently, the August 5-August 30 main period of the strike breaks neatly into two segments: August 5-August 12 was a predominantly repression-free period, while August 13-August 30 was a period of active state repression.

The turnout actions of 1842 represented a "modernized" variant of what Eric Hobsbawm has called (1964: 7-10) "collective bargaining by riot." Lacking the organizational resources of large unions and occurring in a context of high unemployment, a strike was an extremely difficult action to pursue in 1842. The turnout action is a tactic well adapted to this type of situation. It involves a sort of collective organization in active process. Groups of workers on strike attempt to enforce solidarity by marching from factory to factory stopping other workers from working. A central feature of the turnout action is the more or less explicit threat of violence against any workers who might refuse to join the strike.

Of the 48 cases of turnout actions identified in our enumeration, less than one in ten involved direct violence against other workers. The usual pattern was for the turnout "mob" to confront the owner or manager of a mill and demand that he stop production and turn out his employees. This demand would be accompanied by threats to "tear down the mill" or to give the owner/manager a beating if he refused. If the workers turned out either on their own or on their bosses' initiative, then there was no violence done to either property or person. Resistance to the turnout demands led to the smashing of windows and doors, the stopping of machinery by knocking out the boiler plugs (hence, "Plug Plot"), and/or the more or less violent occupation of the mill to drive out the workers. The action did not, however, involve the destruction of machinery; it was primarily and singularly directed at imposing solidarity in the cessation of labor.

Since "labor power" constituted the only significant sociopolitical resource Lancashire workers had at this time, the distribution of control over it was crucial to the pursuit of working-class interests and demands. Our earlier analysis of the strike's diffusion indicates that the turnout action was a means by which an activist core of workers attempted to achieve control over the collective labor power of their class. Their effectiveness in this endeavor rested on their having relatively open or free access to other workers so as to persuade and/or coerce them or their employers into compliance. This, in turn, rested on the relative absence of a countervailing force capable of interposing itself between the turnouts and the other workers. The high levels of unemployment in 1842 meant that there was an enormous potential for strikebreaking. The workers' lack of sufficient strike funds gave the employers a decided advantage, in that, through wages, they controlled access to the means of subsistence.[22] It was probably this situation which directed turnout demands toward the employers, who were, after all, the workers' most immediate rivals in the struggle for control over the collective labor power. In short, the turnout action was a "primitive" form of the very persistent and modern conflict over the distribution of power in the labor market, a struggle which was likely to be particularly intense in an industry with a cost structure like that of textiles at this time.

The August 13 change in repressive policy provided, in the shape of the military presence, a countervailing force capable of blocking turnout access to other workers. In the short run, it returned dominant control over the labor power of the workers to the employers. As we would expect from a liberal state, it enforced a "free" market in labor. It maintained the dominance of property not only in the labor market but also in the state itself. That is, it greatly undermined a serious democratic challenge to the existing liberal state and its restricted property franchise. We can read the record of repression's effects in terms of the turnout actions for which we have evidence. First, some definitions:

(1) A *turnout action* is a collective action by one group of workers on strike to attempt to prevent another employed groups of workers from working.
   (a) A *successful turnout action* occurs when the previously employed workers immediately cease working as a direct result of the first group of workers' turnout action.
   (b) A *turnout failure* occurs when the employed workers remain at work in the face of the turnout action.
(2) An *enforcing turnout action* is a turnout action which occurs at a workplace that had previously been either on strike or the target of a successful turnout action but is now back in operation.

TABLE 5.4   Police Actions and Turnout Actions

Period	Number of Turnout Actions	Number of Turnout Actions with Police Action	Percent of Turnout Actions with Police Actions
8/5-8/12	26	4	15
8/13-8/30	22	14	64
8/5-8/30	48	18	38

(3) *Strikes* begun by workers on their own initiative and without the immediate presence of a turnout mob are not counted as turnout actions.

(4) *Police actions* are defined as any active intervention by the repressive agents of the state into an ongoing turnout action.

Table 5.4 presents the basic figures on the number of turnout actions of all types and the number in which police intervened. The Home Office policy change of August 13 was much more than symbolic. The proportion of turnout actions with active police intervention was more than four times greater in the second, repressive period. The configuration of forces at turnout actions was quite different depending on whether they occurred between August 5 and August 12 or between August 13 and August 30. The problem is to discern what, if any, effect this changed configuration of forces had on the success rate of turnout actions.[23]

We have sufficient information on 38 turnout actions to determine whether they were successes or failures. Table 5.5 presents this information in relation to police action or repression. The evidence is clear: 88 percent of the turnout failures can be attributed to police action. Throughout the entire period, in only two successful turnout actions did police action also occur. The significance of the changed repressive policy adopted by the Home Office is apparent in the drop in the turnout success rate from 75 percent in the August 5-12 period to 39 percent in the second, repressive period. Clearly, the repressive forces of the state operated to deny turnout workers access to and control over the collective labor power of their class.

The distinction between turnout actions and enforcing turnout actions permits a better perspective on the role repression played. Successful turnout actions represented increases in the mobilization of working-class

TABLE 5.5   Success and Failure of Turnouts
            with and without Police Action

Period	Turnouts Without Police Action		Turnouts With Police Action	
	Success	*Failure*	*Success*	*Failure*
8/5-8/12				
Turnout Actions	13	1	0	4
Enforcing Turnout Actions	2	0	0	0
All Turnouts	15	1	0	4
8/13-8/30				
Turnout Actions	4	1	2	6
Enforcing Turnout Actions	1	0	0	4
All Turnouts	5	1	2	10
8/5-8/30				
Turnout Actions	17	2	2	10
Enforcing Turnout Actions	3	0	0	4
All Turnouts	20	2	2	14

resources for collective contention. Enforcing turnout actions, on the other hand, were attempts to maintain an already established level of resource mobilization in the face of actual declines. The effects of the changed repressive policy can now be seen in a somewhat different light. The relatively repression-free period was one in which Lancashire workers achieved impressive gains in resource mobilization for the pursuit of their economic and political demands. There were only two enforcing actions during that period, and both were successful. In short, the nonrepressive August 5-August 12 period mirrored the entire May-July expansion of resource mobilization and contention with little evidence of decline.

The 13 turnout actions which occurred in the second, repressive period occurred between August 13 and 18. Their success rate was 46 percent, compared with 72 percent in the former period. Clearly, mobilization was becoming a more difficult and costly endeavor. In fact, after August 18, the workers were no longer increasing their level of resource mobilization; instead, they attempted to maintain previously achieved mobilization levels. After August 18, enforcing turnouts dominated the scene; and police actions ensured that 80 percent of these efforts to maintain mobilization failed. The lesson had been driven home by the 20th, when speakers at a strike meeting in Middleton warned the workers not to interfere with those returning to work, because "the authorities would come down on them" (NS, August 27). The issue was finally sealed when the Trade Delegates meeting that had declared the strike for the Charter on August 12 issued its final address on August 27, announcing an end to the strike and saying that further action must wait until they had developed greater organization and resources (NS, September 3). That is, after August 18, repression was rapidly demobilizing the Lancashire working class.

How rapidly this occurred can be seen by looking at Figure 5.1. Both class organization and, especially, contention dipped to their lowest yearly levels. This fact goes a long way toward justifying the emphasis we have been placing on political leadership, organization, and agitation as critical to mobilization and contention. Starting on August 17, repression was not only directed against turnouts but was also reflected in the large-scale arrest of trade union and Chartist leaders. These arrests continued into October with trials at Salford, Liverpool, and York involving more than 300 defendants. The core Chartist leadership was bound over for trial at Lancaster in the following spring. When one compares the list of defendants with the list of people who had taken leading roles in the collective gatherings of the year, it is clear that the arrests had emasculated Lancashire's working-class leadership. Agitation and mobilization, in fact, ceased to be the primary concern of the National Charter Association. On September 24, its Executive Council defined the organization's primary task as the raising of defense funds for the arrested (NS, September 24).

CONCLUSION

The overall social geography of working-class contention in 1842 was fundamentally shaped by the economically structured class relations of Lancashire's industrial capitalist order. It was not, however, a direct, unmediated result. Lancashire's 1842 working-class contention waxed and waned in response to the relative power balance between class-based political organizations. Structural relations defined a field of organizational and mobilizational potentialities whose realization rested on more contingent situational and political factors. The 1842 depression-accentuated polarization of labor/capital relations shifted political advantages toward the Chartists. It drew working-class experience closer to the imagery and logic of their political language and program. The economically conditioned success of Chartist agitation, the generally favorable outcomes of their confrontations with the Anti-Corn Law League, and the increasing adhesion of trade unions to the Chartist cause are three good indications of these dynamics. In short, the Chartists were coming to occupy an increasingly singular and central role in the representation and articulation of working-class interests.

Ultimately, however, this process of party/class consolidation depended on the maintenance of a political environment that guaranteed a relatively open field for political action. No matter how great the economically conditioned potential advantages for class mobilization were, they could not be realized independently of the organized process of agitation. Without the inherently political processes of speech, agitation, and collective action that linked activists to workers, potential would remain unrealized. This fact is what gave state repression its critical place in the dynamics of contention during 1842. State-organized repression first succeeded in interposing itself between activists and workers, and then more directly cleared the activists from the public arena. Thus, it succeeded in closing down the opportunities necessary for effective agitation and in eliminating the critical agents in the process of mobilization and class formation. The result was, predictably, the rapid post-September demobilization of Lancashire's working class.

When one recognizes these fundamentally political aspects of working-class formation, one sees the Chartist strategy of placing the democratization of the state at the head of the working-class agenda in a somewhat different light. Our analysis leads to the conclusion that the achievement of a measure of political power at least great enough to neutralize state repression is a necessary, but by no means sufficient, condition for effective working-class formation. In its absence, the organizational and agitational activities critical to building the inherently collective foundations of working-class power will always be subject to severe limitation. In fact, such a situation is likely to result in a pattern of working-class formation similar to the one of 1842: periods of rapid development and consolidation punctuated by short bursts of counterrepression leading to a period of class disorganization, demobilization, and inaction. What the

Chartist challenge represented was an attempt to ensure the limitation of state repression by means of political democratization. By democratically securing the framework of political rights underlying the conditions for successful class formation, the People's Charter would have initiated a period for the progressive development of the collective infrastructures of working-class power. In this sense, worker support for the People's Charter was not only a situationally comprehensible occurrence but also a rationally based action in terms of class interests.

NOTES

1. The many and varied disputes over Chartism's social and political character are excellently reviewed in Morris (1979: 47-56), Mather (1972), and Musson (1972: 36-48). A formulation close to the one presented here is Donnelly (1976: 219-238).

2. The entire range of issues and alternatives in the study of collective action are discussed in Tilly (1975b).

3. A more extensive discussion of the logic of these alternatives is Brown (1979: 3-21).

4. As Kitson Clark puts it, "What the Chartists desired was no doubt to return to a society of small masters and skilled craftsmen, or at least a stay to the development of large factories and high capitalism" (1962: 135).

5. Some "structuralists"-leaning works are Foster (1974) and Rude (1964: 179-191). Harold Perkin (1969) discusses an attempt to synthesize the two perspectives identified here.

6. All correlations reported in the text were done without the parishes of Chipping and Radcliffe, which were extreme deviants. Their small populations (1,675 and 5,099, respectively) meant that when their raw figures were converted into rates per 100,000, they were extremely high. Chipping had three class organization events and one non-Chartist contention. Radcliffe had seven class organization events and one Chartist contention. When converted into rates per 100,000, Chipping's class organization rate was 176.5 and its non-Chartist contention was 58.8. Radcliffe's figures were 137.3 and Chartist contention was 19.6. All these figures were the highest achieved, and those for class organization and non-Chartist contention were extremely high. The average rates for the other 24 parishes were: class organization = 30.4; non-Chartist contention = 6.8; and Chartist contention = 5.5. The way Chipping and Radcliffe distorted the correlations we will discuss in the next few pages can

be seen in the matrix immediately below (the figures in parentheses are the coefficients which were obtained when Chipping and Radcliffe were excluded):

	Chartist Contention	Non-Chartist Contention	Class Organization
Urbanization	-.10(-.07)	-.05(+.16)	-.004(+.17)
Urban growth		Not Applicable	
Urbanism	-.01(+.07)	+.03(+.38)	-.09(+.28)
Industrialization		Not applicable (see note 7)	
Industrialism	+.35(+.52)	+.30(+.61)	+.26(+.64)
Textile Workers per 1,000 acres	+.45(+.60)	+.31(+.80)	+.29(+.79)
Class organization	+.35(+.50)	+.70(+.68)	
Non-Chartist contention	+.05(+.64)		

Since the urban growth variable refers to cities of 10,000 and over, it is not applicable in Chipping and Radcliffe because there were no cities of this minimum size. In light of the small number of their events and their large impact on the overall pattern of relationships, their exclusion seemed warranted. The 24 remaining parishes are Ashton, Blackburn, Bolton, Bury, Chorley, Dalton, Dean, Eccles, Lancaster, Leigh, Liverpool, Manchester, Middleton, Prescot, Preston, Prestwich-cum-Oldham, Rochdale, Sefton, Stockport, Ulverstone, Warrington, Whalley, Wigan, and Ormskirk.

7. Our data on urbanization, urban growth, and urbanism are calculated from Danson and Welton (1856-1859). Data on the rate of change in textile factory workers 1835-1838 are available for the 12 parishes of Ashton, Blackburn, Bolton, Bury, Lancashire, Leigh, Oldham, Preston, Rochdale, Stockport, Whalley, and Wigan in Rodgers (1960: 135-153). The information on textile factory workers 1838 is taken from *Sessional Papers* (HC), 1839, XLII (Returns from Factory Inspectors). The use of factory workers as *indicative* of industrialism perhaps requires some justification over and above the rather obvious one of availability. The first point is that Engels and Smelser formulate their arguments in terms of factory-based textile production. Second, textile factory workers actually are a good indicator of industrialism in Lancashire. D. A. Farnie (1979: 35) argues that the countywide forward and backward linkages of the cotton industry meant that it employed "at least as many hands in its associated manufactures as in the productive process itself." This conservative doubling factor, moreover, applies only to directly linked economic activities; consequently, it greatly understates the degree of indirect dependence. Thus, if we take industrialism to mean the extent to which the economic fate of a population is ultimately dependent on an industrial mode of production, then textile

factory workers are a good indicator. This, of course, leaves out the fact that the cotton industry was largely dependent on a slave-based mode of production for its raw materials. Regrettably, the emancipatory efforts of some are often based on the slavery of others.

8. Perhaps we have been a little unfair to Smelser in dealing only with his generalized arguments about the causes of political turmoil. His more specific argument sees it and other "social explosions" as related to the disruptions of the traditional familial economy of the working class which resulted from the factory employment of women and children. Yet, when we correlate Chartist contention and the proportion of textile factory workers in 1838 who were women, the coefficient is –.22. Thus, even this admittedly crude but nevertheless better-specified test of Smelser's argument contradicts it.

9. We have not pursued a complete partial-correlational-causal analysis for two reasons: (1) the small number of cases and (2) the inability to rule out reciprocal causation.

10. The gloss is of Thompson's remark (1964: 729) that Chartism was the expression of a working class "no longer in the making but already made." No doubt he would resist any "structural" formulation of his arguments which, in fact, entail a great deal more than what we are saying here.

11. A quick sampling of 1843, a relatively good year economically, suggests levels of Chartist contention about one-half to one-third lower than in 1842. Later, however, we shall see that comparative economic conditions were probably not the only reason for this. The courtwoom and the prison played a part as well.

12. The high unemployment parishes were Blackburn, Manchester, Preston, Rochdale, Whalley, and Wigan; the low ones were Ashton, Bolton, Bury, and Oldham. "Unemployment" is defined as number of textile factory workers, 1841, not working divided by number working, 1841 (source: Sessional Papers [HC] 1842, XXII [Returns from Factory Inspectors]).

13. Details on the Anti-Corn Law League's arguments and strategies may be found in McCord (1958).

14. Reports on these confrontations are in the *Northern Star* (January 8, February 5, 12, 19, and 26; March 5 and 19; June 25; July 16 and 23; October 1).

15. John Foster (1974: 115) argues a similar thesis concerning the dynamics and consequences of ACLL/Chartist confrontations.

16. There was considerable debate within the NCA at this time over the question of a middle-class coalition. The point here stands, however, because if such an alliance should have occurred—and it did not—it would have involved difficult negotiations between class leaderships and organizations. This in itself shows that the coalition possibilities had fundamentally altered.

17. A full narration of these events is presented in Rose (1957).

18. The average size of events by time period looks like this:

12/25/41 – 2/4/42:	581.7
2/5/42 – 3/18/42:	2912.8
3/19/42 – 4/29/42:	4900.0
4/30/42 – 6/10/42:	5558.3
6/11/42 – 7/22/42:	6612.7
7/23/42 – 9/2/42:	6137.4
9/3/42 – 10/14/42:	1833.3
10/15/42 – 12/16/42:	1360.6

19. More details on trade unions and Chartism in 1842 may be found in Mather (1974). Musson (1972: 46-48) discusses and criticizes the literature on this question. Obviously, much more research is needed on the specific trades and determinants of their support for Chartism. We are not concerned with this enormous collective biographical task here. What is important to us is to establish the type of situation which influenced union movement toward the Charter; namely, a situation severely limiting their ability to defensively maintain their interests.

20. For an analysis of the close relationship between political conflicts and strike waves in France, see Shorter and Tilly (1974: 104-146).

21. Mather (1966) is a good discussion of the structure and operation of the state's repressive apparatus at this time.

22. The virtual absence of an effective "welfare" system, in itself part of the laissez-faire pattern of the times, made unemployment an extremely difficult experience. J. Garraty (1978: 85-102) provides a brief discussion of this problem.

23. This portion of our analysis combines information from the *Northern Star* and *The Trial of Feargus O'Connor* (1843). The two sources are in general concordance in their event reportage but vary in the completeness of description.

6

Keeping the Navvies in Line:

*Variations in Work Discipline Among
British Railway Construction Crews*

SAMUEL COHN

Recent research has shown that the nineteenth century in the industrialized nations produced a colossal change in the mechanisms of enforcing work discipline. Studies by Marglin (1974), E. P. Thompson (1967), and Pollard (1965) have shown that large-scale production was synonymous with the introduction of rigorous supervision and control of the work force. The revolution in work discipline was as unprecedented and as radical as the revolution in capital and technology. The farthest-reaching transformation, and certainly the most discussed, was the introduction of the factory system with Weberian bureaucracy. This involved the centralization of production, the use of close supervision by foremen, the codification of expected behavior, the introduction of clocks and timekeeping, the devising of rigorous accounting systems, the proliferation of written records, the decline of subcontract, and the development of long-term incentives (such as graded salaries and promotions). The classic statement of this change was Max Weber's (1968); Richard Edwards (1979) has recently rekindled interest in bureaucratization with his study, *Contested Terrain.*

However, bureaucracy was not the only new experiment with industrial discipline. Many solutions were put forward to the problem of the surveillance of workers. Some persisted; others did not. A large set of the archaic nineteenth-century experiments can be grouped together in the category *extramural discipline.* This is discipline that is imposed outside the bounds of the work place. Bureaucracy works entirely within the work place: Workers are watched on the job; their indoor performance is measured; the rewards entail cash or status and authority within the firm. Extramural discipline either monitors outside performance or entails sanctions beyond the confines of the work place. Examples of outside monitoring are company-sponsored recreation or company investigations of employees' private lives. An example of extramural sanctions is company housing which can be rescinded when an employee seriously disobeys. Besides these, the nineteenth century saw company schooling, company-financed religious services, company sick-clubs, and company pension schemes.[1] On the more sobering side, many companies kept private police forces or forced workers to shop at company stores. The extreme case of extramuralism was the company town, in which a worker's life was spent in corporate institutions under constant management scrutiny. Victorian England saw the extensive use of these devices. Hilton (1960) has demonstrated the pervasiveness of the truck system in this period. Many employers supported evangelical missions to their workers (Pollard 1965). Most major railways kept their own private corporate town.[2] Robert Owen's paternalistic community in New Lanark is a well-known extreme case.

EXTRAMURAL WORK DISCIPLINE

Most academic interest is focused on bureaucratic discipline rather than on its extramuralism to one section of a chapter. These books are so rich that we can easily forgive the exclusion. Nevertheless, there are two reasons we may want to expand on these chapters. First, the dynamics of extramural discipline may illuminate the origins of modern work discipline. The adoption of Bureaucracy may have been affected by the viability of the alternatives. Second, an evolutionary focus can undermine our comprehension of the nineteenth century. If we are to appreciate the conditions of the working class, the sources of industrial conflict, or the problems facing mid-Victorian entrepreneurs, we must understand all the available devices for controlling labor. Merely examining those weapons which survived into the twentieth century can distort our perceptions of the arsenals of management.

This chapter is an exploration of how extramuralism worked in one mid-Victorian British industry, railway construction. However, before the analysis begins, it may help to set the stage by discussing some major propositions in the extramuralist literature. This is not a systematic review of the limited literature that exists; nor should it be construed as a list of theories to be directly tested below. Rather, I would like to summarize a limited set of ideas to which I will constantly refer as the discussion progresses.

Efficiency versus Inefficiency

There is an enormous contrast between bureaucracy and extramuralism in the degree to which each is considered effective. Much has been made by Weberians of the "iron law of bureaucracy." Bureaucracy is seen as such an overwhelming tool for generating efficiency that, once introduced, all organizations must bureaucratize or face extermination through competition. Pollard is not alone in explaining the rise of Weberian management by its undisputed superiority to the methods that existed before. Most authors see extramuralism as an ineffective form of discipline which is prone to be eliminated in a drive for greater efficiency. The most explicit statement on this point is by Edwards. Addressing company sick plans, hospitals, housing, and other forms of what he termed "welfare capitalism," he argued that these were ineffectual attempts by management to reduce labor militancy. In the course of undeterred industrial conflict, the feebleness of extramuralism should become apparent; it should then be replaced by bureaucracy and mechanical discipline. Weaker predictions of the withering of extramuralism can be found in the works of Lucas (1971), Hilton (1960), and Pollard (1965).[3]

Truck and Worker Discontent

With good reason, most discussions separate company stores from other extramural measures. Truck shops, another name for company stores, are a blatant and obvious form of exploitation; no other extramural form creates as much worker hostility. Pollard saw the constant friction with employees as draining managerial energy, and predicted that this would lead to trucks' abolition. Hilton noted that exploitation led to government enquiries, which produced legal restrictions on the use of truck. A third consequence of worker discontent, rarely mentioned, is organized conflict and industrial actions. If truck is supported by management and opposed by workers, then some model of labor strength should be able to explain the variance in truck location. Truck shops should exist in those industries and settings where workers are too weak to have it abolished.

External Upper-Class Demands

One might intuit that questions of work discipline would be explained by mechanisms occurring in the work place. Some suggest, however, that considerations beyond the firm play a role in extramural discipline. Entrepreneurs may have altered their disciplinary techniques to placate the demands of elite members in the outer world. Hilton (1960) notes the role of middle-class reformers in eliminating truck. Edwards (1979) believes that welfare capitalism serves as a public relations device. Chaloner's long history of extramuralism in the railway town of Crewe (1950) explains the practice without reference to the internal affairs of the primary employer; rather, the whole account rests on the struggle between various political factions in the town.[4] The social and community life of entrepreneurs may have an impact on the shape of work discipline.

I have raised the general question of nineteenth-century discipline and made some suggestions as to profitable lines of enquiry. The purpose of this chapter is to analyze extramural discipline in railway construction in Britain in 1846. Data were collected on a cross-section of firms to identify and explain variations in the types of extramural discipline used. By means of this immersion in the particular economics of disciplinary decisions in one industry, it was hoped that light might be shed on the questions addressed above. In the course of the investigation, it became apparent that the propositions previously listed had great heuristic value.

Why was railway contracting chosen? First, there exists an excellent source of data on discipline within the industry—namely, the 1846 Report from the House of Commons Select Committee on Railway Labourers. British railway construction boomed in 1846; the demand for railway construction laborers, known as "navvies," was at a level unprecedented in contemporary experience (Lewin, 1936). The House of Commons took an interest in this phenomenon and collected data on over 30 railway construction sites. The material provides a rare opportunity to systematically analyze different firms using standardized testimony obtainable from a convenient, reliable, readily available source. Factual data for 1846 and historical background, unless otherwise indicated, originate from the testimony given in the 1846 House of Commons report.[5]

Railway construction was chosen to study because it used a substantial amount of extramural discipline. This is because railway contractors are generally prevented from using Weberian bureaucracy. The reason will sound familiar to anyone who has read Stinchcombe's classic analysis (1959) of bureaucracy in construction. Bureaucracy requires long-term stable conditions to be effective. Work scattered in multiple locations is hard to supervise or monitor by record. Rulebooks are hard to codify when changing conditions in a continuing progression of new sites requires constant adaptation to local conditions. Most important, bureaucracy depends on the ability of employers to reward employees in the long term. Edwards makes this explicit in his conceptualization of bureaucratic discipline as a cumulating chain of minor promotions. If an employee anticipates imminent dismissal or resignation, the power of these future rewards becomes negligible.

Employment was extremely unstable in Victorian railway construction. The industry was highly cyclical. Most of the British railway net was constructed in two bursts of about four years each. Between the two peaks was a seven-year slump (Lewin, 1936). Individual job tenures were shortened by other considerations. Crews would break up after a given job to move to another section of the line. After the line was finished, the men would disperse to pick up new work on other railways. Labor demand intensified turnover and undercut simple discipline; dissatisfied workers often left knowing they could find jobs with rival contractors.

The result was that discipline frequently broke down. Drinking on the job was rampant enough to become a safety problem. Absenteeism and lateness, while condemned, were entirely commonplace. But the most serious problem was violence. Brawling was also common. Individual grievances about pay were usually settled by intimidation. Ethnic rivalries and personal vendettas led to fistfights with participants numbering in the scores.

The contractors had several tools with which to reassert their authority on the job. Not all of these were extramural. One method—well known to the general reader—is the hiring of "coolie labor," or ethnic minorities. Chinese in America, Italians in France, Irishmen in England: all were at various times economically destitute and desperate for employment. They provided a cheap labor force that was easy to control.

The extramural tactics are less well known. Most railways kept private police with full constabulary powers, who monitored the men and arrested troublemakers. Most contractors kept some form of company housing; this could be ameliorated or rescinded depending on the merits of the tenant. There were two other methods of extramural control: The first, involving truck and the company store, was through the use of indebtedness and the withholding of pay to reduce turnover and create credit dependency. The second was the use of company clergy to monitor the men and to promote religiosity and sobriety.

How did indebtedness work on the railways? Indebtedness is the major device by which truck systems turn from a pettifogging form of minor exploitation into a serious form of extramural discipline. The employer pays his employees at infrequent intervals. When workers run out of cash, they are forced to turn to the employer for whatever subsidies and advances he is willing to offer. The employer then refuses to provide cash, but instead gives credit at the company store. Unable to buy goods in the outside world, the worker becomes bound to the company store and thus to the employer for the period of his debt.

There was enormous variance in the use of debt on the railways. Truck shops were universal, but they were often merely company stores with high prices but no capacity to bind the worker. Hilton has shown from limited but suggestive data that truck shops rarely continued their debts beyond a single payday. Once cash was received, most debts were completely eliminated. However, the length of the pay period varied significantly and, with it, the length of waiting time until the all-absolving payday. On the more humane end, such railways as the Croydon-Epsom or the Peto railways paid weekly or by the fortnight. Debts tended not to accumulate under fortnightly pay, and subsidies thus tended to diminish in importance. On the other hand, many railways, such as the Lancaster-Carlisle paid only once a month. At the far extreme was the Lincoln, Sheffield and Manchester, which paid only once every nine weeks. This implies that a worker would have been paid for his work only five times a year. In this review, the term "short pay" will refer to pay by the week or fortnight; "Long pay," to pay periods of a month or longer.

Railway employers also paid for religion and schooling to be brought to the men. Both preachers and schoolteachers were hired to run services, read the Bible, teach basic literacy, and provide general pastoral aid. Sometimes the company would hire full-time clergy; other times they used volunteer lay Scripture readers. Most of the time the denomination was Church of England, but nondenominational Protestants and the occasional Moravian were known to appear. Although Irish workers were often a substantial minority of the labor force, the companies never took the initiative to hire Roman Catholic clergy. The exact purpose of these clergy is open to controversy and will be discussed in greater detail later. For convenience, both ordained ministers and lay personnel will be lumped together under the term "clergy."

Earlier discussions (Francis, 1851; Williams, 1852; Peto, 1893; Clapham, 1930; Coleman, 1965; Bagwell, 1974) of these phenomena, both from contemporary observers and from the historians who borrowed from them, have focused their attention on the distinctive policies of Sir Morton Peto. Peto was the second largest contractor in England. He used short pay periods and clergy. These two comparatively humanitarian gestures were usually explained by Peto's exemplary moral uprightness; his biographer, for instance, discusses the deep religious sentiments brought on by Peto's fundamentalist Baptist wife (Peto, 1893). Most sociologists are (with good reason) skeptical of "great man" theories of social phenomena. On the other hand, we should not ignore a possible explanation of variance in the data. One way to establish the validity of this explanation is to test the sociological explanations with and without the Peto railways. If the findings prove robust to the exclusion or inclusion of the Peto cases, this weakens the plausibility of "moral influence" as an alternative explanation. If we can find an explanation that is good for all railways regardless of contractors, our approach will have more generality than the "great man" theory.

PATTERNS OF WORK DISCIPLINE
IN RAILWAY CONSTRUCTION

Now to the analysis. The most striking pattern apparent in the 1846 parliamentary data is that pay and, to a much lesser degree, clergy varied strongly by region. It is quite clear from Table 6.1 that short pay is strongly concentrated in southern and eastern England. This is true whether or not Peto railways are included in the sample. There was a southern bias in clergy use as well, but this is explained entirely in terms of Peto's preference for clergy. Thus, regionalism in the clergy will be subsumed in the later discussion of the special problems posed by Peto. Regionalism in pay period can be best explained by the regional distribution of Irish within the labor force. Specifically, I will hold that Northern England and Scotland had a higher percentage of Irish workers, and that Irish workers weakened the bargaining power of the navvies. In the north workers were divided and could not mobilize to attain shorter pay periods.

I have argued that since truck systems were unpopular among workers, a model of the effectiveness of worker agitation would predict the location of truck systems. The same holds for indebtedness and long pay periods. Long pay was extremely unpopular among navvies. Not only did it bind them to the company store, but it increased the likelihood of their not being paid at all. The loss of wages through theft was common along the railways. Defaults have been observed on the Swaffham-Dereham, Great Western, Caledonian, and the Glasgow-Dumfries-and-Carlisle roads (1846

TABLE 6.1   Pay By Region*

Pay	Scotland	Northwest Eng.	Southeast Eng.	Total	
Short	1	2	14 (6)	17	(9)
Long	6	5	2 (2)	13	(13)
Total	7	7	16 (8)	30	(22)

*Figures in parentheses indicate number of southeastern railways with given attributes *not* constructed by Peto. Northwest England represents all of England and Wales north of London and Bristol and west of Southhampton and Leeds. Southeastern England is the remainder.

S.C.; Handley, 1970) Payment was usually made to subcontractors who were responsible for the labor of crews of a few hundred men. Often these subcontractors would employ sub-subcontractors. The money thus passed through several hands on the way from the company to the men. Many of these crew leaders were poor and none too honest, sometimes disappearing with the pay when it came. Often there was no legal recourse for the men when such defaults occurred. The courts tended to hold that the company had filled its legal obligations by having paid a crew leader for his services. Liability rested on the crew leader, who had disappeared. Since the company was under no legal obligation to provide a second packet for the men, the workers were left completely destitute (Handley, 1970). The longer the pay periods, the larger the pay packets, and the larger the temptation to abscond with the lot. Therefore, the men adamantly preferred short pay periods to long ones so they could count on receiving their wages.

However, it is incorrect to assume that because workers sought short pay periods that short pay will be a function of the classic measure of labor strength—labor scarcity. My argument is not that northern workers were weak so much as they were distracted. In the north, workers exhausted their strength in campaigns to ban Irish immigrants from the line. An incredible amount of energy was devoted to ethnic rivalries. The Lake District, the Borderlands, and Lowland Scotland all saw massive riots against Irish navvies. Scotch and Irish navvies each numbering in the hundreds faced each other off at Penrith. In Edinburgh, the Irish were driven off the works by over a hundred Scottish workers. One wave of anti-Irish incidents started on the Lancaster-Carlisle, moved up the west coast of Scotland to Edinburgh, and then moved down the east coast to

TABLE 6.2   Clergy By Region*

Clergy	Scotland	Northwest Eng.	Southeast Eng.	Total
Present	2	4	10 (2)	16 (8)
Absent	4	3	1 (1)	8 (7)
Total	6	7	11 (3)	24 (15)

*Figures in parentheses indicate number of southeastern railways with given attributes *not* constructed by Peto. Northwest England represents all of England and Wales north of London and Bristol and west of Southhampton and Leeds. Southeastern England is the remainder.

Berwick. Treble (1972) and Handley have traced the struggle against the Irish; the history of navvy mobilization in Scotland and the north of England is essentially one of ethnic exclusion. Such incidents were generally absent in the south. This was not the product of the tolerant quality of the English navvy; there were very few Irish in the southern English labor force. Their absence obviated the problem of ethnic hostility. On rare occasions, the Irish did attempt to obtain English employment—as, for example, on the line from London to Birmingham, where they were banned by Englishmen employed on the works. The demographics of Irish scarcity kept ethnic incidents from being more prevalent.

LONG PAY AND ETHNIC DIVISIONS

Why should this preoccupation with the Irish distract workers from the issue of long pay? First, the Irish represented a real source of scab labor that could undercut any serious non-Irish attempts at labor mobilization. Treble has argued that the Irish were paid wages consistently below the British standard. Testimony given before the Select Committee shows the inferior wages, accommodations, and working conditions the Irish had to accept. The Irish Potato Famine was at its height. Thousands of refugees were fleeing Ireland. In their desperation, Irish were happy to accept any conditions that were offered to them. They were present in some districts in very large numbers. In Ayrshire, for example, they represented better than 15 percent of the working population. They provided a massive reserve army of labor that could weaken a campaign against long pay.

Yet, even had the Irish been willing to join with Scottish workers in a combined class-based movement, their vulnerability as targets would have preempted more serious strike action. Suppose mobilized English workers had a choice of actions they could take to improve its lot. They could strike to obtain higher wages or better conditions.

Alternatively, they could move to restrict the labor force by banning the Irish. The latter is a less risky operation that requires a bare minimum of organizational resources. A strike entails the long-term organization of a large body of men. A large number of people must be induced to risk being fired or going without pay. This commitment may have to be maintained over a long period of time. A drive against the Irish is short term and can be almost an impulsive action. It takes large numbers, but these masses are only required for a day or two of sustained violence. Repression is likely to be confined to a small number of leaders, if it is taken at all. No strike fund is required; no long-term incentives to maintain solidarity are needed. Thus, areas with an Irish population will be tempted to divert their energies toward the pursuit of this organizationally easy goal. Ethnic-based distraction from class conflict ends when the weaker group is banned. The elimination of the Irish was thus likely to precede the banning of long pay.

Obviously, this will only hold where the maintenance of long-term solidarity is problematic. A modern construction union can easily pursue ethnic and wage demands simultaneously. However, navvies lacked both the formal organizations and informal ties of association that would have provided the cohesion for a two-front offensive. The weakness of the navvy community stemmed from the mobility of navvy work. Shifting workers from job to job prevented the formation of the informal bonds that come with extended co-residence. The navvies were not linked by common background either: The labor on any line came from a wide variety of disparate locations. The South Devon was built by workers from four southwestern counties. The Knaresborough viaduct in Yorkshire was built by a labor force that was less than 40 percent local. The itinerant majority came from a wide variety of locations: North England, the Midlands, Scotland, and Ireland (Patmore, 1962). No formal organizations existed to help compensate for this fragmentation. Both Peto (1893) and Helps (1874) noted a complete absence of trade unions among navvies. Sick clubs were scarce and hard to maintain. Many would have collapsed without contractor intervention. This did not completely preempt striking: Handley (1970) shows that even in Scotland some strikes did occur. However, they were poorly organized, wildcat attempts. In Irish areas they were totally unsuccessful.

TABLE 6.3   Pay by Irish on Line

Irish	Long Pay	Short Pay	Total
Present	4	0	4
Absent	1	4	5
Total	5	4	9

What empirical evidence can be brought to bear on this explanation?

(1) We should expect a high correlation between long pay and the presence of Irish workers on the line.

(2) We should expect long pay where the Irish constitute a large percentage of the labor force. The Irish will be harder to ban in countries where they are numerous. Thirty Irish can be evicted in a thrice; thirty thousand Irish are tougher to deal with.

(3) We should *not* expect a correlation between labor scarcity and short pay. Ethnic rivalries provide an equal temptation to both strong and weak labor forces, given a low level of organizational sophistication.

(4) We should find labor demands to shorten pay periods concentrated in regions that have few Irish. In highly Irish regions, ethnic demands should predominate.

(5) We should find successful strikes that ban long pay in low-Irish regions.

Were Irish absent on lines with short pay? Data on the ethnic composition of railway construction crews are hard to find. The House of Commons obtained data on nine railways. I dichotomized the railways into, on one hand, those with substantial numbers of Irish and, on the other, those with only trivial numbers of Irish or no Irish.

Table 6.3 speaks for itself. Long pay was overwhelmingly associated with the presence of Irish on the line. There is only one exception to this rule—the Lancaster-Carlisle. Yet this exception is more apparent than real. On the Lancaster-Carlisle, the Irish had been driven from the line immediately before parliamentary evidence was given. The ethnic war was still in flux. The workers were celebrating a recent victory; they had not had time to start pressing for new demands.

TABLE 6.4   Pay by Percent Adult Irish Males in County

Percent Irish	Long Pay	Short Pay	Total
High	12	5	17
Lowa	1	12	13
Total	13	17	39

aLow Irish counties have .015 or less of the male population over the age of 20 Irish. The unit of analysis is the railway.

Was long pay located in counties with heavy Irish populations? The 1851 census gives us the birthplace of the inhabitants of the counties in Britain, which allows inference about which counties had large percentages of immigrant Irish. From this I determined the ethnicity of the counties surrounding each railway.[6] Table 6.4 shows the results of the analysis.

Short pay seems to be located in the counties with negligible Irish populations. Only one railway in a non-Irish county had long periods of indebtedness. Only six railways out of thirty did not fit the general pattern.

I predicted that short pay should not be affected by labor shortage or labor demand. Both strong and weak labor forces should be equally effected by ethnicity. Does this work out? One measure of labor supply is the population density of the county containing the railway. Navvy work is not terribly skilled; anyone who can handle a pick or a shovel can find work in a construction gang. Thus, the labor supply will be unskilled physical laborers—usually men aged 15-50. Since age and sex structures do not vary by county, population density will measure this supply of men.

Table 6.5 shows a trend in the direction of what a labor strength theory would predict. Areas with low density and scarce labor tend to have short pay; areas with surplus labor tend to have long pay. However, the relationship is weak: 40 percent of the cases are exceptions. The table is not statistically significant, even at the .3 level. Controlling for other variables and doing more refined analyses does not alter the basic weakness of the relationship. There is practically no relationship between market labor strength and short pay.

Was the south of England, where Irish were scarce, the location of successful strikes against short pay? Here the evidence is inadequate and contradictory. There are scraps of evidence that support the theory; there

TABLE 6.5   Pay by Population Density

Pop. Dens.	Long Pay	Short Pay	Total
High	8	7	15
Low[a]	5	10	15
Total	13	17	30

[a]Low population density is used for railways whose average county density is less than four people/acre.

is a body of evidence that disconfirms the theory. The data on the whole are not to be relied upon for safe generalization.

On the plus side, we have anecdotal evidence of successful militancy in the south. Peto mentioned a rash of strikes in Anglesey in 1846. In North Wales, navvy combinations were so persistent that machinery had to be developed to replace labor. Furthermore, in the south we do see some mobilization against truck. Navvies struck twice on the South Devon railway: once over long pay and once over safety. Both strikes worked, and the South Devon was forced to shift from monthly to fortnightly pay. There were also strikes against long pay in Ramsgate in Kent. However, this is negative evidence, since all of these strikes failed. Furthermore, we know from Handley that all Scotch strikes failed. Thus, whatever success there was seems to have concentrated in the south.

There are two considerations to the contrary. The first is the systematic denial by contractors that there was any trade-unionism on their lines. Peto, in the 1846 hearings, and Brassey, another large contractor, in his biography, adamantly opposed the suggestion of unionization on their lines. This insistence could mean simply that there were no formal trade unions, or it could be inaccurate. Peto was later contradicted in one case. However, the denial should not be dismissed cavalierly. Second, the literature on construction unions as a whole shows that the 1840s were a weak period for militancy. Masons, the vanguard of any construction worker action, were unable to maintain lodges anywhere in southeast England except in London. There was a dramatic decline in the incidence of strikes. The one known strike, against Peto over the Nelson's Column contract, ended in complete defeat for the masons (Postgate, 1923; Webb and Webb, 1920; Cole, 1932).

None of this evidence is conclusive. The positive evidence is based on only two or three anecdotes. The negative evidence is based on early twentieth-century labor historians, writers who tend to ignore all activity that does not take the form of modern twentieth-century labor organization. Handley (1970) pursued a more satisfactory research strategy: He intensively read the Scottish provincial press, noting every incident of strikes, brawls, or riots concerning navvies. He was able to do this for most of Scotland, which is a considerable achievement. The provincial press picks up a wide variety of incidents that other sources systematically omit or miss. A regional comparison of provincial papers might give us a feeling for how navvy mobilization differed in Irish and non-Irish areas. Until we do this we cannot know if southerners led successful strikes against long pay; our theory is thus only partially confirmed.

CULTURAL MONITORS AS
A FORM OF WORK DISCIPLINE

The use of clergy requires a different explanation than the use of indebtedness. Even though the ministers were extremely unpopular, would this have been the cause of strikes or riots? The worker strength model is probably inappropriate, and we should look elsewhere. Much of our understanding of the use of clergy depends on our assessment of their effectiveness. One might maintain that religion is effective in controlling a company town. However, with a migratory labor force, the disciplinary effect of clergy is likely to be small.

Religious conversion is a slow procedure. It takes long-term exposure to a community of believers and continual support from a circle of dedicated friends. In a settled industrial community, such conversion can occur. A minister could build a few devout workers into a permanent seed community; new converts could then spread their influence among the body of employees. Navvies, however, were characterized by high turnover and geographical mobility. There was no chance to institute the long-term contact required even to produce the first few "seedlings."

Possibly, conversion was not the major goal of the employers. There are a number of more immediate benefits clergy can provide. One possibility is that clergy were used to police the line. The clergy who testified in 1846 claimed success in breaking up brawls and eliminating rough language. Another benefit could come from the religious regulation of leisure time. Time spent in church is time not spent drinking or fighting. On the

Caledonian Railway the pubs were closed on Sunday and used instead for Scripture reading and church services.

Clergy could clearly increase the efficiency of a few; it is not likely that they increased the efficiency of very many. They were rarely hired in sufficient numbers to have an impact on the work force. Scripture readers were usually hired at the rate of one for every 1000-2000 workers. Peto explicitly used the ratio of 1 to 900. Eight readers were given the job of supervising the navvies on the Chester and Holyhead, a line that spans the entire North Welsh coast. The supervision of individual workers cannot have been very close. Most likely, a small body of already tractable navvies had extensive contact with the minister. Most others probably had some casual contact: one or two services attended, a pint of ale hidden as the vicar passed. There were too few clergy to effectively police a navvy force. The majority of workers must have been minimally affected.

What is the point, then, of providing such a token moral presence on the railway? The answer may have less to do with work discipline and more to do with public relations. Clergy may have helped to smooth relationships between the company and neighboring landowners when the cooperation of these landowners was desperately needed.

The railways were very dependent on local communities for a supply of cheap land. The lines ran along routes fixed by strong engineering considerations. A large amount of land was required for construction; the geographic location of this land was relatively inflexible. This left the railways prey to monopolistic pricing. Landlords aware of the situation could inflate the worth of their land. The companies were usually willing to be generous, but only to a point. Acquisitions frequently bogged down in negotiation and arbitration (Francis, 1851; Williams, 1852; Pollins, 1952). The law on these matters was usually on the railway's side. Most railway acts gave the company ultimate legal right to the land after the provision of "reasonable" compensation. Litigation is a time-consuming process, however, and the railways were under pressure to accelerate a settlement. Railways require a colossal capital burden. These debts required steady payment of interest and dividends. The railways required revenue to finance their monetary obligations, which could be provided only after the railway was completed. This meant rapid acquisition of land and rapid construction.

Most railways sought to accelerate the arbitration process by offering as a compromise a number of gratuities. Railways built, at their own expense, a large number of ornamental iron bridges to provide convenient crossing of the right of way. One landlord in Warwickshire demanded and received personal policemen to protect his property from vandalism during construction. There is reason to believe that clergy were used in this way as a concession to landlords during construction.

What was the attraction of offering to provide ministers on the works? There are two main interests which would have found such clergy appealing. The first were those landowners, like the one mentioned above, who feared property damage from navvies on the line. The promise of suitable moral supervision may have helped assuage such fears. The board of the Chester and Holyhead Railway explicitly acknowledged this. In the board minutes that authorized the corporate financing of clergy, they noted that undisciplined navvies posed a continuing grievance to landlords. They sanctioned the hiring of clergy as a step to eliminate this grievance (Coleman, 1965). Of course, a program designed to give the appearance of discipline is not the same as a program designed to provide such discipline. A token presence fulfills one's contractual obligations without incurring much additional expense.

A second beneficiary would have been the forces of organized religion themselves. Railway companies were often approached by clergymen, Sabbatarians, missionaries, and other religious figures seeking a variety of moral concessions. There was an extensive campaign in the late 1840s in Scotland to have railways voluntarily abstain from Sunday travel (Railway Times, 1847). Hospitals often approached the railways seeking philanthropic contributions. In the construction period, by far the most frequent request was for financial support for clergy to minister to the navvies. The religious programs of the South Devon and the Lancaster and Carlisle lines were instituted at the explicit request of local clergymen and community notables. The costs were moderate; the influentials were often landowners. There was a clear opportunity to create community goodwill.

There are two kinds of evidence to support these assertions. The first rests on identifying which companies tended to use this policy. Specifically, the use of clergy should vary directly with the size of the discretionary budget of the company. While clergy may have been a part of such real estate negotiations, they are hardly the main element in such affairs. Land is acquired through diplomacy, legal tactics, and, above all, by compensation being offered. The effects of clergy are unpredictable and inchoate. Ideally, a small fee paid to a Scripture reader will produce a large saving in land prices. However, many landlords may be indifferent to such concessions, while others, though appreciative, may not desist from hard bargaining. In this case, the religious expenditure is essentially wasted. Investment in clergy is an investment in an intangible, not unlike purchases of publicity or goodwill. Expenditure on landscaping, advertising, or philanthropy are all minor but risky investments. When money is readily available, these goods can be purchased on the off-chance that they will be effective. When money gets tight and costs are being cut, only the surest projects can get continued support. In tight periods, intangibles are severely cut. Thus, the total amount of organizational slack should predict the degree of religious expense.

A preliminary example can be given of the relationship between company slack and clergy use. Consider the Muirkirk and Ayr Railway. This was an extension of a larger line into an iron-mining district. Eagerly supported by local business interests, the company began construction before the legal permission had been granted to build. Parliament frequently rejected proposals for railways; construction without sanction was often a risky business (Lewin, 1936).[7] Since construction was preliminary and clearly tentative, one would expect that the company would put a minimum of resources into the building of the branch. Thus, the Muirkirk and Ayr was the typical low-slack line: It did not use clergy or schoolteachers in any form.

Of course, more satisfactory evidence would entail the use of a larger sample. Therefore, for as many railways in my sample as possible, I attempted to find data on the total capitalization of the parent company. This was obtained from published budgets which were available in the contemporary railway trade journals. For the 17 budgets I obtained, I defined the capitalization as being the total historic receipts before expenditure in the capital account. For all railways under construction in 1846, I used an 1846 budget. For railways built in earlier periods (a small minority of the sample) I used budgets a third of the way into the construction process (see Table 6.6).

The data clearly support the notion of a strong correlation between company slack and clergy use. Less than 25 percent of the cases are exceptions. There are no cases of highly capitalized companies without clergy. Furthermore, this finding is not the product of the evangelical drive of Peto. With Peto's railways held out of the analysis, the relationship still holds with 80 percent of the cases being in the predicted cells.

This first test by itself is not wholly convincing. Any intangible purchase would behave this way, including an intangible investment in labor discipline. The public relations interpretation can be bolstered by a second

TABLE 6.6   Clergy by Total Capitalization of Company

Capital	Clergy Present	Clergy Absent	Total
High[a]	8 (4)	0	8 (4)
Low	4 (2)	5	9 (7)
Total	12 (6)	5	17 (11)

[a]High capitalization is greater than £500,000. The Muirkirk and Ayr is coded as low, despite the higher capitalization of the parent company to reflect tentative construction. Figures in parentheses are non-Peto railways with clergy present.

piece of evidence: the source of financing of railway clergy. Most railways were built by subcontract. The railway company would raise the capital and run the finished railway, but farm out the work of actually supervising the construction. Both the company and the contractor are logical sources of funding for clergy. If labor control were the critical issue, both parties might be expected to benefit from clergy; hence, both parties should show an interest in the progress of instruction and both should be willing to contribute financially. On the other hand, if clergy were a device to obtain cheaper land, then only the company would benefit from their use; the contractor would gain nothing. In this case, the company should be apathetic toward clergy and resist having to contribute to their support. In both cases, the company might be expected to support clergy; the attitude of the contractor can identify the main issue.

The Peto railways would at first seem to be an obvious negative case. However, the non-Peto railways clearly fit the land control pattern. They also provide some keys to explaining the Peto deviant case. Unfortunately, we have data on only five non-Peto railways, but on all of these contractor financial support was either nonexistent or capable of being explained away. In three out of the five cases, the contractor provided absolutely no funding for clergy. On the South Devon Railway, the company paid all its own religious bills. On the Lancaster-Carlisle and the Caledonian, the company split the expenses with the outside community. The two non-Peto railways show only dubious contractor support. On the Croydon-Epsom, the contractor and the company split expenses. However, all the initiative and interest seems to have come from the company. The Scripture reader in question testified before the 1846 Committee; he explicitly stated that he was in constant communication with the directors of the company, while the contractor shunned and ignored him. The last case is the Chester and Holyhead, on which the company and the contractor shared expenses. Remember, however, that the Chester and Holyhead was the company mentioned above whose board of directors explicitly hired clergy to placate local landowners. Furthermore, the financial arrangements on this line were very distinctive. On most railways, contractors were faced with the proposals to finance clergy *after* the contract price had been set. The contractor's share would thus have come directly out of his own pocket. The Chester and Holyhead announced their clergy policy *before* bids were submitted. Rather than being a surprise request, these costs were anticipated by contractors. It would have been simple for contractors to add religious costs to the other costs of the work and present the railway company with a higher price for the contract. Thus, the real cost would have been entirely borne by the company, partially through direct contributions and partially through the mechanism of higher prices to contractors. The Chester and Holyhead is an apparent but not a true exception, since the contractor could finance his contribution out of the company's pocket.

The mechanism of cost transfer helps to put the Peto railways in a new perspective. Since Peto fully anticipated using clergy at the beginning of every job, he could easily have added these expenses to his cost estimate. Such additional expenses would not have hurt his competitiveness. Reliable contractors with reputations for speed could command a premium for the quality of their work. Peto had built Nelson's Column and the Houses of Parliament. He was one of the two most prestigious figures in English contracting (Peto, 1893; Helps, 1874); Peto would have had no problem being reimbursed for clergy, since he could obtain a superior price for his work.

But this does not explain why Peto started with clergy in the first place. We know only two other facts about Peto in this period: He started using clergy after having been approached by the City Missionary Society of Norwich, and he was a member of the House of Commons. He sat for Norwich for most of the mid-Victorian era (Peto, 1893). This suggests he was thoroughly integrated with the elite of Norwich. In Victorian times, this entailed strong links with community religious leaders and institutions. An enduring parliamentarian who also runs his own business is likely to be enmeshed in a complex web of social, religious, and political obligations. A large number of influentials both in Norwich and in London would have had powerful claims on Peto's cooperation. Peto would not have been concerned with railway land acquisition—he would not have shared this particular dependency on his community. But he had his own particular obligations stemming from his political and social status. Acquiescence to the City Missionary Society may have been a product of this.

CONCLUSION

What have we learned from all this? With reference to railway construction in England in 1846, we can conclude the following:

(1) The use of indebtedness varied directly with the weakness of the navvy labor force. This was determined to a large extent by the presence or absence of ethnic rivalry on the line.

(2) The use of clergy and religious instruction was an intangible commodity. As such it tended to appear in the larger companies.

(3) The use of clergy and religious instruction was determined less by the internal dynamic of the firms involved and more by entrepreneurs' need to placate critical individuals in the outside world. The need to obtain cheap land was an important source of dependency, but it does not exhaust all the causes of pressure.

The question was raised earlier as to the explanation of extramural discipline as a whole and its relation to bureaucratization and industrialization. These larger questions are of more general interest than the limited questions I discuss here. An attempt to extrapolate to the big questions is worthwhile. Some caution in this enterprise is called for, however. Railway construction is an atypical industry; unique cases make poor bases for generalization.

Railway construction is unusual for two reasons. First, it is technologically stagnant. In most nineteenth-century industries, technological reorganization was of overwhelming importance. Preceding Taylor by a hundred years, early industrial entrepreneurs used mechanical reorganization to radically restructure work organization. Artisans were weakened; work was centralized; technical experts seized power in the heirarchy. The forces of technological change were unimportant in navvy work. Construction continued by pick and shovel through the 1890s—steam shovels did not appear until virtually the end of the century. An 1820s construction site looked remarkably like its 1880 descendant (Coleman, 1965). Thus, one of the major forces of disciplinary change is missing from this study, and this cannot help but bias our results.

The second difficulty was discussed earlier: the highly transitory and unstable nature of navvy work groups. This has several consequences for typicality. The first is that bureaucracy was inapplicable; hence, an evolutionary weeding-out of extramuralism by a hyperefficient bureaucracy would not be likely in this industry. Second, the problems of handling migrant labor forces are different from those of a stable population. No one mentions grape pickers in the same breath with auto workers and steel workers. Thus, if we seek to project our findings onto England as a whole, we cannot use linear extrapolation, but must do a quick turn sideways and laterally project onto a stable and fixed labor force.

Let us now consider the three propositions mentioned at the beginning of the study:

Efficiency versus Inefficiency

This study has obviously been shaped by the frequent assertion that extramural discipline does not work. I conclude that clergy had little disciplinary impact on railways. However, the reader should *not* use this finding as support for the general contention that all extramural discipline is doomed to fail. The mobility of the navvies undercut the hopes of religious effectiveness. In a stable community, the clergy would have had a much better chance of having an effect their following. Who would want to deny the effectiveness of clergy in the social control of a peasant village? Furthermore, we have not spoken to indebtedness at all; whether truck worked or failed is a question that eludes us. My guess is that in most industrial settings truck would have worked and clergy would have failed. However, this is an empirical question rather than a theoretical one, and the data simply are not in yet.

Truck and Worker Discontent

I argued that labor strength models should predict the presence and onerousness of truck. This proved to be the case in railway construction; there are few reasons why it should not apply to other industries. However, in other industries the model of worker strength would have to be readjusted. Labor strength is augmented by artisanal skill, organization, communal solidarity, labor demand, employer tolerance, and lack of employer repression. All of these should decrease truck; which factor is most important is an industry-specific consideration.

Because the labor force studied here was weak, its bargaining power was vitiated by ethnic rivalries. This created a strong regional bias in the location of long pay. Stronger workers—those with an induplicable skill, for example, or those in an isolated community—would be much less threatened by an invasion of unskilled migrants. Campaigns of ethnic exclusion would be less exhausting if undertaken and less necessary in the first place. The responsiveness of work discipline to ethnicity should occur only for weak labor forces. Where ethnicity matters, you should get a strong regional bias in work-discipline.

External Upper-Class Demands

On the railways we found that religious monitoring was shaped by the needs and demands of outside elites. I think we would find comparable patterns in any other industry. In a settled industry, entrepreneurs are of necessity enmeshed in stable community networks. They deal with an unchanging pool of suppliers and customers. They cooperate with other businessmen in the regulation of their community. They work together to solve common problems of the provision of public goods and the governing of the business environment. They join churches, clubs, and political parties and develop networks and alliances based on the internal dynamics of these organizations.

What sorts of demands might a set of outside influentials make? Some could involve narrow self-interest. Shop owners could protest the continuance of truck. Real estate interests could object to company housing. Educators might wish to sell their services to company schools. Religious workers might need extra revenue. There are also reformers with more platonic goals in mind. Many middle-class liberals genuinely pitied the plight of the working class. The effort to abolish crueler forms of exploitation or the call for social services could have been motivated by a Victorian sense of charity. These reforms requests were indeed often backed with legal sanctions: The 1846 Select Committee was investigating the welfare of navvies. The committee's hostility to truck shops was too obvious to ignore. Any railway contractor seeking parliamentary favors, legal concessions, or even the preemption of legal sanctions against truck would have been strongly motivated to at least cosmetic reform after the 1846 hearings.

One should not overestimate employers' responsiveness to these forces. Furthermore, I absolutely do *not* mean to rule out work place dynamics or entrepreneurial economic self-interest as viable sources of explanations. However, for some inexpensive economic concessions, or for some employers with extensive available organizational resources, some responsiveness to these outside demands may be accounted for in this way. These environmental factors could be part of the larger explanation of how extramuralism grew and died.

NOTES

1. Pension schemes persisted, but without the disciplinary edge. Originally, strikers and malcontents could be arbitrarily cut off from the benefits of the plan (Edwards, 1979).

2. The London and North Western controlled Crewe. The Great Western controlled Swindon. The Midland controlled part of Derby.

3. Lucas's analysis is based on company towns in the modern Canadian wilderness. He holds that company housing, churches, recreation, and social institutions are necessary to provide fundamental social services where they do not already exist. He holds that these services are expensive and unremunerative and that corporations seek to unload these obligations when an alternative supplier becomes available. Usually the alternative is town government or an external private sector. The withering prediction should be clear from the summary. Lucas does not consider extramuralism as disciplinary and never discusses it in this light. While one should not impose interpretations on an author, I take this silence to suggest that he considers the disciplinary importance negligible.

Hilton performed a theoretical analysis of truck shops in Victorian Britain. He maintained that trucks' true purpose is to lower wages. Using neoclassical economics, he demonstrates that trucks' true effect in a simplified competitive market is to raise wages. Thus, by the evolutionary logic of such models, truck should be slowly driven from the market. Here, again, the withering prediction is explicit (although questionable). As with Lucas, I take his silence on disciplinary effect as significant.

Pollard is generally vague and ambiguous on this whole issue. The thrust of his discussion of extramuralism is to make the reader marvel at the extreme measures employers had to take to secure discipline. His discussions of bureaucracy, however, are filled with ebullient praise. His attitude toward extramuralism can be inferred from the lack of praise in the section.

4. Chaloner argues that extramuralism in Crewe was part of a larger battle over the provision of municipal services. When all of the population of Crewe worked for the London and North Western Railway, the municipal services were all provided by the company. The company was reluctant to extend these services to outsiders. Over time, the economy of Crewe diversified, creating a set of inhabitants not directly employed by the railroad. These newcomers had no access to municipal services; in

order to obtain them they had to seize political control. The shift of services from the extramural to the public sector was the product of this political struggle.

5. The bulk of my data comes from the Report from the Select Committee on Railway Labourers, House of Commons Sessional Papers, 1846, XIII. This includes nearly all the material on pay periods and clergy use and most of the substantive detail. Demographic data come from the 1851 Census of Great Britain and Ireland. Railway budgets were amassed from the following sources:

Heraphath's Railway Magazine

Railway Chronicle

Railway Record

Railway Times

Scrivenor *Railways of United Kingdom Statistically Considered* (London: Smith Elder, 1849).

Material on militancy in North Wales came from "Richard Roberts of Llaynmynech and the Conway Tubular Bridge," *Byegones* (June 1880).

6. The allocation of railways to counties was actually somewhat complex. When I knew the pay system of the railway at only one point, I coded the railway as being entirely in the county of the point. When I knew the practice along an entire route, I calculated county-level variables for every county along the route and then took the mean.

7. Parliament finally rejected the petition to build. The Muirkirk and Ayr was never completed (Lewin, 1936).

7

Belgian and French Workers in Nineteenth-Century Roubaix

JUDY A. REARDON

NATIVES VERSUS FOREIGNERS

In nineteenth-century France, where a small but significant part of the working population consisted of foreigners, the tension between them and the native French broke into open conflict on many occasions (Perrot, 1974: 170-171). When one of these outbursts of hostility occurred in the early 1890s, the Minister of the Interior ordered a nationwide investigation. The response from Roubaix was surprising—in this textile city on the Belgian border, with its huge foreign population, the police chief reported that no such incidents had taken place (ADN [Archives Departementales du Nord] M610/16). What is more, he added, no preventive measures were needed, since, in his view, "such steps could lead French workers to believe they can free themselves from competition with foreigners." Roubaix's police chief stated what has become a common theme—ethnic differences can act as an effective curb on labor militance.

On at least two occasions, Roubaix showed itself to be the classic case of a city torn by ethnic conflict. In 1819, spontaneous rioting broke out between the French and the Belgians because the preference of the *fabricants* for the more highly skilled foreign spinners enraged the natives. The Belgians reportedly were undercutting wages, a situation the natives judged to be unfair. Feelings ran high for several days, thousands of workers were involved, and the disorder became so acute that many Belgians had to flee across the border for safety (Reboul, 1954). Some years later, in the 1840s, open hostility again broke out in Roubaix. The charges this time were similar to those heard in 1819: Belgians were stealing bread from the mouths of the French by taking jobs at lower pay (ADN M605/3). The background to this problem was the decline of the Flemish linen industry, which had sent a stream of unemployed workers across the border into the Nord (Jacquemyns, 1929: 315, 382). But the economic situation of the '40s affected France as well, exacerbating the scramble for jobs. At the height of the crisis, Roubaix was invaded by hordes of Belgians who came into the city to beg, and these unfortunate people were greeted by harassment from the French (Machu, 1956: 68; ADN M610/5; AN [Archives Nationales] F74106).

Here were two major incidents in which worker turned against worker because one saw the other (quite correctly) as the immediate cause of low wages and unemployment. In both cases the cure appeared worse than the disease, because both times the solution was to rid the city of its foreign work force, if only partially and temporarily. Employers were forced by the riots of 1819 to sign an agreement whereby only natives would be hired as weavers (Reboul, 1954: 349). The problem of the 1840s was solved by a ban on hiring Belgians and by the expulsion of all the unemployed among them (AMRx [Archives Municipales de Roubaix] I II (a), no. 3; I 1 (ba), no. 1). If the presence of foreigners keeps competition alive, it seems illogical that the work force should be purged of them. Obviously, restoration of order became the overriding priority in both cases. In neither case did the initiative for solving the problem come from employers, who benefited by competition among the workers. Ethnic conflict would have adversely affected them only if it either threatened the labor supply or in any other way interfered with production. The flight of the Belgians to safety in 1819 greatly chagrined them.

These two instances of open hostility between foreigners and natives in Roubaix took place during periods of economic distress. The crisis of the 40s is familiar enough. The riots of 1819 occurred within a context of temporary stagnation in the city's cotton industry in a broader period of rapid expansion and easy absorption of both foreign and native labor (Reboul, 1965: 340-341). Analyzing the pattern of ethnic conflict among workers in nineteenth-century France, Michelle Perrot saw a correlation between economic distress and the frequency of outbreaks of hostility

(1974: I, 169). Doubtless, her finding is correct, but is not possible to deduce that whenever overt conflict was absent, social harmony reigned between natives and foreigners. No one would suggest that the absence of race riots in today's cities indicates peace between blacks and whites. The fact that very few recorded outbreaks of open conflict between the French and Belgians of Roubaix took place in the nineteenth century does not mean perfect accord existed between them. To assess whether Belgians and French were alienated from each other, we must look not only at cases of overt hostility, such as those occurring in 1819 and in the 1840s, but at other factors. Beyond this, there are the political implications of ethnic divisiveness: Did it function as a brake on labor militance in Roubaix, and, if so, what happened once the workers mobilized for collective action? Does mobilization mean the disappearance of ethnic conflict?

Although antagonism rarely became overt in Roubaix, an undercurrent of tension seems to have characterized the relationship of native to foreigner. Louis Reybaud, a middle-class observer who wrote about the city's cotton and woolen industry, said he found no instances of open hostility between the Belgians and the French. He added, however, that the foreigners were more tolerated than liked, and that few friendships developed between the two groups (1867: 212, 213). Reybaud made these observations at the height of the period when Belgians were pouring across the border by the thousands to fill jobs in the expanding, mechanized sector of the textile industry. Even when industry was absorbing all the workers it could find and competition for jobs presumably did not pose a problem, antagonism existed below the surface of events. We have the police chief's remark about the efficacy of competition from foreigners as a device to keep the natives in line to remind us that many years later similar feelings could be found.

It is difficult to assess ethnic divisiveness in Roubaix, both because hostility between natives and foreigners rarely surfaced and because evidence from the workers themselves about possible feelings of animosity is virtually impossible to find. However, it is possible to get at ethnic divisiveness by looking at the "social distance" between the two groups. This simply means the extent to which in certain situations or contexts the Belgians were separated, physically or otherwise, from the French. Obviously, social distance is not the same as open hostility or even antagonism. That is, if people are separated from one another, it does not necessarily mean they are antagonistic to each other. In fact, it could be argued that since distance keeps people apart, it therefore reduces the chances for conflict. This claim can hardly be denied, but it does not gainsay the fact that at the same time social distance limits the opportunities for positive social interaction between groups, including the interaction needed as part of the basis for large-scale, organized collective action.

In Roubaix, the foreigners were separated from the natives in at least three ways: culturally, on the job, and in their places of residence. Although in appearance the Belgians were probably not distinct, their language made them visible, since the vast majority came from Flemish-speaking parts of Belgium (Franchomme, 1969: 210). In some areas of France, Flemish was spoken by the natives; but since Roubaix lies just outside French Flanders, native Roubaisians spoke only French, hence the language disparity. Apparently, many of the newcomers from Belgium made little effort to learn French, and in the 1860s and '70s a large number of the city's schoolchildren spoke only Flemish (Anthoine, 1961: 14; Leblond, 1968: 74). The language difference meant that socialists who were organizing in the early 1880s had to hold separate meetings for French and Flemish workers. The appearance of posters in both languages also attested to the persistence of the language duality long after the great wave of immigrants had ceased (ADN M162/6; AMRx I, II (ba), no. 4).

Cultural differences had other aspects. The Belgians were distinguished by the intensity of their commitment to the Catholic faith, a phenomenon that was probably due partly to the support the church traditionally lent to linguistic minorities (Blanchard, 1906: 413). In Roubaix, one form this support took was the assignment of a special religious order to serve the spiritual needs of the Flemish congregation (Franchomme, 1969: 211). It meant that the French and Belgians had separate church communities.

The Belgians' religious ardor not only kept them apart from the French but it also carried political implications. Reybaud ascribed the "good mores" he observed in Roubaix to the devoutness of its people, and he felt this characteristic was particularly strong among the Belgians (1867: 212). Their zeal was cultivated by the *patronat* of Roubaix, which earned a reputation of its own for devoutness and at the same time undertook considerable efforts to instill similar sentiments in their workers, French and Belgian alike (Fohlen, 1956: 83; Landes, 1976). In the era before socialism took root and labor organized successfully in the Nord, these efforts may have been a factor in maintaining a submissive work force. Jules Cambon, who served as prefect of the Nord from 1882 to 1887, suggested this when he said that the electoral victory of the Right in his department in 1885 was due to the force of religion, and that this was rooted in turn in the Flemish character of the area (Trenard, 1974, II: 358).

JOBS AND NATIONALITY

On the job as well, Belgians and French were set apart. In addition, competition for jobs and the related issue of undercutting wages created hostility between them. Job competition meant simply that employers preferred to hire Belgians. That they undercut wages was only one reason they were preferred. Probably the more important reason was docility. If the Belgians were docile, however, it was not because they were inherently so, but because their legal position in the host country virtually required them to be. Foreigners had almost no political rights and as a result could be deported from France by administrative fiat if they caused trouble (Larricq, 1904: 42-43). During the crisis of the 1840s, they were expelled from France on the grounds of being unemployed (technically, the reason was vagrancy). Again, it was their precarious legal position that easily subjected them to exclusionary hiring practices both in 1819 and 1848.

Job competition made the natives docile as well. This is what the police chief meant when he said that French workers should not be led to believe they could rid themselves of competition from foreigners. To what extent the employers of Roubaix exploited their advantage and used foreigners as a threat against the natives is not clear. At one point the socialists accused the city's leading textile magnate, Eugène Motte, of hiring Belgians exclusively in his factories (Egalité, April 8, 1898). The important thing is that even if the employers did not carry out the threat, they had the potential to do so. What is more, they seemed aware of their power. One textile manufacturer declared that he could use job competition to reduce the demands of the natives. Another openly stated that he could purge his work force (of dissidents, presumably) by replacing them with foreigners (ADN M616/7; AMRx F II (c), no. 1). For the employers of Roubaix, foreigners in the labor force were like money in the bank.

The city's chamber of commerce insisted in 1891 that natives and foreigners be paid the same wages for the same jobs (Archives, 1891: 99). Since none of the wage data available for the nineteenth century is broken down by nationality, it is hard to determine whether this claim is correct. We know that during the conflicts of 1819 and the 1840s the French charged the Belgians with undercutting the wage level. Even if they did not, the presence of an immigrant population on the labor market depresses the wage level for all workers simply by increasing the supply of workers. During the latter part of the Second Empire, with the flood of immigrants from Belgium and from other parts of France, wages stagnated in Roubaix.[1] One reason may have been the ready availability of hands, a situation the Belgians helped to create.

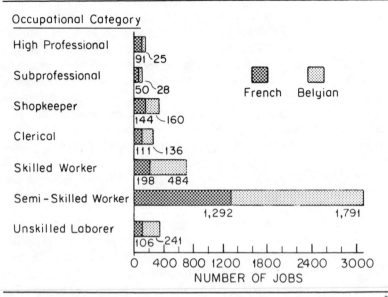

Figure 7.1 French and Belgian Workers by Occupational Category in Roubaix, 1872[a]

[a]Source: Ten percent systematic sample of 1872 census nominal list, coded and put into machine readable form by L. Tilly. Occupational and other codes based on codebook developed by R. B. Litchfield and H. Chudacoff.

Belgian workers may have been preferred, but they were not concentrated in the best jobs. A profile of job distribution by nationality in 1872, based on a 10 percent sample of the manuscript census, makes this clear.[2] This year coincided approximately with the end of the 20-year influx of foreigners and is the point at which the percentage of Belgians in Roubaix was highest, at just over half the population (AMRx F I (a), no. 13). If we first combine specific jobs into broader categories of "occupational status" (Figure 7.1), we get a general idea of what kinds of positions the Belgians tended to fill. There are few surprises. In the "semi-skilled" category," into which most of the textile jobs fell, the Belgians were neither under- nor overrepresented in proportion to their distribution in the labor force. In the two highest-level categories, which included positions such as factory owner and manager, physician, lawyer, and accountant, Belgians were underrepresented. Similarly, in the "clerical" category, where such jobs as office and sales clerk, policeman, fireman, and tax collector were represented, the French dominated. Curiously, a disproportionate share of the skilled jobs (70.5 percent) belonged to the Belgians. In fact, the sample

TABLE 7.1   Concentration of Belgian and French in
Some Unskilled Occupations, 1872

Occupation	Belgian Concentration	Percentage
Laborer (*journalier, homme de peine, manoeuvre*)	151 of 231 jobs	65.4
Firer (*chauffeur*)	19 of 22 jobs	86.4
Earthworks laborer (*terrassier*)	18 of 20 jobs	90.0
Female servant (*servante*)	64 of 95 jobs	67.4
Domestic (*domestique*)	49 of 73 jobs	67.1

shows that almost 18 percent of all the Belgians in Roubaix's labor force were skilled workers at this date, while this was true of only 10 percent of the French. If the situation was similar in 1848, it is no wonder that the French carpenters and joiners voiced their resentment against the Belgians who held these jobs.

Belgian domination was strongest at the unskilled level, where they held more than twice as many jobs as the French. Their domination becomes more apparent when the category is broken down into some of its constituent occupations (Table 7.1). On-the-job contact between foreigners at the unskilled level was limited by the fact that so many of these jobs were the preserve of the Belgians. Sociologist Michael Hechter, analyzing the condition of the *Gastarbeiter* in post-World War II Europe, wrote that the concentration of foreign workers in low-status positions stereotypes those jobs as "immigrant," marks them as inferior, and therefore perpetuates what he calls the "cultural division of labor" along national lines (1976: 217-221). Applied to Roubaix, his interpretation suggests that the Belgians' predominance in the unskilled jobs created not only social distance between them and the natives but perhaps also disdain toward them on the part of the French.

The bulk of Roubaix's workers were employed in textiles. We find some concentration by nationality in certain jobs in this category (Table 7.2), but it was not as pronounced as at other levels. This was because sex and age were at least as important as nationality in the distribution of textile jobs. Women and young people of both sexes were hired to perform such tasks as tying broken warp threads, winding warp yarn, and assisting

TABLE 7.2   Concentration by Nationality in
Some Textile Positions, Roubaix, 1872[a]

Occupation	Percentage of Positions Held by French	Number of Positions	Percentage of Positions Held by Belgians	Number of Positions
Spinner	50.6	87	48.9[b]	84
Warp drawer (*rentreur*)	59.1	13	40.9	9
Warper (*ourdisseur*)	71.4	60	27.4	23
Weaver	34.0	294	65.0	560
Washer	28.9	11	71.1	27
Finisher (*appretêur*)	48.5	48	50.5	50
Comber	26.6	21	73.4	58
Piecer-doffer (*rattacheuse*)	51.0	49	49.0	47
Spool girl (*bobineuse*)	66.3	128	33.7	65
Bobbin girl/boy (*bâcleuse/ bâcleur*)	52.3	34	47.7	31

[a]Sources: *Rapports . . . pendant l'année 1869* (Roubaix, 1870: 71), Renouard
and Moy, (1889: 7-8), Pierreuse, (1972: 78).
[b]The percentages do not total 100 in all cases because foreigners other than
Belgians were not included.

the spinners by replacing full and empty spindles. These were all relatively
low-paying jobs. The higher-paying positions—those in the top half of the
hierarchy represented in the table—were filled largely by men. For
example, men held all but three of the 171 spinning jobs in the sample.[3]
Further down the hierarchy were the jobs filled by women or young
people of either sex. The *bâcleuse* or *bâcleur,* whose job was to replace
spindles, was generally a boy or girl age 10 to 14, irrespective of nationality. Almost half the piecer-doffers were girls and boys under the age of 19,
both Belgian and French. On the other hand, concentration by nationality
as well as sex is apparent in two of the lower-paying jobs, *bobineuse* and
comber. The ranks of the *bobineuses,* whose tasks were similar to those of
the *bâcleuses,* were filled almost entirely by young women, but they
tended to be French. The combers were also likely to be young women,

but they were more often recruited from among the Belgians. Jobs in spinning were about evenly divided by nationality, with the French having a slight edge in these higher-paying positions. Since spinning tended to be carried out in factories, this should have increased the chances for on-the-job contact between natives and foreigners. It would be interesting to be able to determine whether the spinners chose their assistants from people of their own nationality.

Starting around 1870, the weaving of woolen cloth became the basis of Roubaix's textile industry (Franchomme, 1969: 231). This helps explain why, in 1872, the most frequently held job in textiles was weaver. Domination by the Belgians is unquestionable here, for they held almost twice as many of these jobs as did the French. They were also likely to have earned less than the French. This was because the Belgians who migrated to Roubaix tended to enter the mechanized sector, while the natives continued to work at home on their handlooms (Fohlen, 1956: 341). In 1872, handloom weaving still paid more, most likely because at that date, although it was being replaced by power machinery, the manufacturer was still dependent upon it, and the skilled handweaver could earn higher rates.[4] In addition, it is also possible that the availability of foreign workers to fill the less-skilled factory jobs made possible by the use of power machinery explains why wages were lower in this sector. In other words, these jobs paid less simply because there were immigrants to fill them.

The job situation in Roubaix in 1872 thus created or perpetuated ethnic differences in a number of ways. First, the employers' preference for Belgian workers may have caused resentment on the part of the natives. This sentiment was probably felt most acutely among the skilled workers, who were pushed out by foreign domination of these jobs, as they had been in 1848. Second, and paradoxically, Belgian concentration in the unskilled jobs may have led the French to disdain foreigners because they dominated these low-status occupations. Third, because in Roubaix such jobs as day laborer, shoemaker, mason, weaver, and so forth were the preserve of the Belgians, opportunities for on-the-job contact between them and the French were reduced.

THE GEOGRAPHY OF NATIONALITY

Patterns of residence in Roubaix also reveal that there was a certain amount of concentration by nationality. Apparently, the Belgians and the

TABLE 7.3   Distribution of Belgians and French
in Roubaix Street Housing, 1872

Percentage on Each Street	Belgians Number of Streets	French Number of Streets
0- 9	0	0
10-19	0	0
20-29	2	3
30-39	0	1
40-49	2	4
50-59	4	2
60-69	1	1
70-79	4	2
	13	13

French lived in separate parts of the city even in the second half of the eighteenth century (Prouvost, 1974: 24). In the nineteenth century, only Flemish could be heard in certain areas (ADN M176/1). Some of these enclaves remained predominantly Belgian until well into the twentieth century (Lentacker, 1974: 247). With the use of the manuscript census for 1872, a more precise analysis of residential patterns can be made, using a 10 percent sample, or 13 streets.[5] At first glance (Table 7.3), it appears that the Belgians and the French were highly integrated. One thing that leads to this conclusion is the fact that no street in the sample is either exclusively French or exclusively Belgian. Moreover, in four cases, the French and Belgians were represented in numbers proportionate to their distribution in the population as a whole. In addition, households and even families of mixed nationality were not uncommon.

Yet certain streets had an indisputably French or Belgian character. On four of the streets sampled, over 70 percent of the residents were Belgian; and on two others, 70 percent were French. Hence, some of the streets seemed to be the terrain of one or the other nationality. To locate other enclaves, we must literally go *behind* the streets. Roubaix had two types of housing. In 1872 half the population lived in ordinary street housing, while the other half lived in "*cours*" or "*courées*" (Franchomme, 1960: 138). These dwellings were similar to the alley houses in which some of the slaves in U.S. cities lived. They were rows of tiny houses set behind the streets, in some cases all but hidden from view, and accessible only through a passageway off the street. The name derived from the courtyard formed by the rows. This type of housing was far inferior to street housing—much smaller and notorious for inadequate hygienic facilities (Prouvost, 1969: 307-316; Reybaud, 1867: 208-209).

The *cours* had been built specifically to house the Belgians. Most of them were constructed between 1840 and 1860 to accommodate the great number of foreigners who entered the city in that period (Motte, 1946: 82). Since the incoming Belgians tended to enter the mechanized sector of the textile industry, and since the *cours* were built to maximize access to the factories, this made it even more likely that foreigners would live in them. It would also confirm Reybaud's observation that the *cours* of Roubaix were inhabited only by Belgians (1867: 209). One reason the Rue des Longues Haies came to be called "Flemish headquarters of Roubaix" was the large number of *cours* built behind it.[6] It comes as no surprise that the most squalid conditions in the city were found here (Trenard, 1974: II, 404). The Rue des Longues Haies was Roubaix's Belgian ghetto.

Hidden behind the street houses in the above sample were 25 *cours* of varying sizes. Once again, aggregate figures give the impression that natives and foreigners lived side by side, for there were proportionately as many Belgians to French in the *cours* as there were in the population as a whole. But, as with the street houses, examination of individual *cours* (Table 7.4) leaves a different impression. Nine of the *cours* could be considered Belgian terrain, since over 70 percent of their inhabitants were Belgian. In six other *cours,* over 70 percent of the residents were French. This means that Reybaud's observation about the *cours* being inhabited solely by Belgians was not correct. He may have been overawed by places like the Rue des Longues Haies, which probably was the largest street in the city in terms of the number of people living on it.[7] Also, more of the *cours,* especially more of the large ones, were dominated by Belgians.

Needless to say, nationality does not fully explain residential patterns. Residence is also determined by occupation and status, and in Roubaix people with similar jobs tended to cluster on the same streets, regardless of nationality. This explains the considerable mixing of nationalities observed above. Again, it is only by focusing on individual streets and *cours* that occupational and status determination becomes clear. On the Rue de la Potennerie and on Sentier du Pile, for example, there were many weavers and many people who held unskilled jobs, and these workers were fairly evenly divided between the French and the Belgians. The *cours,* of course, were dominated by people in the lower occupational status categories,

TABLE 7.4   Distribution of Belgians and French
in Roubaix *Cours*, 1872

Percentage in Each Cour	Belgians Number of Cours	French Number of Cours
0- 9	2	2
10-19	1	2
20-29	2	4
30-39	4	3
40-49	3	2
50-59	1	2
60-69	3	4
70 and over	9	6
	25	25

French and Belgian alike. Almost no one who held a high-status position lived in the *cours,* which were truly the domain of Roubaix's poor. Other streets were dominated by people in the higher occupational groups. On the Rue de Sebastopol, for example, 40 percent of the heads of household held jobs in the top four occupational status categories, some of whom were Belgian and some French. On still other streets, nationality as well as occupation entered the picture. The most frequently held position on the Rue Nain was manufacturer. Here, however, the French dominated; few Belgians lived on the street. Rue Nain illustrates how in Roubaix occupational status determined a person's place of residence, while at the same time it shows how status was in turn determined by nationality.

CONFLICT AND ETHNICITY

Given the ethnic differences that separated Belgian from French in Roubaix—culturally, on the job, and where they lived—we should expect to find a quiescent town. Presumably, these differences displaced the anger and frustration workers might otherwise have felt toward their employers and directed it instead against each other; and the social distance between the two groups prevented them from forging links of solidarity. In fact, throughout much of the nineteenth century, Roubaix remained quiet; there were few displays of labor militancy. It is tempting to ascribe this situation solely to the divisive effects created by the presence of foreigners. However, since we know that other parts of France, including areas that had few or no foreigners in the labor force, also remained quiet for much of the century, this means that ethnic differences could have played only a partial role in explaining developments in Roubaix.

Starting with a general strike in 1880, the workers of Roubaix mobilized for collective action. A long wave of strikes based on the May Day demand for shorter hours began in 1890 (AN F ^{12}4660; ADN M619/3; Franchomme, 1960: 171-193). Around the same time, the city converted to Marxism, even gaining a reputation as the "Holy City of Socialism." In 1892, the predominantly socialist municipal council chose one of its own as mayor; and the following year Jules Guesde, head of the Marxist *Parti Ouvrier,* was elected to the Chamber of Deputies from a Roubaix constituency (Delory, 1921: 43; Baker, 1966: 69-70). Roubaix also became a strong union town, with a large proportion of the work force organized into the socialist-led *syndicats.*[8]

Paralleling these developments came an acceleration in the integration of foreigners into city life and a breakdown of the barriers between them and the native French. One of the factors in this process not only contributed to the integration of the Belgians but also increased their receptiveness to appeals from the Left. This was the rise of anticlericalism, which weakened the ties of the Flemish to the church and the Catholic *patronat.* Denunciation of the pernicious influence of the clergy was a major theme among the radicals, and the socialists made it an issue in their early organizing efforts in the Nord (Pierreuse, 1969: 251; Willard, 1965: 162). The Ferry laws of the 1880s, by secularizing education, also helped lessen the influence of the church. Free and compulsory education at the primary level helped eliminate cultural differences between French and Flemings because it meant, among other things, that all children learned French in school. Eventually, the anticlerical movement brought about the expulsion of the religious orders, including the one that served Roubaix's Flemish congregation. Finally, a ministerial order of 1890 forbade teaching catechism and preaching sermons in Flemish (Coörnaert, 1970: 323).

More and more Belgians were acquiring French citizenship. A law of 1889 automatically conferred citizenship on a great number of them, so that within a few years the number of people listed in the Roubaix census as Belgian declined by over 16,000 (Statistique générale, 1942: 10-13; AMRx F I (a), nos. 16 and 18). These people became more than de jure French citizens, however, for the "Francization" law applied largely to people who had been born in France. As early as 1872, one-third of

Roubaix's foreigners were French-born. By 1886, that proportion had grown to one-half (AMRx F I (a), nos. 13 and 16). "Francization" merely confirmed an existing fact: Many of Roubaix's Belgians were already French.

A contemporary observer wrote that he believed Jules Guesde owed his seat in the Chamber of Deputies to the votes of the naturalized Belgians of Roubaix rather than to the native French (Lentacker, 1974: 251). This suggests that integration of the Belgians helped lay the basis for the mobilization of labor in the city. There can be no doubt that this development and the breakdown of ethnic differences between foreigners and natives played such a role. But if ethnic differences do not completely explain docility, neither does their decline completely explain the rise of a militant working class, and for the same reason: workers elsewhere in France became receptive to the Left at the same time as the workers of Roubaix.[9] Hence, what happened in Roubaix after 1880 could have been due only partly to the factor of ethnicity.

What casts even more doubt is the fact that ethnic differences in Roubaix did not disappear altogether, but persisted during the time when socialism and organized labor were winning the allegiance of the city's workers. One reason was the arrival, toward the end of the century, of a new wave of immigrants. This was not a new phenomenon, but rather an expansion in the ranks of the commuters who came to Roubaix daily or weekly to work but who lived in Belgium (Lentacker, 1950). By 1903 there were 10,000 "*frontaliers*" in a population of about 100,000 (ADN M154/86). Their numbers increased so fast partly because of improvements in transportation. Another reason was the disparity in wages and cost of living between Belgium and France. Since wages in France were higher than in Belgium, and in Belgium the cost of living was correspondingly lower, it made sense for Belgians to commute to France, since they gained a double advantage (ADN M154/86).

If the natives of Roubaix to some extent had come to accept the resident Belgians as "*frères du travail*," as people with interests the same as their own, they saw the *frontaliers* as somehow more foreign (Egalité, September 24, 1904). For one thing, they created the familiar problem of job competition (ADN M154/86). Even worse in terms of labor solidarity, they were strikebreakers. When the textile workers of the Nord and the Somme went on strike during fall 1903 and spring 1904, trade unionists on both sides of the border tried to coordinate efforts to prevent scabbing.

They were not completely successful, and the workers on strike in Roubaix found themselves compelled to try to halt bodily the worker trains carrying Belgian *supplanteurs* into France. Their attempt failed when police began to provide escorts to protect the "right to work" (Pierreuse, 1972: 271-309; ADN M607/38; *Journal de Roubaix,* March 3, April 1, April 8, 1904). The *frontaliers'* role could hardly have endeared them to the French.

In this period conflict arose not only because of the presence of the *frontaliers* but also as a result of tension between the natives and the resident Belgians. The police chief of Roubaix either erred or lied in claiming that in 1893 no instances of conflict had taken place between natives and foreigners in the city. Just a few months prior to his report, French and Belgian workers employed at a woolen mill exchanged blows in an incident that lasted several days and left a number of people wounded. The reason for the fracas was not known, but apparently animosity had existed for some time between the two groups. The foreigners involved in the incident were not *frontaliers* but Belgians from Verviers who lived in Roubaix (ADN M619/50; Journal de Roubaix, June 22, 23, 1892).

When we discover that in Roubaix not only did new ethnic differences arise with the increase in the number of *frontaliers* but also that old antagonisms persisted, we see a city more divided than ever at the end of the nineteenth century. Some of the reasons are fairly evident. In the 1890s, a resurgence of nationalism was fed by the new imperialism, rivalry with Germany, the decline of the French birth rate, and the rapid growth of the country's foreign population. One expression of nationalism was antiforeign sentiment. Added to this was the factor noted by Perrot: economic distress. Starting in 1897 and continuing through 1901, the woolen industry suffered a severe crisis brought on by protectionism, the loss of markets, and overproduction (Goblet, 1903: 79-91; Pierreuse, 1972: 210-230). In August 1900, 12,000 were unemployed in Roubaix.

Ethnic conflict can be explained by all these causes, but what does its persistence, and what do the other findings on Roubaix, reveal about the equation presented at the outset—divisiveness equals docility? Because the sequence of events in Roubaix—a long period of quiescence for most of the century followed by a sudden and wholehearted embrace of the Left—was repeated elsewhere in France, it is difficult to assess separately the effects of an ethnically divided working class. Further, we should probably recognize ethnicity as a proxy for migration; that is, we should look at Francization of the Belgians and the ties that developed between them and the native French as part of the more general phenomenon whereby immigrants, native and foreign alike, establish themselves in a community and create social bonds with each other.

The continuation of ethnic conflict through the era when labor and socialism won their great victories indicates that the equation cannot be interpreted to mean that once workers shed their docility by aligning with the Left divisiveness will cease. Contradictions persisted in other areas as well following the success of the Left. For example, after the Nord became a bastion of Marxism, it also remained a stronghold of Catholicism, long after the de-Christianization of much of the rest of the French working class (Hilaire, 1966: 188-190). Once they were in power, the socialists of Roubaix, despite their theoretical dedication to the principle of labor solidarity across national lines, did little to unite Belgian and French workers. They were ambivalent at best and hostile at worst toward the foreigners, especially the *frontaliers* (Reardon, 1977: 186-213). The end of docility did not bring about the end of divisiveness, something which suggests either that the triumph of the Left does not immediately resolve all contradictions or that its success in Roubaix was not as great as it appeared.

NOTES

1. Wage figures can be found in the mayor's reports for the period 1864-1871 (*Rapport sur l'administration des affaires de la ville de Roubaix*).

2. All figures on occupation and occupational status are based on this sample, which was gathered by Louise A. Tilly for her work on Roubaix.

3. The domination of men in this traditionally female job was probably due to the use of the mule jenny, a machine that required considerable strength to operate (Raman, 1973: 489).

4. Wage figures in weaving are for 1869 (Rapports, 1869: 170). The mechanization of weaving was making great strides in Roubaix at this time (Fohlen, 1956: 339).

5. No reconstruction of neighborhoods can be made because the available maps do not have street numbers to be matched to the house numbers on the census.

6. In 1872 there were 38 *cours* behind the Rue des Longues Haies, and 75 percent of the people who lived in them were Belgian (AMRx F I (a), no. 13).

7. In 1872, 1,392 people lived in the street houses and the *cours* of the Rue des Longues Haies (AMRx F I (a), no. 13).

8. In 1910, the socialist-led *Chambre syndicale ouvrière textile de Roubaix* alone had 19,363 members (Direction du Travail, 1911: 454).

9. The most cursory glance at the *Statistique des grèves* for the period beginning 1890 demonstrates how extensive the strike waves were in various parts of France.

8

Grapes of Wrath:

Vineyard Workers, Labor Unions, and Strike Activity in the Aude, 1860-1913

LAURA L. FRADER

WINEGROWING IN THE NARBONNAIS

At the beginning of the twentieth century, when the smokestacks of industrial cities darkened the skies of northern France, most of the population of southern France was rural, the vast majority occupied in some way with the wine production for which the Midi was then known. The growth of viticultural capitalism throughout lower Languedoc led to the development of a class of vineyard workers who shared a common experience with their industrial proletariat whose workship was the vines. In contrast to their urban counterparts, however, these workers did not all adopt left-wing electoral politics as a means of expressing their interests; they rejected parliamentary solutions and chose to follow revolutionary

AUTHOR'S NOTE: An earlier version of this chapter was presented to the Center for Western European Studies at the University of Michigan, November 30, 1978. I am grateful to Louise A. Tilly, Henry Peiter, and David Bien for their helpful comments and suggestions.

syndicalism instead. By the turn of the century, they had unionized and ultimately participated in the massive strike wave which swept the entire south between 1903 and 1913. This study of the vineyard workers of Coursan, a small village located about 600 kilometers from Paris and 7 kilometers from Narbonne, provides an example of the development of collective action in the rural setting. It also demonstrates that the work relations between men and women in the vineyard economy may have been more complex than traditional notions of "peasant" life would suggest.

The Narbonnais, once a vast granary in the polycultural regional economy, underwent a major transformation around the middle of the nineteenth century and by 1880 had become an enormous vineyard (Frader, 1978: 50-54, 129-136).[1] During the period of vineyard expansion Coursan's population grew from approximately 2170 in 1850 to just under 3500 in 1881.[2] The growth of vineyards was accompanied by the expansion of accessory industries such as cooperage, masonry, and harness-making. By 1876, the majority (55 percent) of the working population of the village was directly involved with work in the vines (see Table 8.3). The high wine prices of 35 to 50 francs per hectoliter and general prosperity which vintners experienced at this time owed much to the economic crisis experienced by the rest of the Midi in just these years. The sixties and seventies were the years of the terrible phylloxera invasion which destroyed thousands of hectares of southern vines. Between 1865 and 1880, the phylloxera ravaged the vines of the Gard, the Vaucluse, and the Hérault, leaving the Aude's vines temporarily untouched. Thus, vintners in Coursan, whose vines were still producing, were able to profit from the short supply of wine elsewhere in the Midi.[3]

An important characteristic of the agricultural regime in Coursan in the years of prosperity was the coexistence of several forms of vineyard property. The significant productive unit and the largest employer of wage labor in the village was the large *domaine* vineyard. The ten largest *domaines* in Coursan were almost all formed before 1880 and were notable for their large surface area (from 70 to 190 hectares—about 175-475 acres) and their high production of wine, between 1,500 and 15,000 hectoliters per year at the beginning of the twentieth century (Cadastre foncier de Coursan, 1830-1914; Gervais, 1903; 501-502).[4] They were, in the contemporary phrase, *"des vraies usines à vin"* (veritable wine factories).

In addition to the large *domaines* whose land was concentrated in one block, dispersed parcels (*biens du village*), totaling between 21 and 60 hectares, and medium property, between 7 and 20 hectares, were also large employers of wage labor. Finally, small properties of between one and six hectares, which did not generally need to employ wage workers, and "very small" property of less than one hectare were common. Owners of the latter were often vineyard workers (ADA [Archives départementales de l'Aude] 13 M 287, Enquête agricole de 1872 ADA 13 M 61). In fact, between 1871 and 1880, almost one-third of the day laborers (*journaliers*) in Coursan were proprietors; they were known as *journaliers-proprietaires* or *cultivateurs* in the government records.[5] They were able to count on both the products of their own land and on employment as workers in a variety of work settings, whether on the *domaines* or on the smaller, scattered properties in the village. Thus, they could count on a certain security of employment in a competitive situation which served to maintain a relatively high level of wages during the expansion period.

Although property ownership was widespread in this period, one cannot underestimate the power and importance of the *domaine* vineyard in Coursan. The *domaines* resembled the large industrial enterprises of the north. They employed relatively large numbers of workers in a single enterprise (50-70 workers) and were characterized by a hierarchy of work roles and a division of labor. The *domaine* dominated the economic life of the village not only as the primary employer, but also as a consumer, for the masonry, harnessmaking, and cooperage establishments of the village served its needs. Although the labor hierarchy of the *domaine* included a foreman (*régisseur*), an overseer (*ramonet*), and between 10 and 20 farmhands (unskilled laborers, *domestiques*), the majority of *domaine* workers were day laborers (*journaliers:* Augé-Laribé, 1907; Coste-Floret, 1898; Passama, 1906). In the expansion years, most of the day laborers were natives of Coursan (about 70 percent; see Table 8.1) and a majority came from families where one or both parents were day laborers or small property owners (an average of 77 percent during 1861-1880; see Table 8.2). Throughout the period, relatively few children of these workers rose in status to become small proprietors themselves; at no point in the expansion years could a "rags to riches" phenomenon of substantial occupational advancement be detected, although the economic situation of the vineyard laborer did improve over time.[6]

These vineyard workers differed from other agricultural laborers in several ways. First, the day laborer was a skilled worker and considered himself the real artisan of the vineyard. He did the most delicate vineyard work: pruning, chemical treatments, and, later, grafting. Paradoxically, during a period when industrial work became progressively less complex for unskilled and even for some skilled workers, vineyard work became

TABLE 8.1   Geographical Origin of Vineyard
Laborers in Coursan 1861-1910

Place of Origin	1861-1870		1871-1880		1881-1890		1891-1900		1901-1910	
	Num-ber	Per-cent	Num-ber	Per-cent	Num-ber	Per-cent	Num-ber	Per-cent	Num-ber	Per-cent
Coursan or neighboring village in Narbonne arrondissement	66	75.0	78	62.9	42	35.9	73	39.2	88	49.5
Other villages in the Aude or in the Midi	22	25.0	44	33.1	58	49.6	85	45.7	78	43.8
Outside region/ outside France	0	0.0	5	4.0	17	14.5	28	15.1	12	6.7
Total	88	100.0	127	100.0	117	100.0	186	100.0	178	100.0

Note: These figures are based only on individuals for whom place of birth and occupation were given in the marriage records. The 1911 manuscript census (the only available census for this period to list place of birth; the 1906 census for Coursan is missing) was used to check the accuracy of the sample form the marriage records. It was found that 45% of the vineyard workers listed in the census had been born in Coursan or in a neighboring village; 45% came from another village in the department or in the region. Only 1% came from outside the region or outside France. All of the latter were Spanish, with the exception of a few Italian farmhands.
Source: Marriage records of Coursan, 1861-1910.

increasingly demanding, especially after the phylloxera crisis of 1865-1885.[7] Another distinguishing aspect of vineyard work in Coursan was the existence of the *colle,* a team of 10 to 15 skilled workers who circulated from one *domaine* to another, performing specialized tasks such as pruning and grafting. Paid as a group for the tasks they performed, these workers developed a strong sense of collective responsibility. At the same time, by comparison with other workers in the village, they were highly independent, since they were not attached to a particular employer. Finally, in contrast to other forms of agricultural work where workers in the field were often isolated from one another or worked on a seasonal basis (*faucheurs*), the *colle* offered a continuous opportunity for contact between workers and the potential exchange of ideas: a setting in which worker solidarity could develop (Pech, 1975: 417-418; Quilis, 1973).

Work in the vineyards of Coursan, as elsewhere in the region, was clearly divided along sex lines. Female day laborers (*journalières*) gathered

TABLE 8.2   Occupational Mobility of Vineyard Laborers over Two
Generations: 1861-1910

	1861-1870		1871-1880		1881-1890		1891-1900		1901-1910	
	Num-ber	Per-cent	Num-ber	Per-cent	Num-ber	Per-cent	Num-ber	Per-cent	Num-ber	Per-cent
Vineyard laborers whose fathers were also vineyard laborers	25	75.8	58	78.4	47	68.1	94	62.3	84	73.0
N =	33		74		69		151		115	

Note: Women were not included in these calculations because their occupations were only rarely given in the marriage records. Because of the considerable flexibility in the use of the terms *cultivateur* and *journalier* in all government records and the rarity with which individuals identified themselves as *journaliers* at marriage, both occupational categories have been included in these calculations. N is the number of laborers for which both father's occupation and own occupation at marriage were known.
Source: Marriage records of Coursan, 1861-1910.

branches which had fallen to the ground during pruning and tied them in bundles for sale. They carried the heavy sprayer for sulphuring, performed other chemical treatments, and, during the harvest, were primarily responsible for cutting the grapes (Augé-Laribé, 1903: 272, Ministère de l'Agriculture et du Commerce, 1847). With the exception of the harvest, when all hands were needed, the majority of women who worked in the vines were unmarried or widowed (see Table 8.3). Although women's work could constitute an important supplement to the family income, the prosperity of the expansion period may account for the few married women employed during that period.[8]

Indeed, the vineyard laborer's situation during the expansion years was relatively comfortable. Between 1850 and 1880, the daily wages of male workers doubled, reaching 4 francs for an eight-hour day in summer by 1882. During harvest, wages were generally higher, reaching 5 francs per day plus two liters of wine. In fact, the wages of Coursan's *journaliers* were considered high with respect to both village wage levels (skilled masons typically earned between 4 francs and 4 francs 50 per day) and the national average of agricultural wages, in 1882 (3 francs 11 per day, ADA 13 M 282, 13 M 300; AN [Archives nationales, Paris] F[11] 2698; Statistique de la France, 1862, 1882; Augé-Laribé, 1907: 76-77). Women's wages

TABLE 8.3 Occupational Distribution of the Population of Coursan, 1876 and 1911.

Occupation	1876				1911			
	Total		Women		Total		Women	
	Number	Percent	Number	Percent	Number	Percent	Number	Percent
Day laborer/manual laborer	27	2.9	2	1.5	865	47.4	242	52.2
Cultivateur	412	44.8	33	25.0	0	0.0	0	0.0
Proprietor	75	8.2	8	6.1	183	10.0	8	1.7
Rentier	37	4.0	28	21.2	3	0.2	0	0.0
Other agricultural (shepherds, gardeners)	55	6.0	1	0.8	79	4.3	23	4.9
Skilled crafts	141	15.3	7	5.3	237	13.0	60	12.9
Trades (grocers, wine wholesalers)	32	3.5	3	2.3	153	8.4	25	5.4
Professionals (teachers, doctors, pharmacists)	45	4.9	5	3.8	91	5.0	12	2.6
Overseers (*ramonets*)	38	4.1	0	0.0	47	2.6	4	0.9
Servants and farmhands (*domestiques*)	56	6.1	43	32.4	112	6.1	44	9.4
Proprietor/day laborer	0	0.0	0	0.0	1	0.05	0	0.0
Proprietor/*cultivateur*	0	0.0	0	0.0	8	0.5	0	0.0
Ménagère	1	0.1	1	0.8	44	2.4	44	9.5
Wetnurses and midwives	1	0.1	1	0.8	3	0.2	3	0.6
Total	920	100.0	132	100.0	1826	100.2	465	100.1
Married, employed	5		5	3.8	269		269	57.8
Unmarried, employed	127		127	96.2	196		196	42.2

Source: Manuscript censuses of 1876 and 1911.

also increased in this period to 2 francs per day in 1882 (from 90 centimes per day in 1862) and 2 francs 50 during harvests. Yet, their wages remained substantially below those of the men, reflecting the secondary position of women's work in the vines.

The generally favorable situation of vineyard workers in the expansion years, characterized by a high demand for skilled labor, flexibility of employment, and alternative sources of income, changed radically between 1882 and 1890. When the phylloxera finally struck Coursan, one-third of the vineyards were totally destroyed; many of the remaining vineyards were seriously damaged. Day laborers found themselves without work; those who counted upon additional revenue from their small parcels of vines were obliged to choose between tearing out the diseased vines and replanting or selling their land (Barral, 1882; Ministère de l'Agriculture, 1883: 38-39). Most important, over the long term, the phylloxera substantially modified the local economy by establishing the dominance of the large, industrial vineyard.

The prohibitive expenses of reconstitution and replanting, which could run as high as 4000 francs per hectare, put small and medium owners at a distinct disadvantage by comparison with their large competitors (Comice Agricole de Narbonne, 1908: 8; Barbut, 1913; 61-62). Those who lacked the financial resources for reconstitution sold their properties by 1900 (56 percent of those who had newly acquired land in the decades 1850-1880), among them many independent *cultivateurs* and agricultural workers (Cadastre, 1850-1880; Frader, 1978: 234, 238). In addition, the expense of chemical treatments against phylloxera, grafting of French vine stalks to phylloxera-resistant American roots, and submersion drove up the yearly cost of maintenance so that a hectare of vines which cost 340 francs per year to maintain in 1866 cost 1000 francs per year in 1892 (Garidou, 1968: 21-22, 65). It is not surprising that land ownership among workers and small vintners (*cultivateurs*) declined in succeeding years (see Table 8.4). The large *domaine* vineyards, in contrast, each increased their holdings by 20 to 30 hectares each, thereby accelerating the process of vineyard concentration (*Cadastre*). While altering the shape of property ownership in Coursan, the phylloxera and subsequent reconstitution brought other changes for both producers and workers. Vintners now sought to increase production by whatever means possible. They often resorted to *chaptalisation,* the addition of sugar to wine during fermentation to increase the alcoholic content of the final product and also to the addition of sugar to the grapes left in the cistern to produce second wines

TABLE 8.4   Occupational Distribution of Individuals First
Acquiring Land in Coursan, 1861-1910.

| *Occupations* | *Numbers and Percentages of Individuals Acquiring Land* | | | | |
	1861-1870	*1871-1880*	*1881-1890*	*1891-1900*	*1900-1910*
Day laborer/ manual laborer	15 (8.2)	8 (4.2)	10 (6.2)	4 (3.3)	3 (2.7)
Small and medium proprietors (*cultivateurs*)	57 (31.0)	56 (28.9)	11 (6.8)	14 (11.7)	10 (9.1)
Other agricultural (shepherds, gardeners)	21 (11.4)	14 (7.2)	8 (5.6)	5 (4.2)	7 (6.4)
Skilled crafts and trades	49 (26.6)	67 (34.5)	70 (44.0)	43 (35.8)	44 (40.0)
Proprietors and professionals	32 (17.4)	37 (19.0)	53 (33.2)	37 (30.8)	34 (30.9)
Overseers (*ramonets*)	10 (5.4)	11 (5.7)	5 (3.0)	16 (13.4)	12 (10.9)
Farmhands and servants (*domestiques*)	0 (0.0)	1 (0.5)	2 (1.2)	1 (0.8)	0 (0.0)
N =	184 (100.0)	194 (100.0)	159 (100.0)	120 (100.0)	110 (100.0)

Source: *Cadastre foncier de Coursan*, 1861-1910.

or *piquettes*. These practices were facilitated when the government lowered the tax on sugar (Warner, 1960: 13-15). In addition, the crisis period was accompanied by an influx of workers and vintners from other areas of the Midi who had come to Coursan to find work while the phylloxera still spared the Narbonnais and who remained in the village during the late 1880s and 1890s (ADA 11 M 28, 11 M 35, 11 M 37, 11 M 48-49).[9]

These changes ultimately made the situation of the vineyard laborer much less enviable than it had been earlier. The growing ranks of the work force created a more competitive labor market in the very years that declining numbers of medium proprietors reduced an important group of alternative employers outside of the *domaine* vineyards. In addition, the increasing capital requirements of the post-phylloxera vineyard meant that most workers could no longer hope to become property owners, even as holders of small plots, to supplement their income from wage labor. The Coursan day laborer was now more likely to be employed and dependent for wages on the *domaine*.[10] Finally, by 1892, the daily wage of male *journaliers* had fallen to 2 francs 75 from the 1882 level of 4 francs per day; women's wages had also fallen from 2 francs per day to 1 franc 50. Although this was a period in which prices of food and other necessary items of consumption did not rise, rents did increase between 1880 and 1900 (ADA 13 M 30, 13 M 300, 9 M 91-104; Augé-Laribé, 1903: 290-291; Passama, 1906: 100-115, 209-212). In light of these changing conditions, the fact that workers had no formal contract made their position seem doubly insecure. In this context, the appearance of socialism in the Midi held out the possibility of a solution to their problems.

WINEGROWERS MOVE LEFT

The development of the vineyard economy in the Narbonnais was accompanied by a gradual political shift to the left from Bonapartism in the 1850s to republicanism in the 1860s and 1870s (Loubère, 1974; Pech, 1967, M. Pech, 1973). The Narbonne Commune of 1871 was itself a product and symbol of this leftward evolution. During the 1880s, the socialists began to develop a constituency in the Narbonnais and drew support from an alliance of vineyard workers, *cultivateurs,* artisans, and medium vineyard owners—those who had been most seriously affected by the phylloxera.

In 1885 socialists led a campaign to end colonial expansion, for the separation of church and state, reform of land taxes, the repurchase of railroads by the government, and the adoption of "social legislation" (a vague term which usually referred to labor legislation and social security). Their campaigns were marked by fierce attacks on the government and by a regionalism which depicted the Midi as having been sacrificed to governmental and capitalist interests of the north (ADA 5 M 93). In the 1890s, however, the years in which the vineyard workers' situation became increasingly insecure, local socialists—far from painting themselves as a revolutionary workers' party or even speaking directly to the needs of workers—played an active role as the defenders of the interests of vineyard capital. Between 1892 and 1896, for example, Dr. Ernest Ferroul, mayor of Narbonne and member of Jules Guesde's Parti Ouvrier français, spoke out for protective tariffs on foreign wines, repurchase of the Canal du Midi by the government, and the nationalization of railroads and mines (ADA 5 M 9, 15 M 117; Barral, 1968: 155).

The Narbonnais socialists' appeal to the vineyard bourgeoisie rather than to workers was in keeping with the direction political socialism took nationally. The Guesdists' 1892 agrarian program, for example, was aimed primarily at small property owners in its proposals for lifting property taxes and establishing agricultural credit facilities, agricultural education, and retirement programs. The Guesdists carefully avoided references to the class struggle and agricultural collectivization and defended peasant private property as "the tool of the peasant" (Willard, 1965: 363-376). In the Narbonnais, the socialists' almost exclusive attention to the agricultural bourgeoisie eventually cost them the support of the workers. By 1898, in Coursan, worker disaffection from political socialism manifested itself by heavy abstentionism in the national election of that year (ADA 2 M 58, 2 M 67). A major wine market crisis two years later provided the necessary stimulus which forced workers to make the choice between electoral politics and direct action.[11]

The *crise* of 1900, popularly attributed to fraud (the practice of artificially increasing output of wine by methods such as sugaring), was a crisis of overproduction. The department of the Aude produced almost three times its average yield of the preceding ten years. In Coursan, whose vines produced as much as 150 hectoliters per hectare, the price of wine dropped to between 3 and 5 francs per hectoliter after the 1900 harvest. All but the most necessary work in the vineyards stopped; those who continued to work saw their wages reduced by 25 centimes (Ministère de l'Agriculture, 1890-1900; Warner, 1960: 17; Gide, 1907; ADA 15 M 125). From the point of view of the vineyard worker, the struggle for survival had begun. Members of the Narbonne Bourse de Travail (Labor Exchange) and Louis Niel of the Bourse in Montpellier visited Coursan to encourage the workers of the village to unionize. In April 1901 the Syndicat des Cultivateurs et Travailleurs de la Terre de Coursan was formed.

Union membership reflected the now heterogeneous composition of the Coursan working class. The union appealed to the "poor martyr who is called *cultivateur* or terrassier because . . . for a long time we have watered this earth which feeds the capitalists with our sweat" (Gratton, 1971: 13). Not all union members were native villagers. Of the 26 who were arrested during the strikes of December 1904, only four had actually been born in Coursan, although all lived and worked there. A few Spanish workers joined the union, but most foreign workers were reluctant to do so for fear of being expelled from France by the local authorities (ADA 15 M 117, 15 M 125; Quilis, 1973). From an initial membership of 100 (roughly 12 percent of the vineyard workers in Coursan), it grew to 166 members by 1903 (19 percent) and to 350 members by 1904 (41 percent). These numbers, however, only represented a small part of its actual force, since many workers, even if they were not members of the union, supported the strikes when the time came for direct action. Finally, only a handful of women joined the union, despite the fact that growing numbers of Coursannaises worked in the vines after the turn of the century (ADA 15 M 90, 15 M 99).

Although the role of women in agricultural work was considered at early union meetings, the question of women's labor was initially seen only from the standpoint of men's work. François Cheytion, leader of the Coursan union, had argued that women must be permitted to join the unions and participate on union committees in order to educate them about the class struggle and to enlist their support in demanding a higher wage for men. These activities, however, were ultimately designed to lead to the "complete suppression of women's work; women could then return to their domestic duties—the home and the family" (FTAM [Fédération des Travailleurs agricoles du Midi], 1906: 49ff).

Like many unions which were affiliated with the Bourses de Travail, the Coursan union identified itself as revolutionary syndicalist and was marked by the local authorities as "anarchist" (AN F[7] 13599; Maitron, 1951: 271-273). It promoted the self-emancipation of the working class by free association and followed Fernand Pelloutier's (the founder of the Bourses) notion that the ideal society would involve a voluntary association of producers, where the basis of all production would be the union, and where an equal distribution of wealth would provide for the basic needs of all. In keeping with this position, the Coursan union rejected legislation and electoral politics as a means to improve the situation of the workers. Instead, they favored direct action—especially the strike—as the means to initiate social change; they placed special emphasis, in principle, on the importance of the general strike (as opposed to piecemeal struggles).[12] Most of these syndicalist themes were not only adopted by the Coursan union but also dominated the regional agricultural organization with which the Coursan union was affiliated, the Fédération des Travailleurs agricoles du Midi (Gratton, 1971; Matillon, 1908: 256ff; ADA 15 M 101; FTAM, 1903: 10-11).

The character of Coursannais unionism was shaped not only by the union's contacts with the wider national and regional movements but also by the special work experience of Coursan's laborers and by the union leadership as well. First, the team worker (*colle*) system had a subtle effect on the quality of unionism in the village. The special conditions under which the *colle* members worked—in a team, sharing a wage for the work they performed, yet dependent upon one of their members to bargain successfully with the owner or foreman for that wage—made them receptive to the mutualist aspects of revolutionary syndicalism. Reports that *colle* members in Coursan had been responsible for encouraging workers to abstain from voting in the last elections of the nineteenth century suggest that they would easily adopt the revolutionary syndicalist position of political neutrality (Pech, 1975: 418).

Second, suspicion of the central government in Paris, a feature of the regionalist socialist rhetoric with which workers had identified earlier, helped to cultivate antipathy toward the authority represented by the Bourgeois Republic. Finally, the labor union's leader, François Cheytion, was instrumental in bringing revolutionary syndicalism to Coursan. From 1905 to 1914, Cheytion represented the Coursan union in the regional Fédération des Travailleurs agricoles du Midi, where he denounced electoral politics and legislative action and expressed the antimilitarist position of the union, allying himself with the syndicalist Confédération Générale du Travail (Maitron, 1964: II, part 3, 201; Vergnes, 1973, 1974).

UNIONS AND COLLECTIVE ACTION

Unlike many unions in the region which had been formed hastily for the purposes of a specific strike, the Coursan union was in existence for three years before it finally took action. Moreover, it was not during the period of immediate crisis in 1900-1901 that it decided to act, but during the period of recuperation which followed. Although the poor harvest of 1903 caused the price of a hectoliter of wine to climb from the 5 or 6 francs of the two previous years to 20 francs per hectoliter, workers did not benefit from the favorable market situation. On the contrary, wages dropped another 25 centimes, and rains following the harvest led to the firing of numerous workers (ADA 15 M 121, 15 M 125). Some proprietors turned to piece rates to cut costs—a system which required the worker to work harder, faster, and longer for a daily wage and which was uniformly disliked by the French workers.

In the late fall of 1902 and early winter of 1903, several strikes broke out in the region around Béziers, near Coursan. Spurred on by these examples and by their own worsening situation, the Coursan workers presented a list of demands to the *patronat:* a daily wage of 50 centimes per hour, a minimum work day of six hours and a maximum of eight, the suppression of piecework, an increase in wages for work done after a rain, and the promise that no worker would be fired for striking. It was provided that women's wages would be set at at least half of men's wages, with the exception of sulphuring, when they would earn the same wage as the men (ADA 15 M 126). When the vineyard owners of Coursan, who had already formed their own *syndicat patronal,* refused to negotiate with the union, the workers struck on January 12 and marched through the streets, singing the "Internationale" and shouting *"Vive la grève!"*

The timing of the strike was suggestive of the union's intentions and the workers' perceptions of the relationship between the larger market crisis and their immediate situation as wage earners. From one point of view, their decision to take collective action at this time of year was ill-considered. January was one of the less active months of the vineyard work year; a strike at this time could be a much less effective means of applying pressure on the *patronat* than a strike in the spring or early fall. It is likely, however, that Coursan's first strike was less an attempt to smash the system of vineyard capitalism by denying essential labor at a crucial time than a statement about the workers' place in the vineyard economy and a demand for a just wage.

The idea of justice or the moral economy of the workers' position was not articulated explicitly either within their list of demands or in the slogans which they shouted in marching through the streets, but it was evident in the action itself. In January 1904 workers saw the price of wine rise after the harvest of 1903 and fully expected to participate in the profits. They were well aware that the highly competitive market of the twentieth century was substantially different from the "golden age" of the nineteenth century and did not ask that wages return to pre-phylloxera levels. Their demand for a just wage, however, involved the recognition that their employers may have been profiting from the price increase and were "doing so through violations of [their] own duties and other people's rights" (Tilly et al., 1975: 85; see also Thompson, 1971).[13] Into this context must be fit the workers' identification with the small proprietorship which persisted despite the dissolution of their electoral alliance with this group. The support which the striking workers received from them and from others in this and subsequent strikes demonstrated how closely the whole community was bound to the fate of the vineyard economy.

The strike affected the entire village. Official statistics estimated the number of strikers at between 900 and 1000. Since the union membership was approximately 350 at this time, it is clear that nonunion members and even nonvineyard workers lent their support to the movement (Grèves [Statistique des Grèves] 1905; ADA 15 M 99). Merchants and craftsmen closed their shops and workshops; small vineyard owners who had seen many of their friends ruined by the crisis of the preceding years also supported the strike. Finally, family members of the strikers marched through the streets and patrolled the *domaines* (a job assigned especially to women and children) to prevent refractory workers from going out to the vines. Support also came from an unexpected quarter. In one incident, the red flag was hoisted in the bell tower of the village church. This act, though regarded as sacrilege by the departmental subprefect, was not viewed as such by either the parish priest, who sympathized with the strikers, or by Coursan's mayor Theodore Abet, who even gave the strike committee an office in the town hall (ADA 15 M 125, 15 M 126).[14]

Eventually, the strike was a success. In a settlement reached on January 21, nine days after it began, workers won the 3 francs 50 for a seven-hour day eight months of the year, in addition to most of their other demands. For the first time, the *journalier* in Coursan had a work contract and had succeeded in establishing a minimum wage for all workers on all *domaines.* The strike also attracted new members to the union; union membership rose to 450 (Grèves, 1905: 8-11, 32-35; ADA 15 M 125). Finally, the viticultural *patronat* was temporarily put on its guard by a movement whose power lay in the solidarity of the vineyard wage earners and in the support of the nonvineyard population and small proprietorship as well—a demonstration that "property" did not suffice to bind together all factions of the vineyard middle class. Although additional strikes in the same year (1904) were less successful in winning concessions from the *patronat,* they continued to shape the syndicalist character of the Coursan workers.

The general strike of December 1904-January 1905 came on the heels of an abundant harvest when the price of wine fell to close to turn-of-the-century levels: between 3 and 8 francs per hectoliter. In many villages throughout the region, vineyard owners refused to honor the accords of the previous winter; they reduced working hours and in some cases laid off a portion of the work force. In several localities, brief strikes broke out at the end of October, demanding rehiring of workers. This new activity encouraged members of the Fédération des Travailleurs agricoles du Midi who had been arguing for a general strike, and finally a general walkout was proclaimed throughout the region for December 1. The uniform list of demands drawn up by the federation was, for the most part, the same as the demands raised by Coursan workers the previous winter, with one addition. Workers now asked that two liters of "good wine" be given to them daily throughout the year as part of their wage. In the past, it had been customary for proprietors to give workers their second wines (*piquettes*). Workers' refusal to accept this practice now signified their understanding that the production and sale of second wines (which they called "fraud") ultimately worked to their disadvantage by depressing the price of wine and by bringing down their wages as well (FTAM, 1904: 36-38, ADA 15 M 117, 15 M 121; Grèves, 1904: 492-493; Ader, 1905: 130).

Since the Coursan workers had already won most of the demands sought in the general strike, the 700 workers who walked off the job on December 1, 1904 did so in a show of support for their comrades in the region. Soon, however, the sympathy strike turned into a renewal of two demands which had not been satisfied in the earlier strikes of that year: the abolition of piecework and a year-round wage of 50 centimes per hour. The demand for two liters of "good wine" was introduced as well. But the strike, unwisely scheduled for December, was not successful, and unions either reached individual settlements or returned to work.

In Coursan, however, the strike's real impact came from the government's decision to use force to break the strike without consulting the mayor. Even the moderate republican municipal councillors protested against this invasion of local authority (ADA 15 M 120). The spectre of Coursan in a state of near siege did much to inflame resentment against the central government and to awaken workers' hostility to the use of the military as the police force of the vineyard middle class. In the years which followed the general strike of 1904-1905, François Cheytion spoke out vehemently against the government's use of military force to break strikes. The union continued to reject collaboration with the French socialist party on the grounds that it did not represent the working class, and in the legislative elections of 1902 and 1906 abstentionism remained high in the village. The experience of the general strike awakened the antimilitarist sentiments of the union well before the CGT adopted an antimilitarist position at Amiens in 1906 (FTAM, 1906b: 44, 51-54, 89; ADA 2 M 58, 2 M 69; AN F[7] 12544).

THE 1907 MOVEMENT

The first strikes of 1904 and the leadership of François Cheytion both served to educate the workers of Coursan in the use of direct action, but it was not until the regional viticultural crisis of 1907 that they began to develop a clear sense of themselves as a distinct class. The enormous viticultural defense movement which swept through the Midi in 1907 was a direct response to the continuing fluctuations of the wine market and the general failure of Midi viticulture to recuperate from the turn-of-the-century *crise de mévente*. In Coursan, for example, the price of wine by 1906 remained well below pre-phylloxera levels, at 9 and 10 francs per hectoliter. In some villages, prices as low as 1 franc 50 were recorded. The central objective of the movement, the protest against fraud and lack of government regulations of the wine market, attracted a broad, heterogeneous base of support from vineyard workers, small proprietors, merchants, craftsmen, the unemployed, and even numerous farmhands, all of whom were affected by the now perpetual insecurity of the wine market.[15]
In a series of dramatic, peaceful demonstrations—from 5,000 people in Coursan on April 14, 1907 to 500,000 in Montpellier in June—entire towns and villages turned out in force under the joint leadership of socialist chief Ernest Ferroul and Marcellin Albert, an equally charismatic figure in the movement. Finally, a tax strike and the resignation of village governments throughout the south (*la grève bourgeoise*) underlined the gravity and breadth of the regional uprising (ADA 5 M 66, 5 M 67; Frader, 1978; Smith, 1978; Napo, 1971).

The workers of Coursan, like their comrades in other villages, avidly followed the meetings and demonstrations of these months of 1907. Many of them continued to identify their fate with that of small vintners who were also victims of the market crises and who, in 1904, had supported the workers in their strikes. Once more, the idea of social justice came into play. "Fraud" held an important place in the collective psychology of both vintners and workers. The idea that the few benefited from a system which meant ruin for others was one with which workers could easily identify. The picture evoked by the movement leaders, of collusion among the sugar industry, high finance, and the government, had meaning for workers who had borne the material burden and social consequences of the wine market crisis. As one worker said, the demonstrations constituted a "sort of *fronde* against the government" (FTAM, 1907: 44; ADA 5 M 67). In addition, the political neutrality of the movement conformed to one of the syndicalist principles which was strongest in Coursan. However, if the movement attracted many vineyard workers, it also posed a serious problem for the future of the vineyard labor unions.

The turning point for both the viticultural defense movement and the labor unions came in June and July 1907, after government troops in Narbonne shot and killed five demonstrators on June 25. This event shocked the viticultural defense movement into practical action, but the subsequent creation of the General Confederation of Vintners of the Midi (CGVM), headed by Ernest Ferroul, ultimately broke the interclass front of the earlier demonstrations (ANF[7] 1290; Napo, 1971: 113-126).[16]

The CGVM, based in the small vineyard middle class of the region, promoted the solidarity of small vintners against the large and called for minimum prices for wine and an end to fraud. At the same time, it appealed to workers throughout the region for support, offering itself as "the fraternal union of capital and labor" (ADA 5 M 67). Yet, there was nothing in the program of this organization which touched on the specific situation of the agricultural laborer. In fact, the voting power of members was based on the amount of vineland they owned; unless one was a property owner, one had no vote.

The appeal of the CGVM to workers who had so enthusiatically participated in the demonstrations of the preceding months was seductive. Some union militants, such as the head of the Narbonne Bourse de Travail, Vincent Daìdé, saw cooperation with the CGVM as a means of fighting against the "*gouvernment assassin*" who had been responsible for the deaths in Narbonne (ADA 5 M 67).[17] Nevertheless, workers' adherence to this organization threatened the basis of syndicalist unity in the Narbonnais. Membership in the regional agricultural workers' federation had been slipping ever since the abortive general strike of 1904-1905. In Coursan, union membership fell from 487 to 200 between 1907 and 1910 (Matillon, 1908: 69-70; ADA 15 M 102). François Cheytion, who believed that continued cooperation with the small vintners would compromise the position of the federation and its member unions in future labor struggles, waged an energetic campaign to win workers back into the unions and away from the petit-bourgeois CGVM. After a series of heated debates within the Fédération des Travailleurs agricoles du Midi, Cheytion won and the federation eventually voted to oppose workers' adherence to the CGVM (FTAM, 1909: 44-49).

The adoption of this position opened a breach in the workers' movement between the "reformists"—those who saw no incompatibility between membership in both the unions and in the CGVM—and the "orthodox"—those who believed that working-class solidarity required rejection of collaboration with the vineyard petite bourgeoisie. In this split, Cheytion and the Coursan union placed themselves squarely on the side of the "orthodox" revolutionary syndicalists.

OLD PROBLEMS AND NEW ISSUES

Despite declining membership and the collapse of unions elsewhere in the region, the continued activity of the Coursan union in the years after 1907 owed much to the persisting insecurity of the vineyard laborer's material situation. Although wages had risen and working conditions had improved with respect to bargaining power, a 25-30 percent increase in the cost of living since the turn of the century had also eroded some of those gains. The years immediately prior to the war saw protests against the high cost of living throughout the south, and in 1910, the Narbonne Bourse pressured the French and Spanish governments to limit the number of Spanish workers who came to France as harvesters when an anticipated small harvest threatened to reduce jobs. (ADA 5 M 11, 15 M 117; AN F[7] 13599).

Three additional strikes in Coursan in the immediate prewar years demonstrated Coursannais' adaptation to those pressures. These actions also demonstrated the union's willingness to deal more directly with the question of women's work. On February 27, 1911, 600 workers struck for three days and were successful in obtaining two liters of wine for men and one liter for women. Women had not previously been given a separate wine allocation; but now, as the cost of living rose and women's work became increasingly important, so did a wine allocation (ADA 15 M 133; Grèves, 1911: 4-5). A more important strike took place on September 4, 1911, when a similar number of workers stopped work for five days just before the harvest. This time, workers obtained an annually renewable contract which reduced the workday to six hours and provided a uniform wage of 50 centimes per hour for men for all work and two liters of wine for women (ADA 15 M 133). The provision for a yearly contract now gave

Coursan's women workers an opportunity to press for their own terms. When the time came for a contract renewal in October 1912, the men signed their own contract, omitting all clauses pertaining to women. The refusal of the *patronat* to negotiate a separate contract with the women became the occasion of the last and longest strike before the war.

Whereas earlier the regional agricultural worker's federation had envisioned removing women from vineyard work altogether, after 1907 the federation changed its position and began to encourage the unionization of women vineyard workers. This was due in part to the fact that women's work had become an important adaptation to the decline in purchasing power of the agricultural worker in the years around 1910-1911. Since the end of the nineteenth century, the numbers and proportion of women vineyard workers had greatly increased, and the majority of women workers were married (see Table 8.3). In Coursan following the 1911 strikes a women's section was created within the union; by 1912, 108 women had joined, approximately one-third of the total number of the *journalières* in the village (ADA 15 M 102).

The 350 women who struck all the major *domaines* on November 27, 1912 were vine-trimming gatherers (*ramasseuses de sarments*). The wage increase they demanded in their contract would have given them 2 francs 50 per day for six hours of work—an increase of 75 centimes. Thus, their wages would remain half those of the men (ADA 15 M 133; AN F[7] 13626). In addition, they demanded that the traditionally "women's work"—gathering branches, chemical treatments, and harvesting—be reserved for them alone.

From the beginning, the male workers supported the women's strike with the resources of the union's strike fund and a two-day sympathy strike. Later, they continued their support by refusing to clear the vineyards of freshly pruned branches (as scab labor) on the grounds that this was not men's work and had never been specified as such in the contract. The women held out for 58 days. Finally, faced with the *patrons'* continued refusal to negotiate, they returned to work on January 25, 1913.

Although the strike of the *journalières* of Coursan failed, the fact that it had taken place at all was significant. In the past, the women of Coursan had supported the men in their strikes as consumers and as comrades, rather than as producers and workers. Now they struck for themselves, yet they only partially rejected the secondary status which they occupied in the vineyard economy, for they sought to perpetuate both a lower wage scale and the sexual division of labor in the vines. This choice, however, was consistent with the conditions under which they worked; it would ensure future work both for themselves and for their men in an era when the labor market in the Narbonnais was saturated with local and immigrant workers and when the rising cost of living made women's wage work a family necessity.

The emergence of a militant agricultural working class in Coursan, then, was the product of the progressive industrialization of the vineyards which restructured the conditions of employment, reduced the autonomy and mobility of workers, and reinforced their dependence on the *domaine* vineyard. The process of proletarianization was not automatic. In contrast to laborers in the factories of northern France, the workers of Coursan saw neither the erosion of basic work skills nor the massive replacement of human labor with machine labor. Only gradually were they able to come to terms with their specifically worker status and reject cooperation with small proprietors. Indeed, it was participation in collective action which intensified and crystallized class awareness, not the opposite. After the crisis of 1907, as unions throughout the Midi disappeared and union membership dwindled, the workers of Coursan continued to struggle in a world that was both rural and industrial.

NOTES

1. This agricultural transformation was facilitated by poor grape harvests between 1851 and 1856 which drove wine prices up when urban demand for wine was increasing. The opening of the Bordeaux-Cette railroad in 1857, connecting the Paris-Lyon-Mediterranean line to Narbonne and Coursan, decisively opened the Midi to the national market. A fuller treatment of this transformation, as well as a detailed analysis of the structure of the vineyard economy of Coursan, appears in Frader (1978).

2. This growth was due at least as much to immigration as to natural increase. For changing geographical origins of Coursannais, see Table 8.1. The population of Coursan continued to grow through the turn of the century, reaching a peak of 3829 in 1901 and falling to 3793 by 1911. For a more detailed analysis of population trends see Frader (1978).

3. The phylloxera is a small insect which attacks the roots of vines and causes the vine to die over a period of three to four years. It is thought to have been introduced into France from American vines which, although resistant to the insect's damage, nonetheless transported phylloxera.

4. The *domaine*, because it was composed of one concentrated block, was more efficient to work in terms of virtually all aspects of production, including transportation of men and equipment (Pech, 1974: 293).

5. Property of under one hectare could generally provide only a supplement to a family's food supply or income and was usually farmed in a soup garden or a small patch of vines. A family could survive on income from one hectare of vines, however, assuming that the vines were maximally productive (Barbut, 1913: 62-63; ADA 11 M 108). The term *cultivateur* was used to refer to small, independent landowners, worker-proprietors, and even landless workers. This ambiguous usage continued after 1900, even after workers ceased to own much land in Coursan.

6. The picture of low occupational mobility seen in the land records is confirmed by an analysis of mobility in marriage records (Frader, 1978: 244, 372).

7. Vineyard work became more complex after the phylloxera because of the addition of grafting and chemical treatments. On the decline of skilled craft traditions, see Scott (1974). Day laborers in Coursan referred to the unskilled farmhands who did the rough cultivation and digging as *gavots* or *gavaches,* meaning "careless" or "crude." These terms were commonly applied to the mountain folk who came down to the plain around the village to harvest and who eventually found jobs on the *domaines* (Chatelain, 1976: I, 131). Smith (1975), in his study of Cruzy, Hérault, has noted the use of the term *gavaches* in that village as well.

8. It is likely that more women worked in the village than were actually counted. For example, wives of landowning day laborers who did not work for a wage probably helped cultivate the family land. Yet, most local officials considered only wage labor to be productive work.

9. Whereas in 1876 only 26 non-French (mostly Spanish and Italian) villagers were recorded in the census, by 1896 there were 267 foreigners, mostly Spanish, who worked at digging canals for submersion (ADA 11 M 28, 35, 37, 43, 48, 49).

10. In contrast to Coursan, many more workers in Cruzy, Hérault remained property owners at the turn of the century and appear to have been less "proletarianized" by the development of the industrial vineyard than those of Coursan (Smith, 1975, 1978).

11. The case of Coursan suggests that the establishment of socialist politics in southern France was even more complex than Tony Judt has recently argued in his work on the Var (1979). Judt's exclusive focus on electoral politics (despite his appreciation of the relevance of economic and geographical variables in political life) prevents him from teasing apart the class components of the Var's developing left constituency. The workers of Coursan, as distinguished from Judt's "peasants," chose a very different path to the defense of their interests, as seen in the following analysis of their collective action.

12. The principle of political neutrality expressed by the Confédération Génerale du Travail (CGT) with which the Coursan union was associated, was partly based on the recognition that division over electoral politics would undermine worker solidarity.

13. Although the Tillys have applied this concept of justice to violent conflict, I believe it may be appropriately applied to the nonviolent demand for recognition seen in the first strike of Coursan's *journaliers.* As suggested below, it had additional implications for the position they later took on the vintners' revolt of 1907.

14. As Harvey Smith has pointed out, it was not uncommon for republican officials to support the strikes in hopes of obtaining electoral support from workers (Smith, 1978: 107).

15. The emotional impact of the term "fraud" was probably greater than the economic impact of fraudulent wine production. Without neglecting the role of fraudulent production in wine market crises, it is probably true that it accounted for only about five percent of national production (Pech, 1975: 117).

16. The shooting of Narbonne protesters by members of the 139th Infantry occurred during demonstrations to protest the arrest of the leaders of the viticultural defense movement—among them, Ernest Ferroul.

17. Daïdé's position on this question was perhaps responsible for his eventual resignation as general secretary of the Narbonne Bourse du Travail in 1913. The Bourse itself remained affiliated with the CGT and rejected affiliation with the CGVM.

9

Women's Collective Action and Feminism in France, 1870-1914

LOUISE A. TILLY

It was the 27th of May, 1871, in the Parisian suburb of Issy. Victorine B[rocher], an ambulance attendant, accompanied a unit of Fédéres, soldiers of the Commune of Paris, as they attacked an outpost of the Versailles-based French government. She had enrolled, with her husband, two months earlier in a military unit formed for the defense of the republic and the Commune. Her first duty had been as a cook in a caserne in Paris. But now, as Bloody Week drew to a close, her unit was in battle to recapture the fort of Issy. Retreat was called. The red cross flag of the ambulance squad was raised, and Victorine, who had been ordered to stay

AUTHOR'S NOTE: This is a revised version of a paper originally delivered at the International Symposium on the Organizing of Women, Stockholm, February 7-8, 1978. Helpful comments have since been made by Elizabeth Pleck, Ludmila Jordanova, Jane Schneider, Charles Tilly, and audiences at the University of California at Santa Cruz and Los Angeles and at the Ecole des Hautes Études en Sciences Sociales, Paris.

back earlier, went forward. She wrote (Paris, 1976: 177-178) in her memoirs:

> We gathered up our wounded and our dead under enemy gun fire. Although the red cross flag has been raised, the Versaillais continued to fire randomly; more than once we had to drop to the ground, holding our precious burden. . . .
>
> The battle had been terrible, our flag had fallen three times; it was raised once more and this time it was victorious. The Versaillais abandoned the field and fled in all directions.
>
> At the chateau, the scene before our eyes was horrible; dead and wounded were scattered pell mell in the rooms of the first floor. . . . In the midst of this slaughter were three women, the cantinières (of two other units) one dead, one gravely wounded. . . . I was the third, and chance has spared me.

On June 2, 1907, in Nîmes, an administrative and commercial city in southern France, there was a demonstration of 280,000 winegrowers. From all over the south they gathered to march behind a tattered flag which, it was said, had flown in Nîmes in the revolution of 1848 and in the days of the Commune of 1871. The winegrowers demanded that government ease the way for the sale and consumption of their wine by reducing their taxes, lowering transportation charges, negotiating international commercial treaties, and providing daily wine rations to French soldiers. The feminine presence was strong among the demonstrators: "peasant women from Arles in their traditional costume, young women from Portel in the tricolored scarves, those of Carcassone in white blouses with a crepe band, the saleswomen of Béziers in black, women of Marseillan in their work smocks, those of Saint-Thibery in black with tricolored cocades in their hair, those of Antignac with red berets." The speakers at this and other of the massive demonstrations held weekly in the south recognized this in addressing their audience: "Men and women citizens. . . ." (Napo, 1971: 65, 70, 48).

In August 1911, a wave of demonstrations about food prices swept over the industrial northern departments. In several areas there were violent confrontations, such as that at Billy-Montigny, a coal-mining town, on August 30. There a crowd of women and men attacked the wagon of Wils, a baker who was also a municipal council member. He shot one of the demonstrators, and the crowd turned on him in fury. He hid in a house; the crowd smashed the windows, plundered the chicken coops and set a wagon on fire before they were dispersed by gendarmes (Le temps, August 31, 1911, quoted in Hanson, 1976).

In Maubeuge on August 25, a crowd broke the windows of a butter merchant; at Hautmont, three women were arrested in a similar action. On August 31, a large procession of women metal workers and children, wearing red sashes and cockades, protested the high cost of food before the city hall of Maubeuge. A delegation of 12 women petitioned the mayor to bring down prices and to work to free the arrested. The procession continued into the factory district, where the crowd went from plant to plant, turning out the metal workers on strike. Once the heavy sentences levied by the court on the arrested women became known, the strike gathered force. At Hautmont, the crowd in the streets was so unruly that 200 gendarmes were unable to preserve order. On September 2, the Mayor of Maubeuge, negotiating among local farmers and distributors on the one hand and consumer leagues on the other, succeeded in framing an agreement for some price reductions (Le Figaro, August 27, 1911, quoted in Hanson, 1976; newspaper clippings from Le Petit Parisien, September 1 and 2, 1911, found in AN [Archives Nationales de la France] F [12] 7025; see also Flonneau, 1970: 60-61).

On March 10, 1906, a coal mine disaster shook the pits of Courrières in the Pas-de-Calais mine field in northern France. More than a thousand miners were trapped and died. A strike broke out. The miners demanded that the companies pay more attention to their workers' safety. An angry, accusatory song was sung in the mining town, for the strike was bitter, as was often the case in mine strikes:

Yesterday once more, a gas explosion
Trapped hundreds; broken, crushed in the depths of each pit
They died, men who were brave,
Workers transformed into slaves.

Pitiable miners, your face worn,
Your belly empty, your mouth hungry
You cut through the earth
And chisel you own eternal tomb [Luxardo et al., 1979: front page].

There was a dynamite attack on the house of a nonstriking worker. A Paris newspaper (Le temps, April 11, 1906) reports two women's demonstrations in Billy-Montigny on April 10. In the first, a group of 500 women, carrying red and tricolored flags draped in black crepe, went to the train stations to meet a woman thought to be a traitor to the miners' cause. Madame Ringard was believed to be on the train from the *chef-lieu*, where she had given testimony to a judge against three accused dynamiters. Though she was not on the train, the crowd searched the quais, reassembled to sing the "International," and marched off down the street.

Another group of some 200 women had set out from their *coron*, the mine company row housing, for Billy the same day. Carrying black flags, they headed for the house of the mine company director, only to find their way barred by police. Some of them eventually spoke to the director's secretary. They accused the company of letting their husbands starve to death underground, for some of the dead brought to the surface had only recently died. They were calmed by assurances from the secretary, and returned to the street. There they met the women coming from the train station, and the two groups marched together. As police and soldiers hastened to contain the procession, "a great number of rocks were thrown at the soldiers. . . . The two groups broke up and individuals ran through the streets of Billy-Montigny. They threw bricks at the house of M. Bard, the chief engineer of the mine, and broke several windows. Repulsed by the gendarmerie, the demonstrators finally dispersed."

The women cigar makers of the national tobacco monopoly plant of Lille, in the industrial Nord, went out on strike on February 12, 1900. They complained that the administration of the plant was not taking account of the poor-quality tobacco they had to work with when it set wage rates. The tobacco was hard to handle, so they could not produce at their accustomed speed. They demanded supplements to maintain their wages. On the 14th, a general meeting of all workers—union members and nonunion—voted that if the administration did not meet their demands in 12 hours, the entire work force would strike. This they did, starting a long strike.

On February 25, on the occasion of carnival, two floats of women strikers rode in the parade. They sang about themselves:

> Peaceful and courageous workers all, Men, women and girls
> We have but one concern; only one benefit do we seek:
> Bread for our families.
>
> Long days we will struggle on to this end

They collected aid for the 800 strikers from onlookers.

The deputy, mayor, and city counselors were asked to negotiate with the local administration and the government ministry in Paris. A lengthy give-and-take followed, until, after one rejection of an offer, the workers voted to accept a settlement and return to work on March 7 (Mannheim, 1902: 431-434; ADN [Archives Departmentales du Nord], M 621/15, "Grève de 1900").

On July 5, 1914, several thousand women and men gathered at the Orangerie in the Tuilleries Gardens of Paris to hear leaders of feminist organizations celebrate their forerunners and launch their new campaign for votes for women. Séverine, a regional and national leader, apotheosized Condorcet, an Enlightenment figure who supported women's rights. She called for unity among the suffrage groups, a unity without which their cause could not be won and read a poem which ended with these words:

We swear never to break our alliance
Or cease to raise our voices high
Until the words of our hope are chiseled in the marble of the law.

She declared: "It is woman's mission to support justice and promote beauty; if we are trying to reform the world, it is in order to make it a more beautiful world." The group marched solemnly along the quai to the statue of Condorcet, where other speeches were delivered, and then dispersed for a late dinner (Handwritten poem and news clippings in dossier "Manifestation Condorcet [396 Man]" Bibliothèque Marguerite Durand, Paris).

WOMEN'S COLLECTIVE ACTION AND FEMINISM IN FRENCH POLITICS

The incidents described here involved thousands of French women in collective action ranging from rebellion to a public forum. What the incidents have in common are women acting collectively in their self-defined interests. The concept of collective action, as a struggle over control of resources among groups (Tilly, 1978a) is the theoretical framework within which these incidents will be examined. Collective action is defined as the extent of a group's application of pooled resources to common ends. Groups which have identified their interests and see the opportunity to act apply what resources they can muster to other groups or to governments. Political power is the return from the application of resources to governments. Violence occurs when governments or other groups resist the collective action of a mobilizing group, as well as when such a group deliberately chooses violent means. There are five components of collective action: "interest, organization, mobilization, opportunity, and action itself. The components will vary from group to group, place to place, time to time, problem to problem" (Tilly, 1978a: 7; see also 1977b: 484).

Although these incidents all involve women, they differ systematically along two major axes. The first runs from "proactive" to "reactive" collective action. The suffrage movement shared with the labor movement a proactive thrust in collective action, for feminists and workers claimed new rights and sought a redistribution of power. This was in marked contrast to *reactive* protest, the resistance of groups to encroachment on their rights and interests by larger systems—in particular, the consolidating nation state and the widening national market (see Tilly et al., 1975, for discussion of this classification). In this category fit the defense of the commune as experienced by Victorine B. and the winegrowers' movement. Women in their role as workers' wives took part in working-class collective action, such as the coal mine strike and the food price demonstrations, which led to strikes; both actions share proactive and reactive elements. The other axis ranges incidents of collective action in terms of group interest: from those in which women's interests are *incidental,* when they are acting as members of a household, as members of a community, or as wage workers, to those in which women's interests, as women, are *intrinsic.* The defense of the commune, the food protest, the winegrowers' demonstrations, and the mine wives' demonstration, cluster at the end of the continuum where women acted as members of households or communities, in which their interests as women were incidental or subdued. The women tobacco workers' strike comes somewhere in the center of the continuum, for in this case the women acted in their interest as workers, but their association together in work can lead them to be conscious of their interests as women as well as workers. Only in the case of the feminist demonstration were women acting as women on issues usually defined as women's issues.

The history of feminist organization and action in France is not one of easy success. French feminist groups, although they proliferated in the period of the Third Republic, were never as prominent in the political struggles of the time as were such groups in Britain and America; they never gathered a large following; they almost never grabbed headlines with dramatic confrontation tactics. Although women's civil status was somewhat improved by legislation in the period, the fight for suffrage failed.

Female suffrage was granted only in 1945, and other legal reforms came even later. My questions, however, only indirectly address the question of why political feminism was weak in France. I ask instead, around what interests did women in France organize, mobilize, and act collectively? Where, when, and how did the interests of mobilizing feminists intersect with those of other mobilized women?

French politics were highly centralized in the nineteenth century. The period 1870-1914 saw a continuing centralization and concentration of political power. The central government expanded its social programs, for example, providing compulsory and free primary education and the inspection of work places to enforce safety standards and prohibit child labor. Political parties were slow to develop in France, but by the 1880s and 1890s there were political groups which acted collectively on the national level in elections, in legislative voting, and in cabinet ministries. One of the main areas of political agreement among republicans was anticlericalism and secularism. Labor, as a conscious and organized group, worked within various republican and socialist parties in formal politics and through strikes. The nineteenth century saw an alteration of power: "a nationalization of politics, an increased role of special purpose associations, a decline in the importance of communities as the loci of shared interests, a growing importance of organized capital and organized labor as participants in power struggles" (Tilly, 1978b).

The events described above, in all their variety, illustrate that the history of French women and collective action goes far beyond efforts of feminists to bring women into formal politics. Feminist politics in France seldom led women to collective action or to great influence on public policy in the period 1870-1914. Other collective action involving women was much more common. In order to place feminist collective action into the context of other women's activity, let us review first who the feminists were, what were their interests, and what led them to act together at this time.

French feminists were nearly all women of means in the middle or upper classes. Unlike many mainstream American feminists, the leaders of the French movement did not come to feminism through religious reform movements but by way of Free Thought and Masonry—such as Maria Deraismes—minority religious backgrounds—such as Protestants Sarah Monod and Mme. Jules Seigfreid, and Jewish-born Mme. Brunschvicg—or even foreign national origin—such as Jeane Schmahl and Maria Martin, both English (Offen, 1977: 54). They were all women who could afford good educations, who sought control over their wealth and the use of their personal talents.

The programs they articulated called for reform in the civil status of women (particularly through amendment of the Civil Code), political participation for women through the vote, and access to education and employment. Nevertheless, relatively few of these women had to work or did work. The exceptions were journalists, actresses, and schoolteachers. Their movement was more or less contemporaneous with the organization of the working class and the emergence of formal political parties. The typical forms of collective action of these groups were the strike and the demonstration, both of which developed and flourished in the period. French feminists most often adopted the forms of collective action typical of formal politics, oriented toward the national center—the demonstration, the parade, the political meeting, and, occasionally, a symbolic act of disruption of a meeting (see Le Figaro, October 30, 1904 for an account of a disruption of the solemn convocation in the Sorbonne on the centenary of the promulgation of the Civil Code). The various feminist groups of the Third Republic, composed primarily of bourgeois women, acted in the political style of the bourgeois republic, in forms of collective action common to the French political system. Women as well as men tried to influence national politics through petition and other political pressure on legislators and, through litigation, to promote corrective legislation. They met with no success. This relative failure must be understood in terms of politics at the center, in particular the alliances and coalitions of interests in the French Chamber of Deputies and the Senate (Hause, 1977; Hause and Kenny, 1979). The interpretation offered here starts elsewhere, examining the various forms of women's collective action and asking who were the participants, what were their interests, and how changes in economic and political structure from 1870 to 1914 were moving these women to act. The success or failure of feminine politics is not the central focus here; rather, we are concerned with the range of interests acted upon.

ECONOMIC CONTEXT

When politics is understood broadly, women can be seen as political actors trying to influence government authorities and those in positions of economic power in order to protect or promote their interests. The forms of collective action of French women were closely connected to the political system and the economic structures of the time during which they acted. These structures were changing in the process of industrialization, urbanization, and political concentration. In the following sketch of the economic context, it becomes clear that the links among individual women, economic and political structures, and change were mediated by their family position, community membership, or wage labor.

With capitalist industrialization, labor and resources shifted away from primary production (agriculture, fishing, forestry) toward manufacturing and service activities. Capital formation promoted and increased the scale of production, and the factory eventually replaced the household as the locus of productive activity. In France, industrialization was very gradual, and it affected different groups and geographic areas at different rates and times. Over the long run, the decline of small units of production meant a declining number of propertied peasants and artisanal craftsmen and an increase in proletarian propertyless people working for wages, in city or country. Proletarianization, the transformation of former peasant and independent producer populations into wage laborers, was the central experience for ordinary people.

France had its modern industrial region in the north. The smokey red brick textile factories of Roubaix and Tourcoing physically resembled those of Lancashire; the coal mines of the Nord and the Pas-de-Calais resembled those of Yorkshire and South Wales. Yet Bairoch (1965: 1102, 1104, 1107, 1108) shows that although French industry was growing rapidly between 1880 and 1900, it lagged far behind Britain in all indicators of industrial growth.

Even at the end of the nineteenth century, much French manufacturing took place in the households of peasants and craftsmen or in small work shops. France's laboring population lived scattered throughout the country in rural as well as urban areas; as Claude Fohlen (1973: 26) puts it: "the distinction between industrial and agricultural work is often artificial."

In France, in sharp contrast to Britain, the small, family-run peasant farm predominated. There were some regional variations: In the north and around large cities, urban market-oriented farmers hired subsistence peasants and propertyless workers. But Thabault (1971: 21) notes that the tendency toward "an increase in the number of small owners whose assets consisted of no more than a house, a garden, and one or two fields" continued in the period. At the height of this development, in the 1880s, according to Gordon Wright (1964: 6), there were 3.5 million farms in France. At mid-nineteenth century, Marx (1971: 320-321) had described "the great mass of the French nation as an agglomeration of autonomous units. . . . A small holding, peasant and family" In 1959, Alfred Cobban (cited in Wright, 1964: 1) wrote: "In the last resort, and at bottom, France is a Peasants' Republic." Unlike the British farmer, the French peasant continued to depend on the labor of his family, so wives and daughters living and working on small peasant farms were an important part of France's agricultural work force.

The persistence of agriculture in France accompanied a lower level of urbanization than in England. By 1891, Weber (1967: 144) shows, 72.5 percent of the English population lived in places of over 2,000 inhabitants; 32 percent lived in cities of over 100,000. In France, on the other hand, the comparable figures were 37.4 percent and 12 percent, respectively. Over the course of the century, French urban population (in cities over 10,000) increased 2.7 times, which is almost the same rate as the English (2.9 times). Despite the rapid growth of cities, however, France had a much less urban population than England.

Industrial growth had created new kinds of cities in France by the 1870s. (The following description is derived from Tilly and Scott, 1978). The textile city of the Nord and mining cities of the Nord and Pas-de-Calais are examples. These cities, although both products of industrialization, had very different labor force characteristics. In the textile city, there was heavy labor force participation by girls and women, including some married women. In the mining towns, most jobs were held by men. Girls and unmarried women or widows did some auxiliary work around the mines or were servants; married women were seamstresses or store or cafe keepers if they worked. The division of labor by sex in the coal miners' or metal workers' families was especially sharp: Men and boys worked in heavy, exhausting labor removed from the household, while women stayed in the home, responsible for housework and childbearing and rearing. There was little female wage earning. Most French cities did not have the peculiar labor force characteristics of the textile city or the mining town. In other towns and city, public administration, commerce, and small businesses producing directly for consumers were common. In these cities, women worked primarily in the garment industry, food production, domestic service, and tobacco monopoly plants. There were also many urban women in informal, casual labor as carters, petty traders, street hawkers, and laundresses. Women in the cities were more likely than those in peasant households to earn individual wages for their work. The decline of the household mode of production in the urban sector meant that even if they worked at home, women were seldom part of a family productive unit. Instead, they worked for an employer who paid them a wage. Married women in the working class worked intermittently, doing laundry, cleaning, and the like, for they had heavy responsibilities at home. Women's work had changed rather little: The majority of working women had jobs with low levels of skill and low productivity similar to those that had been women's work for centuries.

By the 1890s, however, the development of the tertiary sector was providing new types of jobs for women. As differentiation increased and the scale of organization of the economy grew, bureaucratic and administrative organization expanded. Clerks, typists, and secretaries were needed in increasing numbers to staff company offices and to fill government positions. Larger-scale production was accompanied by larger-scale distribution. The department store, with its army of sales clerks, was born in Paris. Compulsory primary education meant that teachers were needed, while government expansion of communication and social services demanded workers in these areas as well. Relatively high wages in heavy industry continued to draw male workers. The continuation of peasant agriculture reduced the supply of available workers in the urban sector. Confronted with a shortage of male workers and a large demand for white-collar workers, employers began to recruit women. As a result, the twentieth century saw a "migration," as Michelle Perrot (1976: 118-119) puts it, of women from industrial and domestic production into modern tertiary employment. In France this process began as late as 1914. It was to be slowed further by the war years, in which women took men's places in manufacturing. Therefore, the French economy, in the entire period with which this chapter is concerned, was characterized by the continuing importance of peasant agriculture, small-scale manufacture and commerce in cities, large-scale, industrialized enclaves, and a growing tertiary sector.

The family, then, did not disappear as a productive unit in France in this period. The peasant family holding was the typical organization of agriculture. In the middle class, the family managed property and capital. Marriage settlements and contractual arrangements gave a woman a stake in the economic resources of the family she and her husband formed on their marriage. Writing about Paris in the first half of the century, Adeline Daumard (1963: 336) notes:

> The basic cell . . . was the household. At the moment the marriage was performed, it was a business matter, the coming together of two fortunes, or two milieux. Life in common transformed it into a true union, certainly imperfect, surely beset by crisis, but generally solid, at least on the material level.

In the middle classes as well as the peasantry, marriage was an economic alliance and the nuclear family was an institution which protected and developed jointly held resources for the present and the future.

Even among industrial workers where the family economy had disappeared and individual wage earning was the rule, however, the nuclear family was concerned with production in an indirect way: through family decision-making and family strategies through which persons would earn wages in order to accumulate needed cash for consumption needs. Surplus cash, once such needs were satisfied, had to be allocated to other uses. Again, the family unit was the locus of strategy decisions. The organization of production shapes the reproduction of the labor force and affects reproduction decisions. Nevertheless, during industrialization and proletarianization, the family played an active role in determining strategies about wage earning, spending, childbearing, and child nuture (Tilly, 1979). The family, then, continued to mediate between individuals and the large economic processes in which they found themselves.

The continuing centrality of family as an associational reference for the French was not simply a matter of ideology. It was the family's continuing role as an economic productive unit for peasants and craftsmen, and its continuing role as economic resource for propertied and wage earning persons, that makes the family so central in understanding French social relations and French women's collective action.

In summary, in this period the French economy was still decentralized and small scale; peasant agriculture dominated. The household continued to be a unit of agricultural production. Even when the family was no longer a productive unit, it was the guardian and agent of individual economic resources. French politics was centralized and administration and decision-making highly concentrated. These factors defined the structures in which people were located. Any individual's position in these structures shaped his or her interests.

How do women and their interests fit into the structures of power, and how and when do their interests lead women to act collectively? Let us return now to the events of collective action described in the introduction to examine participants, their interests, and the set of opportunities and circumstances which led them to act.

WOMEN'S INTERESTS AND
COLLECTIVE ACTION

When we examine the ordinary participants in the defense of the Commune of Paris, as well as of the leaders, our perspective broadens.

There were women members of the First International, of the several women's organizations within Paris; Edith Thomas (1963) describes these women who spoke in the clubs of the *quartiers* which sprang up following earlier revolutionary custom. There were also lesser-known women, participants in the military defense of the Commune, such as Victorine B. Victorine was a boot sewer; her husband, Rouchy, was a cobbler. (Her father, also an artisan and worker militant, was the son of a bourgeois family.) Relatively well educated and well paid, the Rouchys were active in Paris units of the International in the late 1860s, and they had been among the organizers of a cooperative bakery. Victorine's daily life, like that of many urban women of the popular classes, involved her in wage labor outside the home. Victorine B[rocher] (1976: 61, 66) resented the "pitiful wages" and long hours of women workers, who were "forced to leave their elderly parents and children" in order to work. She pitied the plight of women who, out of necessity for wage work, were unable personally to care for their own children. She herself lost her two sons, despite the fact that she was able to pay for medical attention for the children and although her mother aided her with child care. Even though her own life experience was quite different, Victorine B. seems to express here the craftsman's ideal so often repeated by Proudhon and others of the wife in the home.

In contrast to the occasional feminism, or at least the vigorous individual articulateness of the better-known women militant leaders such as Louise Michel, Victorine B.'s memoirs are politically cautious. She had evidently been asked many times about Louise Michel and the women's groups, for she writes that she met Michel only once, during the Commune defense. Michel asked her to join a defense group. "I didn't know anything about the feminine movement," she wrote (1976: 190). "I never put my foot into a public meeting. It would be impossible for me [to join Michel] for I'd promised my friends never to abandon them." Her loyalties were community-oriented, a community that shared working-class quarters and an organization of work.

Jean Maitron (1972: 104-105) has analyzed the social characteristics of 115 women whose dossiers are in the archives because they were tried and convicted by *jugements contradictoires.* Only two of the women, Louise Michel and Natalie Le Mell, were well-known militants. Demographically and occupationally, these women strongly resemble Victorine B. Most of the women (62 percent) were aged 30 to 50; 75 percent were married or widows. Of those for whom occupations were given, 83 percent were working class, and almost 50 percent of the workers were in the clothing trades. The typical male communard was also a worker, but an "elite worker," according to Jacques Rougerie's analysis (1964: 47). Relatively few of them were true proletarians. Occupational titles may be misleading, however, for the small-scale, craft-organized industries of Paris increasingly were being undermined. Craftsmen and women were on the defensive to preserve control over their own work.

The interests of women and men Communards were those of crafts-people undergoing proletarianization in a changing productive system. Victorine B. (1976: 160-161) defined the goal of the Commune as a desire for freedom of political association for workers and a republican govern-ment as a means to guarantee that their voices would be heard:

> By establishing the republic, one could achieve an improved society by means of government action, not by means of the social republic [for only a minority of the Communards favored this].

> The Communards wanted a more equitable, more humane Republic. The Commune would concern itself with local affairs.

Victorine B. spoke for a "reactive" interest within the defenders of the Commune. She did not voice the radical program which was debated in the clubs: the social republic, the criticism of the church, the defense of common law relationships, and protection of illegitimate children's rights. As in most revolutions, there was a convergence in Communard collective action of a range of interests which intersected temporarily. The interests and ideas of Victorine B. may have been typical of the majority.

In any case, the opportunity—and indeed the necessity—to act joined radicals and others when the central government attacked the Commune. Everyone was needed in the defense of the city, although some fought to promote the social republic, some for local urban autonomy, some for declining craft positions, and some in hopes of far-reaching economic and political change. The women of the popular classes had long been inte-grated into a world of work outside the home, oppressive as wage work often was. They were little affected by the civil code's definition of their dependent status in the family. Many had worked in the interests of their families, and many fought so, alongside family and companions of *quartier* and work (see Perez, 1974). Class, community, and family interest inter-sected in the collective action of these women in defense of the Commune of Paris.

The wine growers who rose to protest conditions of the Languedocian wine industry in 1907 were men and women who owned small holdings and did skilled labor in the vineyards of larger landowners. Harvey Smith

(1972; see also Frader, this volume) has shown that in many ways the winegrowers were cultivators with artisanal characteristics—skill, the spirit of independence, and corporate identity. Competition from larger, more efficient vineyards increasingly put the smallholder/skilled worker under economic pressure. The smallholders allied themselves with propertyless laborers in 1907, thus producing a huge audience for protest meetings and thousands of marching demonstrators. According to Smith (1972: 227), 1907 was the culmination of about ten years of mobilization, "the result of efforts taken by the body of skilled agricultural workmen in the village to defend their position from further deterioration, while attempting simultaneously to prepare a reorganization of the village community along the lines that would ensure the security of their children in the future." The wives and daughters of the smallholder winegrower took an active role in cultivation. Their work and their future was closely tied to the success or failure of the family holding. As had occurred among the women of the crafts families of Paris who fought in the Commune, the household organization of work and the communal links among working households brought them to collective action. Many of the wage laborers who were involved in 1907 demonstrations acted because of their own poor harvests. A speaker at the agricultural workers' congress that year noted, "we are all both workers and small holders" (Smith, 1972: 269). Proletarianization of smallholders, like proletarianization of artisans, mobilized all members of the household for protest.

The wine growers' collective action was primarily reactive, but the form of action—the demonstration—developed in proactive protest such as that of organized labor or political parties. The gigantic demonstration, with its sea of people, banners, and placards, had little in common with rural protest of the past. At appointed times, speakers addressed the assembled throng, and units organized by communes marched past. They had come in by special train; at the end of the day they dispersed to their villages to plan their appearance at the next, and largest, demonstration in Montpellier on June 9, 1907. Their demonstrations and petitions were directed at the Parliament and the premier, Clemenceau. They acted in the context of politics at the center.

Food protest by the women of Maubeuge and its region was class-based women's collective action. The actors were women who lived in households with a strict division of labor. The food price demonstrations began in metal working and mining areas in which the labor market situation meant little wage work by wives and a primarily familial role for them that emphasized the management of consumption. The labor force was overwhelmingly male in these towns; work was heavy and exhausting. Such workers left housework and child rearing to their wives, who were expected, in turn, to use male wages to purchase a comfortable standard of consumption. The contemporary motto, "the miner in his home" ("*le mineur chez soi*") summed up the notion of the home as a haven from work, a haven into which his wife's energy and time was to be invested. The "*homme de fer*" (Bonnet et al., 1976: 150-152; 1977: 77-78, 164, 165) acted similarly. In such a household division of labor, the wife's role as wise consumer was salient.

It was just such women, acting as consumers, who launched the food protest in 1911. This consumer interest recalls the role of women in grain and food riots in the eighteenth and early nineteenth century. Women had a special concern with the consumption needs of their families. They had to make scarce cash stretch to buy food when prices rose. Yet there were important differences between the protest of 1911, and that of, for example, 1789. Old regime food protest consciously referred to the system of paternalistic economic market regulation by local or royal government. The crowd in the eighteenth or early nineteenth century claimed to be defending the traditional right or custom of local consumers to the product of their community. Informed by these beliefs, men and women food rioters invoked an earlier justice of consumer protection (see Thompson, 1971; L. Tilly, 1971, 1977; C. Tilly, 1975a), and tried to block grain shipments out or set prices on bread.

The 1911 food protest broke out first in industrial areas, not in areas whose products were being shipped out, driving up prices. (From the metal and mining areas of the Nord, the protest spread to the textile industrial area; from there it moved to nonindustrial, specialized farm areas, such as Burgundy, and finally to areas in the west where there were arsenals and navy yards, in which urban and familial division of labor were again similar to that in mines and metal working). Demonstrations were only tardily launched in cities, such as Paris, where women worked in consumer industry and services. They occurred primarily in industrial areas around which little food was produced and in which consumption was highly differentiated from production (for the geography of the movement, see Hanson, 1976: 10-20; Flonneau, 1970: 60-62; Perrot, 1974: 130-132).

The object of price fixing was less often bread and grain, basic diet items, and more often butter, meat, and eggs. The form of protest was also quite different from the old food riot. The protesters often resembled strikers more than food rioters, organized strikers who bargained with producers and merchants in the marketplace. Once a price was agreed upon, they sought to police the agreement. Those who resisted their demands or who tried to elude the set price were attacked. They also, as we have seen, used the strike as an additional form of pressure and to gather a large crowd. The correspondent of *Le Figaro* (August 27, 1911, quoted in Hanson) who filed a report from Maubeuge wrote that the protest was "more than a strike but not quite a crusade." Michelle Perrot (1974: 131) writes, "For doubtless the first time, the strike became, in a massive way, a form of protest against high prices."

Labor unions moved to catch up with the protest and perhaps lead it. Some of the later incidents, such as those at Creil, near Paris, and Charleville and Mezières in the Meuse valley, followed the efforts by CGT speakers to spread the word about resistance to high prices. In Paris, formal demonstrations were organized by the Union des Syndicats de la Seine (Hanson, 1976: 18-29; Flonneau, 1970: 61).

Even before the unions moved to take the lead, however, aspects of the collective action differentiated it from old regime food riots. The demonstration of women in Maubeuge followed new forms of protest. The delegation which met the mayor was more formal and more bureaucratic than anything in the old regime food riots. Then rioters had shared a sense of justice and of communal rights but no formal organization. The "turn out" of workers on strike borrowed a labor form of collective action. Part of the difference with the old form of food riot was the influx of men into the demonstrations, men who "marched with red flags, sang the International, and held meetings" (Flonneau, 1970: 61), but many of the incidents show that women also called upon the demonstration and strike as their model of collective action.

It was the consumer interest of working-class wives which led them to protest in 1911; the high prices and shortages of that year gave them the occasion for expressing their interest in forms of collective action—the strike and the demonstration—which were available in the repertoire of contemporary political struggle.

The coal miners' wives action was also class-based, but their class collective action was shaped by the paternalistic environment in which mine families lived and worked. The mine wife was exceptional among workers' wives in her active participation in work-connected struggles. More often than not, she had herself worked at the mine when a girl, as a carrier or sorter of coal: She knew mine work. As a miner's wife, she had to deal with the company as landlord and as owner of the store, distribu-

tor of health services and even sometimes schooling. Michelle Perrot
(1974: 505) writes that the mine strike was an

> affair of the tribe: committed, the women demonstrated unequalled
> tenacity, seeking contributions for aid, collectively organizing the
> slim resources of strikers, boosting the flagging morale of the men,
> involving themselves with the policing of the strike. At the time the
> shift of workers changed, they stood across the roads, blocked access
> to the pits.

Some of women's policing strikes resembled an older form of collective
action, the *charivari.* The banged on pots outside the door of scabs living
in the *coron,* accosted miners who worked during the strike, pulling down
their pants and spanking them. At Lievin on April 15, 1906 (Luxardo et
al., 1979: 133) women forced another woman who had bragged that her
husband was not striking to carry a flag around town shouting, "Long live
the strike!"

The women demonstrating at the train station of Billy-Montigny were
collectively seeking to discipline the woman who they believed had
betrayed the striking workers. Yet the second women's demonstration
illustrates another aspect of mine wives' lives: the extreme division of
labor in the household, and the dependence of the wife on her husband as
a wage earner (See Vuillemin, 1872: 31; Delcourt, 1906, 204-220; Michel,
1891: 25ff; Condevaux 1928: 8, 16, 50). Her own responsibility for the
house and children was time-consuming, but the death of her wage earner
was a severe blow to the mine wife, living in a community where it was
likely to be difficult for a woman to support herself. These two interests,
then—the solidarity among workers, and the dependence of the mine wife
and family on male wage earning—were present in the demonstrations in
the streets of Billy-Montigny in March 1906. Although there are elements
of defensive or reactive collective action in the demonstration of the wives
who protested the slowness of mine rescue operations, the other demonstration was proactive in its effort to police class solidarity. The form
chosen for both actions was a familiar one in turn-of-the-century France—
the demonstration-procession. This time the women marched behind flags
draped in black, recalling the disaster which provided the occasion for the
strike.

Women tobacco workers in Lille were very different from the Parisian
garment workers and craftsmen, although they, too, were workers. The

factories of the tobacco monopoly employed thousands of people in one institution, 90 percent of them women who earned wages far removed from their households for hours each day. Although women tobacco workers were primarily unmarried, as were most women workers, there were proportionately more married women than in other occupations, for the job was relatively secure and skilled. Women apprenticed and trained for several years to become cigar makers, shorter periods for other specialities. The daughters of workers sought to enter the profession, for although tobacco working conditions gave plenty of cause for complaint, the industry was superior to many others (see Mannheim, 1902). The government, which held the monopoly of tobacco production and sales, was a relatively responsible and responsive employer. In many ways (Zylberberg-Hocquard, 1978), workers in the tobacco factories were peculiarly privileged.

Apprenticeship, parent and child links to the same occupation, and lifetime commitment to the occupation suggest the opportunity for the development of solidarity and association among women tobacco workers similar to that of male craftsmen. In fact, the tobacco workers had mutual aid or friendly associations before they formed unions, just as did many artisanal groups. The Marseilles union, founded after an 1887 strike, was the first local; by 1891, 40 percent of tobacco workers were in unions. One consequence was a relatively high (for women workers) propensity to strike. Perrot (1974: 129) writes, "Although they accounted for 5 percent of the female labor force [in the period 1871 to 1890] they [tobacco workers] supplied 16 percent of female strikers."

The tobacco workers were proletarians who, like many other workers, organized in their interests *as workers* to guarantee or improve wages and conditions of work and claim benefits for themselves. They acted in a decisively proactive mode. These women at times called for maternity leave but, interestingly enough, they never objected to unequal pay for women workers (Colin, 1975: 46). The large scale of their industry, which grouped many women together, the skill and security of their jobs, the segregation of women in certain jobs and units and collaborative work teams promoted association. The tobacco workers developed organization in female or predominantly female groups. Theirs was one of the few unions in which women were a substantial proportion of the leadership. (There were 13 women out of 21 delegates to the trade union congress in 1891; this proportion declined thereafter, but it was high again after 1910, with 24 female delegates out of 49 in 1913. The tobacco workers' unions had much higher proportionate women's membership and female leadership than did textile unions.) This level of female association with other women in work and organization contributed also to the strong individualism seen in some tobacco workers' public statements. Marie Jay, of the Marseilles union, spoke thus (Colin, 1975: 42) at the union congress of 1892: "No matter what her physical characteristics, a women must not be considered a slave or a servant; she must achieve her independence by her own work." Jay, along with other working women, did not see the legal provisions of the civil code, which assigned a woman's wages to her husband, as a serious issue. In everyday life in the popular classes, a woman's wage most likely was not spent for her personal needs; rather, her earnings went into a family wage pot to be allocated for family needs. The proletarian wife, who spent most of the family's earnings on necessities, was little concerned about her husband's claim on her wages, except when he appropriated them unfairly for his own leisure or drink.

Collective action by women tobacco workers was both more common and more effective than that of other women workers. The interest they were defending and the rights they were claiming were those of skilled wage earners who were incidentally women. The form of their association, the union, and the form of their collective action, the strike, were those developed in contemporary industrial struggles.

FRENCH WOMEN'S INTERESTS AND FEMINISM

This *tour de France* of women's collective action has shown how women participated when their interests were involved and when opportunity or need to defend old rights or make new claims for these interests occurred. French-women's collective action was linked to their class position, to their role in the productive process, to their consumer role in the household division of labor, and to their involvement in community or formal associations.

We return to the Parisian feminists to ask again when and how other women's interests intersected with the feminist program. Women in peasant and artisan households earned influence in the household through their contribution to the common economic enterprise. They played their part in the household division of labor. Public, formal political involvement of the household unit was by way of its head. To the feminists, this was an abomination; to the peasant wife, this reflected her husband's public responsibility for the household as an agricultural production unit, as a taxpaying unit, as a contributor of young men to military conscription. Each person in the household contributed to family goals by doing his or her work. This is illustrated by the enormous effort on the part of all household members that went into saving the cash that would rent or buy an extra field or buy a substitute for military service for the son of the family needed on the farm (Guillaumin, 1919). Peasant and artisan women, working members of a household productive unit, most often acted in the interest of the unit rather than themselves as individuals with autonomous needs.

Wives in the industrial households, where wage earning was the male's activity, also had little chance to develop concepts of themselves with individual needs. These women lived in households where activities were highly differentiated but in which both husband's and wife's activities were crucial and mutually respected. Control over property was simply not an issue in these households; nor, usually, was control over the intermittent wages a wife might earn. If a woman did do wage work, it was likely to be because of great need; her wage then went for necessities. At other times, she was needed in the management of the household, childbearing and child rearing, and saving through sacrifice of her own time.

Women who were themselves skilled workers and who maintained wage work commitments over their lifetimes, like the tobacco workers or primary school teachers, in practice usually chose to work within the labor unions rather than to reach across class lines to feminist women of another class. However, these women workers were the only group among those examined here whose position and interest offered something of a choice of strategies for collective action. Continuing verbal opposition of some male skilled workers, such as printers, to women as competitors and continuing ideological commitment of male industrial workers to the concept of strict household division of labor gave some organized women workers pause. These were the women with a lifelong career, not the young, unmarried women who were working at one stage of their lives who would later marry and do wage work only intermittently.

A teacher militant (quoted in Albistur and Armogathe, 1977: 362; see also Hunt, 1978) wrote in 1913,

> The class struggle will be effectively carried on only if there is absolute agreement between men and women marching to the attack against the privilege of their bosses; this will come about when both receive the same education, when they have the same rights, when they treat each other as comrades, friends, and equals.

Hélène Brion, also a teacher, went much further: "Women are still more exploited by males than they are as producers exploited by capital" (quoted in Albistur and Armogathe, 1977: 363). Brion argued that class-based organizations, such as unions, in no way protected women in their everyday family relationships. Any feminist-worker alliance was sure to be uncertain because of the areas in which interests did not coincide, as Sowerwine (1978: 75-80, passim) has shown. The 1900 Congress on Women's Rights, planned by Marguerite Durand, first showed how little the bourgeois feminists knew about working women. Durand recruited women workers in 1901 for a printing firm whose male workers were on strike, thus opening herself to accusations of dividing the working class. In 1907, she presided, as government-appointed head of the Office of Women Workers, over a congress on women's work (Colin, 1975: 44). Women unionists who attended were offended by the condescension of the invitation they had received and of the feminist speakers. One Mme. Roques, a unionist, noted, ironically, "Comrades, mesdames, we have the good luck of having the bourgeois women come ask us what we think." She ended by accusing the feminists of being "handmaidens of Capital." On the other hand, socialist and union women were unable (unwilling?) to build feminist issues into their organizations (See Sowerwine, 1978: 85-168). Some women teachers opposed the tentative alliance of one of their groups with a feminist organization, the National Council of French Women, in support of suffrage. Marie Vidal of Marseilles condemned the council as bourgeois, backed by Rothschilds, welcoming teachers only because they could "be valuable when it comes to leading the people into paths favorable to the interests of capitalism" (Hunt, 1975: 83). The syndicalist schoolteachers moved away from the feminists in mutual recriminations over feminist intervention in a union disagreement, again over female printers.

The story of feminist labor unions and socialist interaction is much more complex than this brief sketch suggests. Women workers definitely benefited from feminist support and intervention in some areas. Overall, however, most working women, although they could benefit from parts of the feminist program, were reluctant to join forces with this interclass interest group. To the extent that they were integrated into the productive process—and skilled workers with career commitments were strongly so—most women chose to work within class-based organizations to define and expand their interests and rights as workers.

THE BOURGEOISIE AND FEMINISM

Under most circumstances, then, there was relatively little intersection between the interests of many groups of French women ready to defend their interests and the middle-class feminists who promoted female suffrage. But what of the bourgeoisie? Why were French feminists apparently less successful in garnering support even from women of means than were the American and the British? (No one has attempted a quantitative estimate of the proportionate numerical importance of feminist supporters in the three countries. The French were less successful politically than the other women, but that was at least partly a matter of the French political context, and not a function of the amount of support for feminism among women. A suffrage law was voted by the Chamber of Deputies in 1919 but rejected by the Senate, where a combination of anticlerical radicals, alarmed by Catholic support for suffrage, and conservatives feared the effect on the family. It is generally assumed, on impressionistic grounds, that French feminists were proportionately fewer in number than were American and British.)

Here we must examine the differences between the middle class in France and in England and the United States. In all these countries in the nineteenth century, there was increased differention between the public world of work and the private world of the household, most markedly in the upper classes. There was less involvement of middle-class women in the world of production. At the same time, more of these women were educated and had the leisure to read and talk about politics. They had occasion to develop networks of friendship and companionship in causes such as charity or moral reform movements. Women in earlier periods, due to their greater involvement in small-scale units of production, were more isolated from other women and did not act collectively in these ways. The networks middle-class women developed were voluntary; they were not built on mutual needs for assistance, as were networks among peasant or urban working-class women whose networks were more often built on family connections (see Rossi, 1974: 241-281; Cott, 1977; Smith-Rosenberg, 1975; Anderson, 1971; Young and Wilmott, 1957).

Many middle-class women, furthermore, had relatively weak class identification, little consciousness of class interest, compared to women of the working class and peasantry, for they were not personally involved in production or relations of domination and submission outside their families. It was middle-class women such as these who transformed a feminist ideology, based on universalistic concepts of equality of the sexes, into a concrete program in the national political arena.

Many French bourgeois women shared these characteristics with American and British middle-class women. They believed that women should organize to claim equality in the political sphere, an end to patriarchal authority over wives and children in the family, and access to education and jobs. The majority of these women have not been studied, although their leaders are well known; they were the demonstrators and activists in the French suffrage movement and militants in other struggles for women's rights. Their story lies outside the scope of this study, which focuses on other bourgeoises, probably in the majority, who identified their interests in very different ways from those of French or Anglo-Saxon feminists. There were at least two factors in French bourgeois women's experience which militated against feminist orientation (see Smith, 1975).

First, Frenchwomen's education and participation in charity and moral reform movements were likely to be under the auspices of the Catholic Church. Although education, privilege, and church-linked reformist activism were part of the background of British and American feminists, Catholic education and activism contributed little to participation in French feminist action, but rather in church-dominated female political associations. A French Catholic or Christian feminist review, *Feminisme chretien,* founded in 1896, editorialized in favor of women's education, women's right to work, equal pay for women, and married women's property rights. The newspaper's position, however, envisioned both education and charity rising out of women's family roles; it proposed no individual choice or autonomy, no universal claim of sexual equality. The Catholic women's suffrage movement, activated by Pope Benedict XV's endorsement, urged the vote in order to defend family interest (Hause and Kenny, 1979). Neither peasants nor workers practiced Catholicism as fervently as did the bourgeoisie, and Catholicism offered an alternative universal ideology and limited feminism for the bourgeois woman.

Second, many women of the French bourgeosie maintained connections to production through their contribution of property to the marriage and their share in family business. The marriage settlement was the crucial institution, although the importance of family-owned business also played a role. Every bourgeois daughter and wife had a stake in family property. A bourgeois woman brought wealth to the family she formed at marriage. Individual choice and autonomy were not part of this marriage system, but loyalty to the nuclear family. A large share of influence over decisions about property and children—over the future and the economic well-being of those aspects of the family—came to a bourgeois woman with marriage. A marriage that worked was an economic agreement according to the social rules of the class. That was the interest that many bourgeois wives wished to guard and protect. Protecting it meant careful management of investment and resources, having few children and raising them in a family-oriented way. Individualism could tear the fundamental unit of the family apart; with her economic stake in it, the bourgeois wife had no interest in doing any such thing. Thus, even the perceived interest (here, of course, a distinction could be made with their real interest) of many a bourgeois woman was not congruent with the farther-reaching aspects of the feminist program.

No wonder Louise Weiss, French feminist leader of the interwar years, exclaimed in despair, "Peasant women kept their mouths tightly closed when I spoke to them about the vote. Working women laughed, shopkeepers shrugged their shoulders, and the *bourgeoises* pushed away horrified" (quoted in Albistur and Armogathe, 1977: 383).

This historical overview of French women and collective action from 1870 to 1914 has shown that women were participants in group politics, whether or not they had formal political rights. Occasions for collective action were shaped by interest and organizational bases rooted in the economic and social structures in which they lived. Political relationships and contemporary repertoires determined the forms of collective action. The long- and short-run political situation provided, or denied, opportunities for action. Louise Weiss was correct that suffrage interested few French women; but the vote is only one of the ways in which people act collectively on their interests, as French women most assuredly did.

10

Conclusion

LOUISE A. TILLY

You have before you an ambitious variety of social history. The contributors to this volume have disciplinary homes in sociology, political science, and law, in addition to history. Yet they all practice structural historical analysis. Their topics fall into the twin rubrics of class conflict and collective action. The study of class conflict asks in what ways, and to what degree, classes or parts of classes act against other classes. The study of collective action focuses on a more inclusive category, the commitment of pooled resources to common ends. The authors ask to what extent modern Europeans acted together on the basis of class, and under what conditions class interests led to collective action. Those are old historical questions, and ambitious ones.

NARRATIVE OR ANALYSIS?

Historians are a contentious group of scholars; they debate method, goals, and issues vigorously even as they practice their craft. In a recent exchange about writing history, Lawrence Stone announced a revival of narrative—which he defines as "the organization of material in a chrono-logically sequential order and the focusing of the content into a single coherent story, albeit with subplots" (Stone, 1979: 2). He continues: "Many historians now believe that the culture of the group, and even the will of the individual, are potentially at least as important causal agents of change as the impersonal forces of material output and demographic growth." The revival of narrative signals the bankruptcy of "economic and/or demographic determinism."

What caused the revival of narrative? What caused the decline of analytic history? Stone suggests three causes: the "intellectual decline of Marxism" (Stone, 1979: 9); revived awareness of the centrality of questions of political power; and the paucity of significant or important findings from quantitative work, especially computer-based analyses which model or manipulate enormous quantities of data.

Yet, in quoting Carlo Ginzburg, Stone suggests some dissatisfaction with his own evaluation of the trend toward narrative:

> The quantitative and antianthropocentric approach of the sciences of nature has placed the human sciences in an unpleasant dilemma: they must either adopt a weak scientific standard so as to be able to attain significant results, or adopt a strong scientific standard to attain results of no great importance.

Is it necessary that historians choose between significant results and rigorous method? Stone's apocalyptic announcement of the "end of an era: the end of the attempt to produce a coherent scientific explanation of change in the past" (p. 9) is a dismaying abandonment of the historian's mission.

E. J. Hobsbawm, another of the pioneers of social history, published a commentary on Stone's essay. Hobsbawm questions whether there is such a swing to narrative as Stone suggests. He argues that the changes in historical presentation embodied in the "new narrative" are most often efforts to present the *results* of complex historical analysis in new ways rather than new ways of performing historical analysis. Today's historians, Hobsbawm believes, use narrative in writing "which embodies and exemplifies the stratified structure of a society but concentrates . . . on the complexities and interconnections of real history, rather than with the study of the structure itself" (Hobsbawm, 1980: 7). Hobsbawm concludes that "it is possible to explain much of what he [Stone] surveys as the continuation of past historical enterprises by other means" (p. 8)—an elaboration of the historian's craft.

Thus, Stone's irritable disillusionment is countered by Hobsbawm's optimism. Yet Stone is not alone in his criticism; some of his irritation is mirrored by other historians. The structural analysts and quantifiers may have oversold themselves on the explanatory powers of the social sciences. They have not realized that these disciplines are more effective in specifying what has to be explained and in ruling out superficial explanations than in producing explanations that could satisfy the average historian. Although they have produced and analyzed much new data, they have not been as successful in interpreting their findings to their fellow historians. Structural studies which "take up new subjects, materials [and] methods [need to show] how the results bear on questions about which other historians already care" (C. Tilly, 1980b).

"WHY" QUESTIONS

Lawrence Stone puts forward a demanding agenda for structural historians when he provides examples of the big "why" questions, as he calls them, "the causes of 'great revolutions' or the shifts from feudalism to capitalism" (Stone, 1979: 7, 9). The essays in this volume report studies in search of answers of these and similar "why" questions; their authors proceed in systematic ways, by different methods and with different styles, to rephrase and specify the questions, amass appropriate evidence, and apply "reflection disciplined by theory" (C. Tilly, 1980b).

The essays by Charles Tilly and Wayne Te Brake address the central eighteenth-century meaning of the great revolution, or its absence. They agree on several important points. The Dutch Revolution, the American Revolution, and the Wilkite collective action (which never became a revolution) all incorporated principled challenges to oligarchical indirect rule. These challenges to perceived injustice were not disinterested but were firmly rooted in the collective interests of those who made them: on one hand, the urban commercial and manufacturing populations of cities like London or Charleston, South Carolina, and, on the other, rural inhabitants of Bathmen whose livelihood was being undermined by large landowners enclosing common lands. Both C. Tilly and Te Brake show that collective action in periods of extraordinary ferment, such as the Wilkite or Stamp Act agitation or the Dutch Revolution, were often a continuation of past politics and an acceleration or increase in scale of old disputes. The new context enflamed familiar issues. Conceptualization of revolution as a sharp break in political process suggests otherwise. C. Tilly and Te Brake show that the revolutionary process embodies some continuity; the revolutionary *outcome* is the sharp break. The revolutionary libertarian political challenge in the Netherlands and Britain and its North American colonies successfully destroyed the legitimacy of corporate claims. It opened the way for concentration of power in national states and eventually formalized electoral and interest group politics.

These chapters answer the question of the causes of revolutions by showing how revolution grows out of everyday political struggles on the local level; how these struggles interact with events at the political center and become integral to the revolutionary process.

The political process of concentration of power in national states and their institutions was accompanied by capital concentration consequent to the development of industrial capitalism. Although they do not go back to the transition from feudalism to capitalism, Munger, Brown, Cohn, Reardon, and Frader all examine major transitions of the establishment of industrial capitalism in different settings. Rather than placing political revolution at the center, they focus on specific cases of popular contention—primarily strikes and demonstrations—which accompanied these transitions. A picture emerges of principled, purposeful popular action within a context of economic concentration, proletarianization, ethnic rivalry, and competing ideologies. Contention was no simple reaction to misery or disequilibration; it was an integral part of political process shaped by changing economic structures.

Louise Tilly's essay provides another overarching comparison, that of differences and likenesses in collective action by sex. Her focus, as elsewhere in the volume, is on interests: Women's interests vary in systematic ways which grow out of their structural position, in addition to whatever common interests they have based on their sex. She moves the problem of understanding the intersection of politics and economics out of the public sphere and into the family in order to clarify women's collective action. Women were by no means passive bystanders, but actors in economic and political struggles. Their patterns of participation were different from those of men because women's interests often were more defined by a combination of individual socioeconomic structural position and family position and their action shaped by household division of labor.

In addressing these "why" questions, then, the authors of this volume all take the politics of ordinary people seriously. They see the form of collective action, as well as its intersection with large-scale structural change, as problematic. Ideology is a subject of inquiry; it is not assumed.

The variation in specific groups' participation in different forms of collective action over time and space becomes salient, as opposed to levels of action in broad evolutionary schemes at the level of a society or a national state.

METHOD, STYLE, AND ISSUES

Styles of presentation vary. The two Tilly essays use narrative extensively to forward systematic analysis. In these essays, the description of events prompts questions and points up contrasts. They range widely in space for their examples and examine long periods to illuminate large-scale structural changes and the consequences for collective action. Munger introduces his essay with a narrative of sharply contrasting events, then moves on to quantitative analysis. The other studies are organized and written in a more purely analytic style. Hobsbawm's position, rather than Stone's, more accurately describes the practice of this group of social historians.

The essays vary considerably in other aspects of style. There are three local case studies which examine aspects of change in a community setting. There are two regional comparisons of the same region, Lancashire, but with different time perspectives. Munger compares not only cross-sectionally but over a long time period; Brown concentrates on the geographic variation of events in one year. Cohn has written a case study of an industry in a short period; his findings report an ingenious analysis of limited sources. Most of the authors use quantification when appropriate to test alternative explanations or study differences in structural position of occupations, ethnic groups, or the two sexes. Most often, however, the statistics are descriptive rather than analytic, and the papers (C. Tilly and L. Tilly) that take the longest chronological perspective and broadest geographic frameworks eschew it all together. Analytic quantification tests carefully specified theories for Brown, Cohn, and Munger. Case study, comparison over long time periods and over space, quantification, narrative: The historical methods represented here are several. The authors have not moved in methodological lockstep but have chosen methods of analysis and presentation appropriate to their questions.

Within the general rubrics of the "why" questions, the authors of this volume discuss a series of common issues. Such problems as changing forms of collective action, the role of repression, occupational variation in collective action, the significance of ethnic divisions, and the role of ideology emerge over and over in the essays.

FORMS OF COLLECTIVE ACTION

Typical forms of collective action change over time, with several forms clustered together in each period. The studies in this volume dispute the belief that increased *levels* of contention are a response to disequilibrating effects of rapid social or economic change. They draw attention instead to disputes surrounding changes in the *forms* of contention.

One of the main thrusts of C. Tilly's contribution is that the "rich, varied, expressive, and purposeful" vocabulary and typical forms of action rise from the setting of both revolution and lesser events: the eighteenth-century city, its distinctive economic activities, its social relation and public routines. These aspects of urban life were informed by the commonly accepted concept of corporate collective rights which authorities were expected to respect. The same kind of corporate identity, rights, and obligations attached to the Dutch rural community, or *mark,* as described by Te Brake. Even as they report on the continuity of eighteenth-century forms of collective action, both C. Tilly and Te Brake identify forms of action and groups which would become predominant in the nineteenth century. The spread of capitalist property relations was undermining the assumptions of corporatism, and noncorporate special interest groups were emerging and acting collectively.

Frank Munger, whose time period also spans the turn of the century, likewise identifies a change in form of contention. Munger identifies a permanent and dramatic shift in the issues of contention from those concerning community claims on food supply, embodied in the form of the food riot, to those concerning control over conditions of work. Much of this discussion concerns the struggle over the form that disputes over workers' rights should take. At first, elements of the Lancashire working class mobilized to petition Parliament through the demonstration of which "Peterloo" is the outstanding example. This was followed by a shift to more narrowly economic forms of conflict—strikes. (Strikes, of course, had political meaning and import, as Brown's essay demonstrates so clearly.)

Issues of commodity supply disappeared in Lancashire in Munger's period, but the issues crop up again in later periods, as L. Tilly and Frader, for example, note for France in 1911. Although the issues reappear, the form of collective action against high prices changed. In 1911, French protesters made no corporate claims of the sort made in the Lancashire potato riot of 1800. Rather, they staged political demonstrations which sometimes offered the occasion to play out personal grudges. Munger shows that the disappearance of the food riot in early nineteenth-century Lancashire and the eventual emergence of the strike as a preferred form of collective action were the result of dialectical interactions among new interests (those of wage earners in industrial capitalist production), demographic change (urbanization), and state repression.

In his study of Lancashire in 1842, Brian Brown shows how limited and problematic strikes could be without political democracy for workers. By this period, both strike and demonstration were established forms of working-class contention. The emphasis must be that they were forms of *contention,* of deploying resources and making claims, not that they were fully legal or ordinarily successful. Brown closes his essay with an illuminating discussion of the "turnout." This is the march of striking workers from factory to factory, an attempt to enforce strike solidarity. The turnout is a familiar elaboration of the strike in the early history of worker collective action in other nations and other periods, from Lowell, Massachusetts, in the 1840s, to Milan in 1898 (Dublin, 1979; L. Tilly, 1972).

Brown joins Munger in showing how often working-class action was directed against fellow workers—a stage, he argues, in the development of the strike form. The central struggle was between the liberal state's effort to protect nonstrikers' "right-to-work" and striking workers' efforts to enforce worker solidarity. Munger and Brown argue that labor power itself was the object of contention, for it was the only significant "sociopolitical resource" of workers, a resource that workers claimed the right to control themselves. This claim is a manifestation of the interest of the working class in its reproduction, an issue currently under debate by scholars of women's and family history (Humphries, 1977).

By the end of the nineteenth century in France, the strike was the preferred form of urban and rural work place collective action, as Frader and Reardon show. Louise Tilly, in turn, notes the set of conditions under which women workers were more likely to strike. She shows also how workers' wives sometimes supported strikes with their own demonstrations or picketing. Coal miners' wives, living in households with a strictly defined division of labor, participated in working-class collective action about the conditions of work and the sale of *men's* (their husbands' and sons') labor power. On the other hand, women's action in individual sex-based interest was limited by wives' material interest in maintaining a household, whether as productive unit (peasant farms), a unit dependent on shared wages (the proletarian family), or an economic alliance for holding and transmitting property (the bourgeois family). Women's collective action, though more decisively shaped by their household position than that of men, nevertheless took the typical nineteenth-century forms.

OCCUPATIONAL VARIATION

The timing of participation in collective action varied in patterned ways among occupational or social groupings. Te Brake shows that it was primarily the smallholders of Bathmen who fought the defensive battle against enclosure and later joined the Dutch Patriot Revolution against the urban oligarchs. They lost both struggles. Munger demonstrates the uneven effects of the early Industrial Revolution on various categories of workers and similarly patterned consequences for their collective action. His systematic comparisons of contentious gatherings show that factory spinners were in the forefront of the early textile strikes in Lancashire. The scale of their work place—industrialized spinning mills—favored their mobilization; changes in the organization of work provided them with grievances. In her discussion of forms of collective action related to the proletarian condition, Frader shows that vineyard strikes were typical of wage-earning vineyard workers. These workers eschewed the electoral socialism of small producers of Languedoc in the same period. In 1907, however, Coursan's syndicalist workers joined the regional interclass front which gathered to defend the viticulture of the Midi. When the front was broken, most Coursan workers returned to class-based syndicalist work place action. Their proletarianization was a major factor in their largely independent course, their faithfulness to strike tactics, and their distrust of party and parliament.

REPRESSION

Forms of collective action were not shaped merely by structural factors; repression also played its part. Te Brake shows that the corporate defense of their communal rights by Bathmen smallholders was repressed by state forces. Munger argues that the food riot disappeared in Lancashire as the corporate vision, and reality, of community interest dissolved and as law and repressive policy increased the costs for food rioters and reduced the freedom of local officials to respond. Working-class public petitioning was bloodily rejected as a legitimate form of contention at "Peterloo."

State repression of the more overly political challenges forced working-class collective action into the narrow form of the strike.

When, as Brown shows for the turnouts of 1842, the economic program of strikes and political program of the People's Charter merged, military repression was launched by royal proclamation. The result was a short-circuit of collective action and the process of class formation, a massive demobilization. Brown argues that the Chartist strategy of placing the democratization of the state high on the working-class agenda, if successful, would have provided a necessary condition for working-class formation. Until that condition was obtained, state repression regularly followed worker mobilization and action.

In France, state support of employer intransigence to workers' claims extended well beyond the period (1848) when democratic political participation in the form of universal manhood suffrage was permitted. The use of force against strikers, food protesters, and demonstrators is amply illustrated in L. Tilly's article examining the first 30 years of the French Third Republic. Forceful repression reappeared in England in the decade before World War I. Working-class victories and legitimation of strikes were not a necessary prelude to regularization of working-class access to state institutions. In turn, democratization did not end state or employer efforts to limit strikers' tactics and frequent use of state repression in the interest of employers.

ETHNIC DIVISIONS

Less strictly repressive employer efforts to control their work force are discussed by Cohn and Reardon. Sam Cohn presents another view of the complex interaction between worker and employer interest in a systematic comparison of variations in work discipline among British railway construction crews. This essay differs from the others in this volume in that it concerns not worker collective action but employer disciplinary policy. The question is whether discipline varies inversely with worker bargaining strength. His analysis shows that long pay and truck were more common in the north of England railway construction sites. Cohn suggests that native workers were slow to mobilize and unsuccessful in strikes in the North because of the competition of Irish workers; successful strikes and labor militance were positively correlated with geographic areas where there were few Irish. Cohn has established an interesting set of links among labor discipline, labor militance, and ethnic divisions in a particular industry in which extramural disciplinary schemes were common employer strategies. His labor strength argument, with its implications for possible "preventive disarming" of worker contention in cases of ethnic rivalry, needs to be tested in other situations. As he notes, variations in discipline may not be comparable across industries or across long periods of time because too many factors come into play. Among these are skill, opportunities for building solidarity, the legal status of unions and strikes, and the relative strength of labor in national politics.

Judy Reardon's study of French and Belgian workers in nineteenth-century Roubaix, the French textile city, starts with the question with which Cohn ends: Do ethnic rivalries act as an effective curb on labor militance? In Roubaix there were relatively few incidents of overt conflict between immigrant Belgian and French workers. Nevertheless, Reardon shows that in 1872 and later, the two groups lived and worked in separate spheres. Belgian workers were vulnerable by virtue of their structural position, just as Cohn shows Irish workers were vulnerable. Irish and Belgians both share this characteristic with immigrant workers in other nations and other periods. When the workers of Roubaix mobilized to act collectively in 1880 and later, the factors which promoted this mobilization—concentration of workers in large production units, a densely populated political community in which working-class and socialist culture and ideology flourished—outweighed ethnic divisions, at least temporarily. Ethnic isolation and segregation, however, did not disappear. The growth of unions and the rise of militance did not end ethnic divisions but proceeded alongside them.

Here Cohn's suggestion is relevant: In practice, class coalitions cannot overcome structural vulnerability on the part of some groups of workers. Were the incomplete and temporary victories of Roubaix unions the consequence of employers' ability to hire Belgians? To answer this question would require much more detailed information about hiring at the level of the shop; such data are simply not available. What is known is that antagonism flared even as mobilization proceeded. The factors which facilitated working-class mobilization, many of them linked to national conditions, were more powerful—at least for a time—than ethnic division. Labor strength—to the extent of overcoming ethnic divisions—is connected with historic circumstances such as the strength and maturity of a working class and trade cycles, as well as the competitive position of an industry and organization of work within that industry.

IDEOLOGY

The links of ideology and collective action are addressed in the essays by Brown, Frader, Reardon, and L. Tilly. Brown emphasizes the popular democratic political program to which the Lancashire working class was committed in addition to its work place economic claims. Frader insists on the appropriateness of syndicalist ideology and practice of vineyard wage workers, skilled and accustomed to teamwork. Their rejection of party-based parliamentary action went so far as widespread abstention from voting. Frader's syndicalist militants seem to have become more conscious of common interests with women workers and worked in coalition with them more readily than did socialists, whose base was male skilled workers. The socialist culture of Roubaisien textile workers was a male culture from which women were most often excluded. Socialist ideology emphasized international class solidarity, but it did not make it easy for women to move into party or union hierarchies. Women's cooperation might be welcome in some strikes; in others alleged substitution of women workers for men was an object of the strike. The uneasy relationship between feminist ideology, largely couched in terms of middle-class women's issues, and working-class women's collective action is discussed by Louise Tilly. Class, ethnic, and sex divisions were hard to reconcile in ideology or practice, except in short-term, narrowly focused struggles.

CONCLUSION

The studies of collective action in this volume start from a commitment to take ordinary people's politics seriously, to examine the logic and rationality of such action on its own terms. The authors think politically about events which have often been seen in social-psychological or narrowly economic perspectives. They have located their studies in time and space, and they temper and test theory with the complexity of history. The abundant data they put forward support several fundamental generalizations about the history of collective action and the transition to industrial capitalism. Large-scale structural change—capital concentration, the growth of wage labor, and the centralization and bureaucratization of states—undermined and eventually destroyed old bases for action (the corporate community, the household) and replaced them with new ones (the factory, the differentiated city) in which new interests were identified and new forms of action were taken. Formal organization, special interest groups, and centralization of popular politics were the result. Forms of collective action have changed in patterned ways along with the politically mediated consequences of shifting economic structures.

Traditional political history defined the triumph of bourgeois politics as the core of history; the study of class conflict gives the opposition to bourgeois domination its due and shows in what ways the outcome was contingent and problematic; the study of collective action views class conflict in historically particular cases and, at the same time, in a wide comparative perspective of variation in time, space, and form. This is our contribution to that history of the working class Barrinton Moore saw emerging.

REFERENCES

ADER, P. (1905) "La Grève générale des travailleurs agricoles du Midi." Mouvement Socialiste 147 (15 Janvier).

ALBISTUR, M. and D. ARMOGATHE (1977) Histoire du féminisme français du moyen âge à nos jours. Paris: Éditions des femmes.

ANDERSON, M. (1971) Family structure in nineteenth century Lancashire. Cambridge: Cambridge University Press.

ANTHOINE, M.-E. (1878) L'instruction primaire dans le département du Nord, 1868-1877. Lille: Robbe.

AUGÉ-LARIBÉ, M. (1903) "Les ouvriers de la Viticulture languedociènne et Leurs Syndicats." Musée Social: 265-328.

––– (1907) Le Problème Agraire du Socialisme. Paris: Giard et Brière.

BAGWELL, P. (1974) Transport Revolution from 1770. London: Clowes.

BAIROCH, P. (1965) "Niveaux de développement economique de 1810 à 1910." Annales: Economies, Sociétés, Civilisations 20 (November-December): 1091-1117.

BAKER, R. P. (1966) "A regional study of working-class organization in France: socialism in the Nord, 1870-1924." Ph.D. dissertation, Stanford University. (unpublished)

BARBUT, G. (1913) Etude sur le Vignoble de l'Aude. Carcassonne: Polère.

BARRAL, J. A. (1882) Conférence sur le Phylloxéra, faite le 1er avril 1882. Paris: Tremblay.

BARRAL, P. (1968) Les Agrariens français de Méline à Pisani. Paris: A. Colin.

BERCÉ, Y.-M. (1974) Croquants et Nu-Pieds. Les soulèvements paysans en France du XVIe au XIXe siecle. Paris: Gallimard/Julliard Series "Archives."

BLAADJE zonder titel voor burger en boer in Overijssel. (1785) No. 8 (3 November) Deventer: G. Brouwer.

BLANCHARD, R. (1906) La Flandre: Etude géographique de la plaine flamande en France, Belgique et Hollande. Dunkirk: Société dunkerquoise pour l'avancement des lettres, des sciences et des arts.

de BODEM van Nederland (1965) Wageningen: Stichting voor Bodem-Kartering.

BOHSTEDT, J. (1972) "Riots in England 1790-1810, with special reference to Devonshire." Ph.D. dissertation, Harvard University. (unpublished)

BONNET, S. avec la collaboration E. de KAGEN et M. MAIGRET (1976-1977) L'homme du fer. Volumes I and II. Nancy: Centre Lorrain d'Etudes Sociologiques.

BOSERUP, E. (1965) The Conditions of Agricultural Growth. Chicago: AVC.

BREWER, J. (1976) Party Ideology and Popular Politics at the Accession of George III. Cambridge: Cambridge University Press.

B[ROCHER], V. (1976) Souvenirs d'une morte vivante. Paris. Maspéro.

BROWN, B. (1979) "Lancashire Chartism and the mass strike of 1842: the political economy of working class contention." Working Paper No. 203. Center for Research on Social Organization, University of Michigan.

BYTHELL, D. (1969) The Handloom Weavers: A Study in the English Cotton Industry During the Industrial Revolution. Cambridge: Cambridge University Press.

CHALONER, W. H. (1950) Social and economic history of Crewe. Cambridge: Cambridge University Press.

Chambre de Commerce de Roubaix (1891) Archives. Roubaix: Reboux.

CHAPMAN, S. J. (1904) The Lancashire Cotton Industry: A Study in Economic Development. Manchester: Manchester University Press.

CHATELAIN, A. (1976) Les Migrants temporaires en France de 1800 à 1914, 2 vols. Lille: Publications de l'Université de Lille.

CLAPHAM, J. H. (1926-1938) An Economic History of Modern Britain. Cambridge: Cambridge University Press.

——— (1930) Economic History of Modern Britain: Early Railway Age 1820-50. Cambridge: Cambridge University Press.

CLARK, G. K. (1962) The Making of Victorian England. New York: Atheneum.

COLE, G.D.H. (1932) A Short History of the British Working Class Movement 1789-1927. London: George Allen and Unwin.

——— and R. POSTGATE (1961) The British People, 1746-1946. London: Methuen/ University Paperbacks.

COLEMAN, T. (1965) Railway Navvies. New York: Hutchinson.

COLENBRANDER, H. T. (1897-1899) De Patriottentijd, hoofdzakelijk naar buiten-landsche bescheiden, 3 volumes. 's Gravenhage: M. Nijhoff.

COLIN, M. (1975) Ce n'est pas d'aujourd'hui. Femmes, syndicats, luttes de classe. Paris: Éditions sociales.

COLQUHOUN, P. (1788) An Important Crisis in the Calico and Muslin Manufactory in Great Britain, Explained. London.

CONDEVAUX, J. (1928) Le mineur du Nord et du Pas-de-Calais. Sa psychologie, ses rapports avec le patronat. Lille: Danel.

COÖRNAERT, E. (1970) La Flandre française de langue flamande. Paris: Éditions ouvrières.

COSTE-FLORET, P. (1898) Le Travail au Vignoble. Paris: Masson.

COTT, N. (1977) The Bonds of Womanhood: Women's Sphere in New England, 1780-1835. New Haven, CT: Yale University Press.

DANIELS, G. W. (1930) "Samuel Crompton's census of the cotton industry in 1812." Economic Journal (Economic History Supplement) 2 (January): 108-111.

DANSON, J. T., and T. A. WELTON (Parts 1-3, 1856-1857; 1857-1858; 1858-1859) "On the population of Lancashire and Cheshire and its local distribution during the fifty years 1801-51." Transactions. Historic Society of Lancashire and Cheshire, 9: 195-212; 10: 1-36; 11: 31-70.

DARVALL, F. O. (1934) Popular Disturbances and Public Order in Regency England. London: Oxford University Press.

DAUMARD, A. (1963) La bourgeoisie parisienne de 1815 à 1848. Paris: SEVPEN.

DELCOURT, R. (1906) De la condition des ouvriers dans les mines du Nord et du Pas-de-Calais. Paris: Giard et Brière.

DELORY, G. (1921) Aperçu historique sur la Fédération du Nord du Parti Socialiste (1876-1920). Lille: Dhoossche.

De VRIES, J. (1974) The Dutch Rural Economy in the Golden Age. New Haven, CT: Yale University Press.

Direction du Travail (1911) Annuaire des syndicats professionnels: industriels, commerciaux et agricoles. Paris: Imprimerie nationale.

——— (1889) Associations professionelles ouvrières. I. Paris: Imprimerie nationale.

DONNELLY, F. K. (1976) "Ideology and early English working-class history: Edward Thompson and his critics." Social History 2 (May): 219-238.

DUBLIN, T. (1979) Women at Work: The Transformation of Work and Community in Lowell, Massachusetts, 1826-1860. New York: Columbia University Press.

DUMBAR, G. (1732-1788) Het Kerkelyk en wereltlyk Deventer, 2 vols. Deventer: H.W. van Welbergen.

DUPAQUIER, J., M. LACHIVER, and J. MEUVRET (1968) Mercuriales du pays de France et du Vexin français (1640-1792). Paris: SEVPEN.

EDWARDS, R. (1979) Contested Terrain: Transformation of the Workplace in the Twentieth Century. New York: Basic Books.

Égalité de Roubaix-Tourcoing (1898, 1904) Roubaix.

ÉGRET, J. (1962) La pré-révolution française. Paris: Presses Universitaires de France.

ELIAS, N. (1974) "Toward a theory of communities" in C. Bell and H. Newby (eds.), The Sociology of Community: A Selection of Readings. London: Frank Cass.

ELLISON, T. (1886) The Cotton Trade of Great Britain. London: Wilson.

ENGELS, F. (1973) The Condition of the Working-Class in England. Moscow: Progress.

FABER, J. (1972) Drie eeuwen Friesland, 2 vols. Wageningen: A.A.G. Bijdragen, No. 17.

——— et al. (1965) Population Changes and Economic Development in the Netherlands. Wageningen: A.A.G. Bijdragen, No. 12.

FARNIE, D. A. (1979) The English Cotton Industry and the World Market, 1815-1896. New York: Oxford University Press.

FTAM [Federation des Travailleurs agricoles du Midi] (1903) Compte Rendu du Ier Congrès national des Travailleurs agricoles du Midi et partis similaires. Béziers: Imprimerie J. Perdrault.

——— (1904) Compte Rendu du IIe Congrès, 1904, Narbonne: Boulet.

——— (1906a) Compte Rendu du IIIe Congrès, 1905. Perpignan: Muller.

——— (1906b) Comte Rendu du IVe Congrès, 1906. Paris: Maison des Fédérations, Service de l'Imprimerie.

——— (1907) Compte Rendu du Ve Congrès, 1907. Béziers: Imprimerie des ouvriers de Centre des Ouvriers syndiqués et fédérés.

——— (1909) Compte Rendu du VIe Congrès, 1908. Montpellier: Imprimerie coopérative ouvrière.

FLONNEAU, J. M. (1970) "Crise de vie chère et mouvement syndical, 1910-1914." Le Mouvement Social, 72 (July-September): 49-81.

FOHLEN, C. (1956) L'industrie textile au temps du Second Empire. Paris: Plon.

——— (1973) "The Industrial Revolution in France, 1700-1914," pp. 7-75 in C. Cipolla (ed.), The Emergence of Industrial Societies, vol. 1. London: Collins/Fontana.

FORMSMA, W. J. (1948) "Vormen van bestuur ten plattelande in de noordoostelijke provincies voor 1795." Bijdragen voor de Geschiedenis der Nederlanden, vol. 3.

FOSTER, J. (1974) Class Struggle and the Industrial Revolution: Early Industrial Capitalism in Three English Towns. London: Weidenfeld and Nicolson.

FRADER, L. L. (1978) "The working class in the wine industry of lower Languedoc: Coursan, 1850-1914." Ph.D. dissertation, University of Rochester. (unpublished)

France, Direction du Travail (1905) Statistique des Grèves et des recours à la Conciliation et à l'arbitrage survenus pendant l'année 1904. Paris: Imprimerie nationale.

FRANCHOMME, G. (1960) "Roubaix de 1870 à 1900." Thesis for the Diplôme d'études supérieures, University of Lille.

――― (1969) "L'evolution démographique et économique de Roubaix de 1870 à 1900." Revue du Nord 51 (April-June): 201-247.

FRANCIS, J. (1851) History of English Railways. London: Longman, Green and Longman.

FRANKLIN, B. (1972) The Papers of Benjamin Franklin (W. B. Wilcox, ed.). Volume 15, January 1 through December 31, 1768. New Haven: CT: Yale University Press.

GARIDOU, J. F. (1968) "La Viticulture audoise, 1870-1913." Travail d'Études et Recherches, Faculté des Lettres de Montpellier. (unpublished)

GARRATY, J. (1978) Unemployment in History. New York: Harper & Row.

GASH, N. (1979) Aristocracy and People. Britain 1815-1865. Cambridge: Harvard University Press.

GAYER, A. D., W. W. ROSTOW, and A. J. SCHWARTZ (1953) The Growth and Fluctuation of the British Economy, 1790-1850, 2 vols. Oxford: Clarendon.

GERVAIS, C. (1903) L'Indicateur des Vignobles Méridionaux. Montpellier: Firmin, Montagne et Sicardi.

GEYL, P. (1947) De Patriotten-beweging, 1780-1787. Amsterdam: P.N. van Kampen.

GIDDENS, A. (1975) The Class Structure of the Advanced Societies. New York: Harper & Row.

GIDE, C. (1907) "La Crise de Vin dans le Midi de la France." Revue d'Économie politique XXI (July): 481-512.

GILES, P. M. (1959) "The felt-hatting industry, c. 1500-1850 with particular reference to Lancashire and Cheshire." Transactions of the Lancashire and Cheshire Antiquarian Society 69: 104-124.

GOBLET, A. (1903) Le peignage de la laine à Roubaix-Tourcoing et son évolution économique et sociale. Lille: Tricot.

de GRAFF, J. (1946) "Sallandsche Markedagen." Verslagen en Mededelingen betreffende Overijsselsch Recht en Geschiedenis 60: 52-60.

GRATTON, P. (1971) La Lutte de Classes dans les Campagnes. Paris: Éditions Anthropos.

Great Britain, Parliament (1830) Report of the Select Committee to Consider Means of Lessening Evils Due to Fluctuations in Employment in the Manufacturing Districts. Parliamentary Papers, X, 221.

――― (1835) "Reports of factory inspectors." Parliamentary Papers, XL, pp. 689-704.

GUILBERT, M. (1966) Les femmes et l'organisation syndicale avant 1914. Paris: CNRS.

GUILLAUMIN, E. (1919) The life of a simple man (M. Holden, trans.). London: Selwyn and Blount.

GURR, T. R. (1969) Why Men Rebel. Princeton: Princeton University Press.

GUSFIELD, J. (1963) Symbolic Crusade. Status Politics and the American Temperance Movement. Urbana: University of Illinois Press.

HAMMOND, J. L. and B. HAMMOND (1970) The Skilled Laborer, 1760-1832. New York: Harper & Row.

HANDLEY, J. E. (1970) Navvy in Scotland. Cork: Cork University Press.

HANSON, P. R. (1976) "The 'vie chère' protests in France, 1911." (unpublished)

HAUSE, S. C. (1977) "The rejection of women's suffrage by the French Senate in November, 1922: a statistical analysis." Third Republic/Troisieme République 3-4: 205-237.

––– and A. R. KENNY (1979) "The development of the Catholic women's suffrage movement in France, 1896-1922." (unpublished)

HAY, D. et al. (1975) Albion's Fatal Tree: Crime and Society in Eighteenth-Century England. New York: Pantheon.

HECHTER, M. (1976) "Ethnicity and industrialization: on the proliferation of the cultural division of labor." Ethnicity 3 (September): 214-224.

HELPS, A. (1874) Life and Labours of Mr. Brassey, 1805-70. Boston: Roberts.

HILAIRE, Y.-M. (1966) "Les ouvriers de la région du Nord devant l'église catholique (XIXe et XXe siècles)." Le Mouvement Social 57 (October-December): 181-201.

HILL, C. (1969) Reformation to Industrial Revolution. London: Weidenfeld and Nicolson.

HILTON, G. (1960) Truck System. Cambridge: Heffer.

HOBSBAWM, E. J. (1959) Primitive rebels. Studies in Archaic Forms of Social Movements in the Nineteenth and Twentieth Centuries. Manchester: Manchester University Press.

––– (1964) Labouring Men: Studies in the History of Labour. London: Weidenfeld and Nicolson.

––– (1971) "From social history to the history of society." Daedalus 100 (Winter): 20-45.

––– (1980) "The revival of narrative: some comments." Past and Present 86 (February): 3-8.

HOERDER, D. (1977) Crowd Action in Revolutionary Massachusetts, 1765-1780. New York: Academic Press.

van HULZEN, A. (1966) Utrecht in de Patriottentijd. Zalt bommel, The Netherlands: Europese Bibliotheek.

HUMPHRIES, J. (1977) "The working class family, women's liberation, and class struggle: the case of nineteenth century British history." Review of Radical Political Economics 9 (Fall): 25-41.

HUNT, L. A. (1978) Revolution and Urban Politics in Provincial France: Troyes and Reims, 1786-1790. Stanford: Stanford University Press.

JACQUEMYNS, G. (1929) Histoire de la crise économique des Flandres (1845-1850). Brussels: M. Lamertin.

Journal de Roubaix (1892, 1904) Roubaix.

JUDT, T. (1979) Socialism in Provence 1871-1914. A Study in the Origins of the Modern French Left. Cambridge: Cambridge University Press.

KELSALL, R. K. (1938) Wage Regulation under the Statue of Artificers. London: Methuen.

KRONENBERG, H. (1921) "Schepenen, Raden, en Gezworen Gemeente te Deventer." Verslagen en Mededelingen betreffende Overijsselsch Recht en Geschiedenis 38: 79-87.

LANDES, D. (1976) "Religion and enterprise: the Case of the French textile industry," pp. 41-86 in E. C. Carter II, R. Forster, and J. N. Moody (eds.), Enterprise and Entrepreneurs in Nineteenth- and Twentiety-Century France. Baltimore: Johns Hopkins University Press.

LARRICQ, P. (1904) Des mesures législatives proposées pour la protection du travail national. Paris: Jouve.

LEBLOND, M. (1968) "La scolarisation au XIXe siècle dans le Nord." Mémoire de maîtrise, University of Lille.

LEMISCH, J. (1968) "The American Revolution seen from the bottom up," pp. 3-45 in J. Bernstein (ed.), Towards a New Past: Dissenting Essays in American History. New York: Pantheon.

LENTACKER, F. (1950) "Les frontaliers belges travaillant en France: caractères et fluctuations d'un courant de main-d'oeuvre." Revue du Nord 32 (April-September): 130-144.

——— (1974) La frontière Franco-belge: étude géographique des effets d'une frontière internationale sur la vie des relations. Lille: Morel et Corduant.

LEWIN, H. G. (1936) Railway Mania and Aftermath, 1845-52. London: Railway Gazette.

LIPSON, E. (1915-1931) The Economic History of England, 3 vols. London: A. and C. Black.

LIUBLINSKAYA, A. D. (1966) Vnutriennaia politika frantsuskovo absolutismo. Moscow/Leningrad: Izdatel'stvo "Nauka."

LOUBÈRE, L. A. (1974) Radicalism in Mediterranean France. Its Rise and Decline, 1848-1914. Albany: State University of New York Press.

LUCAS, R. (1971) Mill Town, Mine Town, Rail Town: Life in Canadian Communities of Single Industry. Toronto: Toronto University Press.

LUXARDO, H., C. C. RAGACHE, and J. SANDRIN (1979) Courrières-1906: Crime ou catastrophe? Paris: Floréal.

LUXEMBURG, R. (1971) The Mass Strike. New York: Harper & Row.

MACHU, L. (1956) "La crise de l'industrie textile à Roubaix au milieu du XIXe siècle." Revue de Nord 38 (January-March): 65-75.

McCORD, N. (1958) The Anti-Corn Law League, 1838-1846. London: George Allen & Unwin.

MACPHERSON, C. B. (1962) The Political Theory of Possessive Individualism: Hobbes to Locke. Oxford: Clarendon Press.

MAIER, P. (1963) "John Wilkes and American dissillusionment with Britain." William and Mary Quarterly 3rd series, 20 (July): 373-395.

——— (1970a) "The Charleston mob and the evolution of popular politics in revolutionary South Carolina, 1765-1784." Perspectives in American History 4: 173-196.

——— (1970b) "Popular uprisings and civil authority in eighteenth-century America." William and Mary Quarterly, 3rd series, 27 (January): 3-35.

MAITRON, J. (1951) Histoire du Mouvement Anarchiste en France. Paris: Société Universitaire d'Éditions et de Librairie.

––– (1964) Dictionnaire Biographique du Mouvement ouvrier français. Paris: Éditions ouvrières.

––– (1972) "Étude critique de Rapport Appert. Essai de 'contre rapport.' " Le Mouvement social 79 (April-June): 95-118.

MANN, M. (1973) Consciousness and Action among the Western Working Class. London: Macmillan.

MANNHEIM, C. (1902) De la condition des ouvriers dans les manufactures de l'état (tabacs-allumettes). Paris: Giard and Brière.

MANTOUX, P. (1962) The Industrial Revolution in the Eighteenth Century. New York: Harper & Row.

"Dat MARCKENBOECK van Bathmen" (1892) Overijsselsche Stad-, Dijk-, en Markeregten 3, no. 9. Zwolle: J. J.Tijl.

MARGLIN, S. (1974) "What do bosses do?" Review of Radical Political Economics (Summer).

MARSHALL, D. (1968) Dr. Johnson's London. New York: John Wiley.

MARX, K. (1971) "The Eighteenth Brumaire of Louis Napoleon Bonaparte," in S. K. Padover (ed.), On Revolution. New York: McGraw-Hill.

––– (1976) Capital, Vol. 1. New York: Vintage.

MATHER, F. C. (1966) Public Order in the Age of the Chartists. Manchester: Manchester University Press.

––– (1972) Chartism. London: Historical Association.

––– (1974) "The general strike of 1842: a study in leadership, organization and the threat of revolution during the Plug Plot disturbances," pp. 115-135 in J. Stevenson and R. Quinault (eds.), Popular Protest and Public Order: Six Studies in British History, 1790-1920. London: George Allen & Unwin.

MATILLON, R. E. (1908) Les Syndicats ouvriers dans l'Agriculture. Paris: Bonvalot-Jouve.

MATTHEWS, R.C.O. (1954) A Study in Trade-Cycle History. Cambridge: Cambridge University Press.

MICHEL, G. avec la collaboration de A. RENOUARD (1891) Histoire d'un Centre ouvrier (les concessions d'Anzin). Paris: Guillaumin.

MILIBAND, R. (1977) Marxism and Politics. Oxford: Oxford University Press.

Ministère de l'Agriculture et du Commerce (1847) Agriculture française par MM. les Inspecteurs de l'Agriculture. . . . Département de l'Aude. Paris: Imprimerie royale.

Ministère de l'Agriculture (1868) Résultats généraux de l'Enquête décennale de 1862. Strasbourg: Imprimerie administrative de Berger-Levrault.

––– (1883) Compte Rendu des Travaux de la Commission supérieure du phylloxéra (1882) et Rapport de M. Tissérand, Conseiller d'État. Paris: Imprimerie nationale.

––– (1887) Résultats de l'Enquête décennale de 1882. Strasbourg: Imprimerie administrative de Berger-Levrault.

––– Bureau de Subsistances de Secours et de la Statistique agricole. (1890-1900) statistiques agricoles annuelles. Paris: Imprimerie nationale.

MITCHELL, B. and P. DEANE (1971) Abstract of British Historical Statistics. Cambridge: Cambridge University Press.

MOFFITT, L. W. (1964) England on the Eve of the Industrial Revolution: A Study of Economic and Social Conditions from 1740-1760. New York: Barnes and Noble.

MOORE, B., Jr. (1978) Injustice: The Social Bases of Obedience and Revolt. White Plains, NY: M. E. Sharpe.

MORRIS, R. J. (1979) Class and Class Consciousness in the Industrial Revolution, 1750-1850. London: Macmillan.

MOTTE, G. (1946) Roubaix à travers les âges. Roubaix: Éditions de la Société d'émulation.

MOUSNIER, R. [ed.] (1964) Lettres et mémoires adressés au Chancelier Séguier (1633-1649), 2 vols. Paris: Presses Universitaires de France.

MUSSON, A. E. (1972) British Trade Unions, 1800-1875. London: Macmillan.

NAPO, F. (1971) La révolte des vignerons. Toulouse: Privat.

OFFEN, K. M. (1977) "The 'woman question' as a social issue in nineteenth-century France." Third Republic/Troisième Republique (3-4): 238-299.

OZOUF, M. (1976) La fête révolutionnaire, 1789-1799. Paris: Gallimard.

PALMER, R. R. (1959) The Age of the Democratic Revolution, vol. 1: The Challenge. Princeton, NJ: Princeton University Press.

PASSAMA, P. (1906) La Condition des Ouvriers viticoles dans le Minervois. Paris: Giard et Brière.

PATMORE, J. E. (1962) "Navvy gang of 1851." Journal of Transport History (February): 182-189.

PECH, M. (1973) "Les Luttes politiques à Narbonne à la fin du XIXe siècle," pp. 95-105 in Narbonne: Archaeologie et Histoire. Montpellier: Féderation historique du Languedoc-Meditérranéen et du Roussillon.

PECH, R. (1967) "La vie politique dans l'Aude, 1891-1902." Diplôme d'Études supérieures, Faculté des lettres, Paris.

――― (1975) Entreprise Viticole et Capitalisme en Languedoc Meditérranéen de la Crise Phylloxérique à la Deuxième guerre mondiale. Toulouse: Université de Toulouse-Le Mirail.

PEREZ, R. (1974) "Women in the commune: the persistence of tradition and its adaptation to modern conditions." (unpublished)

PERKIN, H. (1969) The Origins of Modern English Society. Toronto: University of Toronto Press.

PERROT, M. (1974) Les ouvriers en grève: France, 1871-1890 (2 vols.). The Hague: Mouton.

――― (1976) "L'éloge de la menagère dans le discours des ouvriers français au XIXe siècle." Romantisme, numero special: 105-121.

PETO, H. (1893) Sir Morton Peto: A Memorial Sketch. Private print.

PIERREUSE, P. (1969) "L'ouvrier roubaisien et la propagande politique, 1890-1900." Revue du Nord 51 (April-June): 249-273.

――― (1972) "La situation économique et sociale à Roubaix et à Tourcoing de 1900 à 1914." Thèse pour le doctorat, 3e cycle, University of Lille.

POLLARD, S. (1965) Genesis of Modern Management. Cambridge: Harvard University Press.

POLLINS, H. (1952) "Note on railway constructional costs." Economica (December).

POSTGATE, R. W. (1923) Builders' History. London: Labour Publishing.

PROUVOST, E. (1974) "Les ouvriers du textile à Roubaix dans la seconde moitié du XVIII siècle." Mémoire de maîtrise, University of Lille.

PROUVOST, J. (1969) "Les courées à Roubaix." Revue du Nord 51 (April-June): 307-316.

QUILIS, J. (1973) Interview with former *colle* leader, conducted with the assistance of R. Pech. Coursan, June 29.

RAMAN, M. (1973) "Mesure de la croissance d'un centre textile: Roubaix de 1789 à 1913." Revue d'histoire économique et sociale 51(4): 470-501.

Rapports sur l'administration des affaires de la ville de Roubaix (1964-1871). Roubaix.

REARDON, J. A. (1977) "Belgian workers in Roubaix, France, in the nineteenth century." Ph.D. dissertation, University of Maryland. (unpublished)

REBOUL, P. (1954) "Troubles sociaux à Roubaix en juillet 1819." Revue du Nord 36 (April-June): 339-350.

REDDY, W. M. (1977) "The textile trade and the language of the crowd at Rouen, 1752-1871." Past and Present 74 (February): 62-89.

RENOUARD, A. and L. MOY (1889) Les institutions ouvrières et sociales du département du Nord. Lille: Danel.

RESTIF de la BRETONNE, N. (1930) Les nuits de Paris (Henri Bachelin, ed.). Paris: Editions du Trianon. L'Oeuvre de Restif de la Bretonne, vol. I.

REYBAUUD, L. (1867) La laine. Paris: Michel Lévy frères.

RODGERS, H. B. (1960) "The Lancashire cotton industry in 1840." Transactions and Papers, Institute of British Geographers 27: 135-153.

ROSE, A. (1957) "The Plug Riots of 1842 in Lancashire and Cheshire." Transactions, Lancashire and Cheshire Antiquarian Society 67: 75-112.

ROSSI, A. (1974) "Social roots of the women's movement in America," pp. 241-281 in A. Rossi (ed.), The Feminist Papers. From Adams to de Beauvoir. New York: Bantam.

ROSTOW, W. W. (1948) British Economy of the Nineteenth Century: Essays. Oxford: Clarendon Press.

ROUGERIE, J. (1964) "Composition d'une population insurgée. L'exemple de la Commune." Le Mouvement Social 48 (July-September): 31-47.

RUDÉ, G. (1959) The Crowd in the French Revolution. Oxford: Clarendon Press.

——— (1962) Wilkes and Liberty. Oxford: Oxford University Press.

——— (1964) The Crowd in History, 1730-1848. New York: John Wiley.

——— (1971a) Hanoverian London, 1714-1808. London: Secker & Warburg.

——— (1971b) Paris and London in the Eighteenth Century. Studies in Popular Protest. New York: Viking.

——— (1978) Protest and Punishment. The Story of the Social and Political Protesters Transported to Australia, 1788-1868. Oxford: Clarendon Press.

SCHAMA, S. (1977) Patriots and Liberators: Revolution in the Netherlands, 1780-1813. New York: Alfred A. Knopf.

SCHWEITZER, R. A. (1980) "A study of contentious gatherings in early nineteenth-century Great Britain." Historical Methods 12 (Summer): 1-4.

——— C. TILLY, and J. BOYD (1980) "The texture of contention in Britain, 1828-1829." Working Paper 211. Center for Research on Social Organization, University of Michigan.

SCOTT, J. (1974) The Glassworkers of Carmaux. Cambridge: Harvard University Press.

SENNETT, R. (1977) The Fall of Public Man. New York: Alfred A. Knopf.

SHELTON, W. J. (1973) English Hunger and Industrial Disorders: A Study of Social Conflict During the First Decade of George III's Reign. London: Macmillan.

SHORTER, E. and C. TILLY (1974) Strikes in France 1830-1968. Cambridge: Cambridge University Press.

SLICHER van BATH, B. H. (1946) "Manor, mark and village in the eastern Netherlands." Speculum 21.

——— (1957) Een samenleving onder spanning. Geschiedenis van het platteland in Overijssel. Assen, The Netherlands: Van Gorcum.

——— (1963) Agrarian history of Western Europe, 500-1800. London: Arnold.

SMELSER, N. J. (1959) Social Change in the Industrial Revolution: An Application of Theory to the British Cotton Industry 1770-1840. Chicago: University of Chicago Press.

SMITH, B.G.S. (1975) "The women of the Lille bourgeoisie, 1850-1914." Ph.D. dissertation, Rochester. (unpublished)

SMITH, J. H. (1972) "Village revolution: Agricultural workers of Cruzy (Herault)." Ph.D. dissertation, Wisconsin. (unpublished)

——— (1975) "Work routine and social structure in a French village: Cruzy, Herault in the nineteenth century." Journal of Interdisciplinary History 5: 352-387.

——— (1978) "Agricultural workers and the French wine-growers revolt of 1907." Past and Present 79 (May): 101-125.

——— (1979) "Peasant proletarians: work structure and labor organization in rural Languedoc 1880-1910." Presented at the 25th Annual Meeting of the Society for French Historical Studies, Pittsburgh, Pennsylvania, April 30.

SMITH, W. A. (1965) "Anglo-colonial society and the mob, 1740-1775." Ph.D. dissertation, Clarement Graduate School and University Center. (unpublished)

SMITH-ROSENBERG, C. (1975) "The female world of love and ritual." Signs I: 1-29.

SOBOUL, A. (1958) Les sans-culottes parisiens en l'an II. Paris: Clavreuil.

SOWERWINE, C. (1978) Les femmes et le socialisme. Paris: Presses de la Fondation Nationale des Sciences Politiques.

Statistique générale (1942) Études démographiques, No. 3: Les naturalisations en France (1870-1940) Paris: Imprimerie nationale.

STEVENSON, J. (1974) "Food riots in England, 1792-1818," in J. Stevenson and R. Quinault (eds.), Popular Protest and Public Order. Six Studies in British History 1790-1920: London: George Allen & Unwin.

——— (1977) "Social control and the prevention of riots in England, 1789-1829," in A. P. Donajgrodzki (ed.), Social Control in Nineteenth Century Britain. London: Croom Helm.

——— (1979) Popular Disturbances in England, 1700-1870. New York: Longman.

STEVENSON, J. and R. QUINAULT [eds.] (1975) Popular Protest and Public Order: Six Studies in British History, 1790-1920. London: George Allen & Unwin.

STINCHCOMBE, A. (1959) "Bureaucratic and craft administration of production." Administrative Sciences Quarterly (May): 168-187.

STONE, L. (1979) "The revival of narrative: reflections on a new old history." Past and Present 85 (November): 3-24.

van STUIJVENBERG, J. H. [eds.] (1975) De economische geschiedenis van Nederland. Groningen: Wolters-Nordhoff.

TAYLOR, W. C. ([1842] 1968) Notes of a tour in the manufacturing districts of
Lancashire. New York: A. M. Kelly.

TE BRAKE, W. (1977) "Revolutionary conflict in the Dutch Republic: the patriot
crisis in Overijssel, 1780-1787." Ph.D. dissertation, University of Michigan. (unpublished)

THABAULT, R. (1971) Education and Change in a Village Community, Mazières-en-
Gâtine, 1848-1914 (F. Tragear, trans.). New York: Schocken.

THOMAS, E. (1963) Les pétroleuses. Paris: Gallimard.

THOMPSON, D. (1962) The Early Chartists. London: Macmillan.

THOMPSON, E. P. (1964) The Making of the English Working Class. London: Victor
Gollancz.

——— (1967) "Time, work-discipline and industrial capitalism." Past and Present 38
(December).

——— (1971) "The moral economy of the English crowd in the nineteenth century."
Past and Present 50 (February): 76-136.

——— (1975) Whigs and Hunters: The Origin of the Black Act. New York: Pantheon.

TILLY, C. (1974) "Town and country in revolution," pp. 271-302 in J. W. Lewis
(ed.), Peasant Rebellion and Communist Revolution in Asia. Stanford, CA:
Stanford University Press.

——— (1975a) "Food supply and public order in modern Europe," pp. 380-455 in C.
Tilly (ed.), The Formation of National States in Western Europe. Princeton:
Princeton University Press.

——— (1975b) "Revolutions and collective violence," in F. T. Greenstein and N.
Polsby (eds.), Handbook of Political Science, Vol. 3. Reading, MA: Addison-
Wesley.

——— (1977a) "Collective action in England and America, 1765-1775," pp. 45-72 in
R. M. Brown and D. E. Fehrenbacher (eds.), Tradition, Conflict, and Moderniza-
tion: Perspectives on the American Revolution. New York: Academic Press.

——— (1977b) "Getting it together in Burgundy, 1675-1975." Theory and Society 4
(Winter): 479-504.

——— (1978a) From Mobilization to Revolution. Reading, MA: Addison-Wesley.

——— (1978b) "Studying social movements/studying collective action." (unpublished)

——— (1979) "Repertoires of contention in America and Britain, 1750-1830," pp.
126-155 in M. Zald and J. McCarthy (eds.), The Dynamics of Social Movements.
Cambridge, MA: Winthrop.

——— (1980a) "How (and, to some extent, why) to study British contention."
Working Paper 212. Center for Research on Social Organization, University of
Michigan.

——— (1980b) "Two callings of social history." Theory and Society 9: 679-681.

——— and R. A. SCHWEITZER (1980) "Enumerating and coding contentious gatherings in nineteenth-century Britain." Working Paper 210. Center for Research on
Social Organization, University of Michigan.

TILLY, C., L. A. TILLY, and R. TILLY (1975) The Rebellious Century. Cambridge:
Harvard University Press.

TILLY, L. A. (1971) "The history of the grain riot as a form of political conflict in France." Journal of Interdisciplinary History 2 (Summer): 21-57.

――― (1972) "I Fatti di Maggio: the working class of Milan and the rebellion of 1898," pp. 124-158 in R. Bezucha (ed.), Modern European Social History. Lexington, MA: D. C. Heath.

――― (1977) "Women and collective action in Europe," pp. 31-44 in D. McGuigan (ed.), The Role of Women in Conflict and Peace. Ann Arbor, MI: Center for Continuing Education of Women.

――― (1979) "The family wage economy of a French textile city, Roubaix, 1872-1906." Journal of Family History 4 (Fall): 381-394.

――― and J. W. SCOTT (1978) Women, Work and Family. New York: Holt, Rinehart & Winston.

TREBLE, J. H. (1972) "Irish navvies in the north of England 1830-50." Journal of Transport History (December).

TRÉNARD, L. (1972-1974) Histoire des Pays-Bas français, 2 vols. Toulouse: Privat.

USHER, A. P. (1929) A History of Mechanical Inventions. New York: McGraw-Hill.

VERGNES (née CHEYTION), A. (1973) Interview conducted with the assistance of R. Pech. Coursan, June 28.

――― (1974) Interview conducted with the assistance of R. Pech. Coursan, August 20.

VESTER, M. (1970) Die Entstehung des Proletariats als Lernprozess. Die Entstehung antikapitalistischer Theorie und Praxis in England 1792-1848. Frankfurt a/Main: Europäische Verlaganstalt.

VIJLBRIEF, I. (1950) Van Antiaristocratie tot Democratie, een bijdrage tot de politieke en sociale geschiedenis der stad Utrecht. Amsterdam: Querido.

VUILLEMIN, E. (1872) Enquête sur les habitations, les écoles et le degree d'instruction de la population ouvrière des mines de houille du Nord et du Pas-de-Calais. Comité des houillères du Nord et du Pas-de-Calais.

WADSWORTH, A. P. and J. de L. MANN (1931) The Cotton Trade and the Rise of Industrial Lancashire 1600-1780. Manchester: Manchester University Press.

WALSH, R. (1959) Charleston's Sons of Liberty. Columbia: University of South Carolina Press.

WARD, J. T. (1970) "Introduction," in J. T. Ward (ed.), Popular Movements c. 1830-1850. London: Macmillan.

WARNER, C. K. (1960) The Winegrowers of France and the Government Since 1875. New York: Columbia University Press.

WEARMOUTH, R. F. (1945) Methodism and the Common People of the Eighteenth Century. London: Epworth Press.

WEBB, S. and B. WEBB (1920) Industrial Democracy. New York: Kelley.

WEBER, A. F. (1967) The Growth of Cities in the Nineteenth Century. Ithaca, NY: Cornel University Press.

WEBER, M. (1968) Theory of Social and Economic Organization. (A. M. Henderson and T. Parsons, trans.). New York: Free Press.

WILLARD, C. (1965) Les Guesdistes: Le mouvement socialiste en France, 1893-1905. Paris: Éditions sociales.

WILLIAMS, J. (1852) Our Iron Roads. London: Longman, Green and Longman.

de WIT, C.H.E. (1974) De Nederlandse revolutie van de achttiende eeuw, 1780-1787. Oirsbeek, The Netherlands: Lindelauf.

WOLF, E. (1966) Peasants. Englewood Cliffs, NJ: Prentice-Hall.

WOOD, G. H. (1910) The History of Wages in the Cotton Trade during the Past Hundred Years. London: Sherratt and Hughes.

Van der WOUDE, A. M. (1972) Het Noorderkwartier, 3 vols. Wageningen: A.A.G. Bijdragen, No. 16.

WRIGHT, G. (1964) Rural Revolution in France. Stanford: Stanford University Press.

YOUNG, M. and P. WILMOTT (1957) Family and Kinship in East London. London: Routledge & Kegan Paul.

ZYLBERBERG-HOCQUARD, M.-H. (1978) "Les ouvrières d'état (tabacs-allumettes) dans les dernières années du XIXe siècle." Le Mouvement Social 105 (Winter): 87-107.

ABOUT THE AUTHORS

Brian R. Brown is a graduate student in the Department of Political Science, University of Michigan. He is currently engaged in writing a doctoral dissertation on "The Political Economy of Working Class Contention in Lancashire, England, 1837-1842."

Samuel Cohn is a graduate student in sociology at the University of Michigan. He is currently investigating the origins of work discipline, regional economic inequality, and occupational sex-typing in Britain.

Laura L. Frader received her Ph.D. from the University of Rochester in 1978 and is Assistant Professor of History at Northeastern University. She is completing a book, *Peasants and Protest: Agricultural Labor and Collective Action in Southern France,* and is working on a study of women's work and fertility in rural France. At Northeastern she teaches courses in European social history and women's history and has published articles on these subjects in both the United States and France.

Frank W. Munger, Jr. is an attorney and Professor of Law at Antioch School of Law in Washington, D.C. The chapter which appears in this volume is part of a larger study of the suppression of collective action in Industrial Revolution England. Professor Munger is currently engaged in a longitudinal study of social conflict and civil litigation in the United States. His recent publications include "Suppression of Popular Gatherings in Lancashire, England, 1800-1830," forthcoming in the *American Journal of Legal History.*

Judy A. Reardon studied modern French social history at the University of Maryland during 1970-1977. Her dissertation, "Belgian Workers in Roubaix, France, in the 19th Century," focused on a textile city in the industrial Nord, demonstrating that a labor force of mixed nationality created certain advantages for employers and the state. She has taught at the University of Maryland, George Washington University, and Catholic University of America. Dr. Reardon is currently developing instructional resources for teaching history at high school and college levels, and is a consultant on historical documentation for the Department of Education, Washington, D.C.

Wayne P. Te Brake is Assistant Professor of European History at the State University of New York, College at Purchase. He received his Ph.D. in history from the University of Michigan and has been a research fellow of the American Council of Learned Societies in 1980-81. His research interests include the social and political development of the Low Countries during the *ancien régime* and the revolutionary political movements there at the end of the eighteenth century. He is presently completing a monograph on the Dutch Patriot Revolution in Overijssel.

Charles Tilly is Professor of Sociology and History and Director of the Center for Research on Social Organization at the University of Michigan. His main interest is in the historical study of collective action and its changes under the impact of capitalism and the growth of national states. His most recent books are *From Mobilization to Revolution* and *As Sociology Meets History.*

Louise A. Tilly is Associate Professor of History at the University of Michigan, where she has directed the Women's Studies Program. She is a specialist in nineteenth- and twentieth-century Western European history, with special emphasis on industrialization, work, and family in Italy and France. Her most recent books are *The Rebellious Century* (with Charles and Richard Tilly) and *Women, Work, and Family* (with Joan Scott).